NEW FORMATIONS

MW00978586

PRODUCTI(
For enquiries   iart.

SUBSCRIPTIONS:
UK: Institutions £125, Individuals £40.
Rest of world: Institutions £125; Individuals £40.
Single copies: £14.99 plus £2 post and packing.
Back issues: £14.99 plus £2 post and packing for individuals;
£34.99 plus £2 post and packing for institutions.
Payments can be made by Visa and Mastercard.

CONTRIBUTIONS AND CORRESPONDENCE:
Send to Scott McCracken: The Editor, *new formations*
School of Cultural Studies, Montgomery House,
32 Collegiate Crescent, Sheffield Hallam University,
Sheffield, S10 2BP
s.mccracken@shu.ac.uk

BOOKS FOR REVIEW:
Send to: Timothy Bewes, Reviews Editor
new formations, Department of English, Brown University, Box 1852,
Providence, Rhode Island, 02912 USA.
Timothy_Bewes@brown.edu

new formations publishes themed issues, themed sections and discrete articles. Contributors are encouraged to contact the editor to discuss their ideas and to obtain a copy of our style sheet, which can also be obtained on our website at http://www.newformations.co.uk

Manuscripts should be sent in triplicate; experts in the relevant field will referee them anonymously. The manuscripts will not be returned unless a stamped, self-addressed envelope is enclosed. Contributors should note that the editorial board cannot take responsibility for any manuscript submitted to *new formations*.

ISSN   0 950 237 8
ISBN   1 905007 035

Printed in Great Britain at the University Press, Cambridge.

new formations is published three times a year by
Lawrence & Wishart, 99a Wallis Road, London E9 5LN
Tel: 020-8533 2506 Fax: 020-8533 7369
Website: www.newformations.co.uk

Orders and Subscription payments to:
Lawrence and Wishart, PO Box 7701
Latchington, Chelmsford CH3 6WL
landw@btinternet.com

NOTES ON CONTRIBUTORS

Deborah Cameron is Rupert Murdoch Professor of Language and Communication at the University of Oxford, and is author of *Good To Talk? Living and Working in a Communication Culture* (Sage 2000).

Mary Baine Campbell teaches medieval and early modern literature and culture at Brandeis University. She is the author of two scholarly books, *The Witness and the Other World: Exotic European Travel Writing 400-1600* and *Wonder and Science: Imagining Worlds in Early Modern Europe*, and two collections of poetry.

Phil Cohen is Director of the London East Research Institute and Professor of Cultural and Innovation Studies at the University of East London. One of his current obsessions is how to create and sustain forms of critical intellectual practice whose purchase outside the Academy does not depend on cultural snobbery, administrative utility, or market values. Another is the need to hitch such a practice to a popular culture of curiosity. This essay is from work in progress.

David Cunningham is Lecturer in English Literature at the University of Westminster and an editor of the journal *Radical Philosophy*. He is currently writing a book on the concept of an avant-garde, as well as co-editing a collection of essays on Adorno and Literature.

Andrew Gamble is Professor of Politics and co-Director of the Political Economy Research Centre at the University of Sheffield. He is the author of *Politics and Fate* and *Between Europe and America: The Future of British Politics*.

Keya Ganguly is an Associate Professor in the Department of Cultural Studies and Comparative Literature at the University of Minnesota. She teaches critical theory, the sociology of culture, film, and postcolonial criticism. She is the author of *States of Exception: Everyday Life and Postcolonial Identity* (University of Minnesota Press 2001) and is currently finishing a book on Satyajit Ray and Indian avant-garde cinema.

Andrew Gibson is Professor of Modern Literature and Theory at Royal Holloway, University of London. His books include *Joyce's Revenge: History, Politics and Aesthetics in Ulysses* (Oxford University Press 2002). He has published widely on contemporary French thought, and contributed the Afterword to the English translation of Alain Badiou's writings on Beckett. He is currently completing *The Pathos of Intermittency: Alain Badiou and Samuel Beckett*.

Jon Klancher teaches literary and cultural studies at Carnegie Mellon University, and is currently completing a book about Romanticism and the modern discourse on cultural institutions. He has published widely on the formation of reading audiences and public spheres in the eighteenth and nineteenth centuries, the sociology of culture, and the history of criticism.

Scott McCracken is Editor of *new formations*. He is Principal Lecturer in English at Sheffield Hallam University. Publications include, *Pulp: Reading Popular Fiction* (MUP 1998). He is co-author with Peter Buse, Ken Hirschkop and Bertrand Taithe of *The Arcades Project: an Unguided Tour* (MUP 2005).

Jacqueline Rose teaches in the English and Drama Department at Queen Mary University of London. Her most recent publications are *Albertine*, a novel and *On Not Being Able to Sleep - Psychoanalysis and the Modern World*. She was the writer and presenter of the Channel 4 documentary, 'Dangerous Liaison - Israel and America'. *The Question of Zion* will be published by Princeton University Press next Spring.

Jani Scandura is Assistant Professor of English at the University of Minnesota and the co-editor of a collection of essays, *Modernism, Inc: Body, Memory, Capital* (NYU 2001). Her book, *Down in the Dumps: Place, Modernity, American Depression*, is forthcoming from Duke UP.

Peter Scott is Vice-Chancellor of Kingston University and formerly Pro-Vice-Chancellor at the University of Leeds and Editor of *The Times Higher Education Supplement*. His most recent book (with Helga Nowotny and Michael Gibbons) is *Re-Thinking Science: Knowledge and the Public in an Age of Uncertainty* (Polity 2001).

Stephen Shapiro, a former active member of ACT UP/NY, now teaches in the Department of English and Comparative Literature at the University of Warwick. Co-editor of *Revising Charles Brockden Brown: Culture, Politics, and Sexuality in the Early Republic* (Tennessee 2004), he is working on a study of Atlantic capitalism and the Early American Novel and another on homoerotics in eighteenth-century Anglo-America.

Judith Surkis is Assistant Professor of History and Literature at Harvard University and, in 2003-2004, Nancy L. Buc Fellow at the Pembroke Center for Teaching and Research on Women at Brown University, where she is working on a history of public indecency in modern France. She is also completing a book on citizenship, masculinity, and the family in the French Third Republic.

CONTENTS
NUMBER 53 SUMMER 2004

Intellectual Work

ii   Notes on Contributors

7   *Scott McCracken*   Editorial

12   *Phil Cohen*   A Place to Think?: Some Reflections on the Idea of
                                      the University in the Age of the 'Knowledge Economy'

28   *Peter Scott*   Prospects for Knowledge Work: Critical Engagement
                                      or Expert Conscription?

41   *Andrew Gamble*   Public Intellectuals and the Public Domain

54   *Deborah Cameron*   Talking Up Skill and Skilling Up Talk

65   *Scott McCracken*   Idleness for All

77   *Stephen Shapiro*   Marx To The Rescue!: Queer Theory And The Crisis
                                      of Prestige

91   *Keya Ganguly*   The Work of Forgetting: Raymond Williams and the
                                      Problem of Experience

103   *Jani Scandura*   Cinematic Insomnia

115   *Jacqueline Rose*   The Body of Evil

            REVIEWS

130   *Mary Baine Campbell*   Strategic Universalism?

136   *Andrew Gibson*   The Rarity of the Event: On Alain Badiou

143   *Jon Klancher*   The Modern Prints

146   *David Cunningham*   Making It Newer

149   *Judith Surkis*   Queering the Spheres

In Memory of

EDWARD SAID

1 November 1935 – 25 September 2003

University of Warwick

Department of English and Comparative Literary Studies

Invites you to the inaugural

Edward Said Memorial Lecture

to be given by Professor Timothy Brennan
University of Minnesota

on Tuesday 5 October 2004 at 6pm
at the Warwick Arts Centre Conference Room
University of Warwick

For more information nearer the time contact:

Neil Lazarus   *N.Lazarus@warwick.ac.uk*
Benita Parry   *B.Parry@warwick.ac.uk*
Rashmi Varma   *Rashmi.Varma@warwick.ac.uk*

EDITORIAL

Scott McCracken

On 18 February 2004, the French weekly *Les Inrockuptibles* published a petition signed by 8,000 members of the 'intellectual professions' - teachers, researchers and lawyers, actors, theatre directors, artists, psychoanalysts and students - against the Gaullist administration's 'war on intelligence'.[1] Signatories included Jacques Derrida, Etienne Balibar and Alain Touraine. If more evidence were needed of the difference between the intellectual culture of France and that of the Anglophone world this was it. A concerted and political campaign in favour of intellectual workers seems unimaginable in Britain or the United States. Nor was the campaign the voice of an elite, two weeks later *Les Inrockuptibles* claimed 70,000 signatures and, despite the petition's denunciation of both Left and Right, it quickly won the support of the Communist and Socialist parties as well as number of minor parties on the Left. As befits a society that still has an active revolutionary tradition, the campaign was a product of the professional classes as organised labour, bringing together workers in scientific laboratories and universities, and protests against the regulation of psychotherapy, the judicial system and the entertainment industry. Yet if the militancy was startling, the diagnosis was familiar:

1. Nicolas Weill, 'Le gouvernement accusé de mener une "guerre à l'intelligence"', *Le Monde*, 18/02/04.

> A politics of impoverishment and destabilisation of all those spaces that are considered unproductive in the short term, or useless or dissident, of all the invisible work of the intelligence, of all those places where society thinks itself, dreams itself, invents itself, cares for itself, judges itself, repairs itself.[2]

Such spaces are increasingly under threat in a globalised system - or rather, globalisation is the excuse for closing down such spaces, which have always been viewed with suspicion by instrumentalist views of the world. In an echo of Andrew Gamble's analysis of the deterioration of the public domain in this issue, the petition condemns a simplifying tendency in public discourse, a reduction of complexity into binary oppositions of arguments for or against (*Les Inrockuptibles*, 18/02/04). And it is clear from where the threat comes:

2. 'Appel contre la guerre à l'intelligence', *Les Inrockuptibles*, 18/02/04.

> This war on intelligence is without precedent in the history of the nation. It is the end of a French exception: a simple look at some of our European neighbours, post-Thatcherite England or Berlusconi's Italy, permits us however to see what happens to schools, hospitals, universities, theatres, publishing houses, as a consequence of those policies which, carried out

in the name of economic sense and budgetary rigour, have an exorbitant human, social and cultural cost and irreversible consequences (*Les Inrockuptibles*, 18/02/04).

If this is an example of elitism, then it is one that holds that the 'production and diffusion of knowledges is as indispensable to us as the air we breath' (*Les Inrockuptibles*, 18/02/04).

It is easy perhaps to get carried away with the invigorating rhetoric of French political discourse, the calls to: 'participate in struggles and mobilisations' and 'to address a solid and unified protest to the government coming from all the sectors under attack from this anti-intellectualism of the state'. And perhaps too easy to forget - despite the rhetoric - the institutionalised elitism of French society, a key factor in the protests of 1968 against the education system, and one which has still not been properly addressed. There is a danger too of engaging in what a former of editor of this journal described to me when I first proposed this issue, as 'Golden Ageism': the illusion that a better environment for intellectual work once existed in an earlier time or another place. Yet all of the articles in this issue are wary of these dangers. Their concern is rather the politics of intellectual work in an age when some of the larger concepts used to describe it - postmodernism, neo-liberalism, globalisation, Empire - have become too easy a shorthand for the complexity of the current conjuncture.

Recent issues of *new formations* have intervened in key debates in cultural politics ranging from the legacy of Fanon to the position of modern African art. Issue 52, *Cultures and Economies*, edited by Mandy Merck, addressed the re-recognition of the importance of economics in cultural studies. The aim of this issue is to take some time - time not devoted to short-term objectives and outcomes - to think about the labour of thinking itself. The first three articles discuss the state of the academy. In Britain, universities have been subject to an unprecedented regime of regulation and central control. As the French petition recognises, Thatcherism's project of deregulating capital was matched by a move to rein in the semi-autonomous parts of the public sector: schools, universities, the legal and medical professions. New Labour has continued and in some cases intensified that project, recently turning on the BBC, which is now threatened by the new body for regulating the privately owned broadcasting media 'Ofcom'.

In an opening salvo, Phil Cohen analyses the market pressures on academic life and the student experience, tracing the metamorphosis of the radical protests of the 1960s into a culture of deregulated knowledge, the aim of which is to service the immediate demands of the job market. Cohen offers the first of a series of alternatives, tracing an intellectual legacy that goes back to the mendicant friars of the middle ages - a peripatetic tradition that proposes an anti-systemic approach to knowledge and suggests a productive form of interdisciplinarity rather than the two alternatives currently on offer: either hermetically sealed disciplines and an 'ivory tower' approach to knowledge; or a pick and mix approach to education.

Peter Scott has a similar diagnosis: identifying the pressures of the market and the importance of higher education as a form of social distinction in the context of the fluidity of contemporary societies. He argues that this leaves the Left with a 'cruel dilemma', welcoming the expansion of higher education, but wary of the market-driven imperatives that have replaced the social democratic assumptions that underpinned its support. Yet, Scott is optimistic about the positive effects of mass higher education which, despite the coercive mechanisms introduced to manage change and the current political atmosphere of anti-intellectualism (nothing new on the British Left), point towards new and more open knowledge systems. There is, he argues, the possibility of a democratic rather than a market solution.

The state of democracy - never a 'finished system' capable of withering as well as growing - is the subject of Andrew Gamble's article on public intellectuals. Gamble defines the crisis of democracy as one where the key institutions that constitute a public domain cannot fulfil their function. Competitive pressures on journalists mean that the media operates against the public interest, encouraging populism and panic rather than informed debate. Reductions in academic freedom limit the role of academics as public intellectuals. In contrast to the narrow expert in a specialised field of knowledge, Gamble identifies Bernard Crick and Stuart Hall as examples of intellectuals who move between the academic and the public, civic and political spheres. It is this traffic that makes the organic intellectuals a genuine democracy need.

A lack of informed public debate is also at the root of Deborah Cameron's identification of a gap between rhetoric and reality in the 'knowledge economy'. Cameron argues for a distinction between intellectual work and knowledge work. So-called knowledge work has been ill defined and its meaning has spread to include functions in the service sectors that differ little from Taylorisation. Taking call-centres as a case study, Cameron argues that much of what is described as education or training for the knowledge economy is actually the opposite of intellectual work - the imposition of a tighter grid of control on work both in the service sector and within institutions of education.

Cameron's piece suggests that the question of intellectual work cannot be disaggregated from the larger context of the dominant culture of overwork that has become the norm in Anglo-American capitalism. Scott McCracken proposes that rethinking intellectual work means rethinking the nature of work and the division of labour itself, a process for which Walter Benjamin's concept of *Müßiggang* or idleness offers a productive starting point.

In contrast to idleness, activism is the focus of Stephen Shapiro's article on the relationship between radical theory and political practice. Shapiro argues that the anti-systemic potential of queer theory was rooted in the political protests generated by the AIDS crisis in the 1980s. Decoupling the link between the academy and the street emptied out that radical potential. Prestige in the academy for queer theorists led to a waning of their power to critique American society and left them ill-prepared to engage with the anti-capitalist protests of the 1990s. Shapiro advocates a re-establishment of the links between critical theory and political activism.

The speed with which the connections between political engagement and intellectual work can be forgotten is the subject of Keya Ganguly's timely return to the work of Raymond Williams. The market mode of theory as a kind of sweet counter from which intellectuals can pick and mix is countered by Ganguly's critique of the kinds of misunderstandings of Williams that both forget and deny his contribution to how we think now. This is, as she points out, not only bad intellectual history, but at odds with Williams own generous engagement with his critics during his lifetime.

In a further exploration of intellectual states, Jani Scandura examines not forgetting, but insomnia. The power of film has meant its effect on the mind has often been treated with suspicion. Hollywood was described as a 'dream factory' from its earliest days. Scandura traces the history of film's relationship to sleep, suggesting that insomnia rather than dreaming is the more productive concept to work with when trying to understand the medium.

The issue concludes with an important new contribution from Jacqueline Rose. Rose's work has never been confined to the narrow discourses of the academy. In this essay she moves from the uses of the word 'evil' in the current international crisis to its avoidance by the perpetrators of crimes under the apartheid regime in South Africa. Returning to Arendt's 'banality of evil' Rose analyses the ethics of representation in J.M. Coetzee's most recent work, including his extraordinary new novel, *Elizabeth Costello*, as a way back into the politics of the present, messy conjuncture. As much as anything, Rose's essay is an example of the kind of intellectual work we need. In contrast to the tendency to look for simple alternatives identified by Gamble, it refuses to give simple answers to complex problems. Controversial, it provokes debate rather than closing it down. It stands in opposition to the tendency recognised by Cohen for the academy to evade the public and political spheres.

The success of the 'war on intelligence' in Britain and the United States has, as Jenny Bourne Taylor has suggested, been partly because the work ethic has been so crucial to the identity of the intellectual left in terms of its sense of its own relevance and effectiveness. The success of the British Research Assessment Exercise (RAE)[3] or the US academic star system as disciplinary devices to be incorporated by a whole generation of intellectuals who might have been expected to stand more firmly against them. Instead, because of the breakdown of any meaningful collective action in that generation, it has made its own work projects stand in place of these wider political meanings.[4]

If that is the case, then this issue will only have succeeded if it starts a

3. The RAE is a peculiarly British form of academic audit where certain kinds of research 'outputs', articles, books etc. are calibrated and valued to decide future funding. For more on its consequences see Cohen, Scott and Gamble in this issue.

4. The ideas in this paragraph are taken from an email to me on 6 June 2004 from Jenny Bourne Taylor that was part of a discussion of this issue within the Editorial Board of *new formations*.

process that recognises the public and political intellectual work that needs to be done outside as well as inside the academy so that, indeed, the 'production and diffusion of knowledges becomes as indispensable to us as the air we breathe'.

This issue is dedicated to the memory of Edward Said who lent his name to new formations *from the journal's inception in 1987 and remained a member of its Editorial Advisory until his death. He leaves a body of intellectual work that will continue to resonate in the pages of* new formations *and elsewhere.*

A Place to Think?: Some reflections on the idea of the university in the age of the 'Knowledge Economy'

Phil Cohen

EVERYONE NEEDS A PLACE TO THINK

Susan Sontag does it in Times square, Ian McEwan does it in the Chilterns. Naomi Klein does it on horseback. Archimedes did it in the bath and a lot of people I know say they do it on the loo. Everyone needs a place to think, but none of the ads in the launch campaign for BBC4 with this strapline featured anyone doing it in Academia. All the people chosen were public intellectuals, they were well known writers, artists, musicians, or cultural commentators but none of them were academics as such. Unsurprisingly they were also extremely photogenic. And sharply dressed. In the era of what Regis Debray has called the Mediocracy, the dishevelled egghead look (aka John Bayley or Sir Patrick Moore) is most definitely out. Now that iconography has replaced ideology in the public authorisation of ideas you have, it seems, to be a fully fledged knowledge power dresser to stand a chance of getting your arguments across to a public wider than your immediate intellectual peers. This shift towards the impression management of knowledge and its implication for sustaining some kind of critical intellectual practice inside and outside the university is one of the themes I want to address.[1]

1. This is a shortened version of a much longer study of changing modes of intellectual production and their relation to popular cultures of knowledge. A version of the present paper was given at the Festschrift for Mike Rustin at the University of East London. I am also very grateful to Ien Ang, George Morgan and other staff at the Centre for Cultural Research at the University of Western Sydney for an opportunity to give a version of this text at a public lecture and for the contributions of the discussants, Michael Singh and Bronwyn Davies. None of the above should be held responsible for the views expressed here.

There is another more material aspect to this. One of the commonest refrains amongst academics is that we can never get any 'work' done when we go into work. In other words we are so busy and stressed out by our ever increasing teaching and admin loads that we literally have no time or place to think - let alone to do anything approximating sustained research. That is saved up for 'the sabbatical'. The sabbatical has become the holy grail of Academic Life - the promised land where all the ideas that have laid dormant will come to fruition, all the scattered fragments of writing will be brought together into a coherent whole, and we will return to the academic treadmill refreshed and with a renewed sense of intellectual purpose.

The reality is somewhat different. The original meaning of the sabbatical, from the Hebrew *Sabat* entailed the principle that one year in seven the field lies fallow, so that it may be more productive on the eighth. And indeed the notion of a latency period in the gestation of ideas is one that is strongly endorsed by research into the nature of creativity. However, the groves of Academe have long ago been cut down to make way for the multi-site campus. These days sabbaticals are definitely not about lying fallow; they are part of the 'publish or perish' ethos which has come to dominate so much of our intellectual life. So we have a university research culture held together by the desire to get the hell out of the university into some kind of privatised sanctuary where there is, at last, time and space to think. Yet once people get there they often promptly collapse into lethargy or ill health, bodies and minds so addicted to the routine stress of academic life that they simply cannot cope with its sudden absence.

Of course there are always individuals who successfully buck these trends. We all know colleagues who are productive in ways that go far beyond what could ever be measured by the audit culture and the British Research Assessment Exercise (RAE), whose research interests combine breadth and depth in a way that both contributes to disciplinary innovation and opens up conversations between disciplines and who combine the avocations of the public intellectual and private scholar. But the question is why are they so few and far between and getting scarcer by the year? What is it about the way our universities are currently organised that militates against sustaining a culture of intellectual innovation?

As soon as we ask a question like that, one of the traps we can fall into is thinking that at some point, once upon a time, things were a lot different and better. Someone is sure to start talking about the great lost idea of the university as a community of scholars. Take for example the recent furore in the UK over the Education Secretary's attack on some of our Ivory Tower dwellers for failing, as he saw it, to help our economy and society deal with the negative effects of globalisation. In the comments page of the *Times Higher Educational Supplement* there was not a Vice Chancellor who did not protest and declare allegiance to the idea of the university as a privileged site for the unfettered pursuit of knowledge and truth. Those same VCs who have been the most enthusiastic in ensuring that every aspect of university life conforms to corporate norms of management accountability, who are the keenest promoters of business links and the commercial applications of research, are the very ones who with shining eyes conjure up images of the mediaeval cloisters where scholars pursue their studies uncontaminated by the ways of the world.

The mediaeval historians whom Charles Clarke seems to think should be retired early or retained merely as an ornament to the new edifices of knowledge transfer, will tell you that European universities in the middle ages were very far from being ivory towers; they were disputatious, often violent places, centres of intrigue enmeshed with the workings of both church and court, where academic backstabbing might involve physical injury as well as intellectual insult, and heretical ideas might be punished by banishment, or torture at the hands of the Inquisition, while student riots and street brawls frequently ended in death. Nevertheless I don't think we should see the invoking of a romanticised ideal of the university as community of scholars as pure hype. The fact is that so called blue sky thinking is precisely what the knowledge managerialists who have taken up residence in the boardrooms of global capitalism want most of all. And this is not exactly new.

My best friend at Cambridge in the 1960s got a First in Classics and a special prize for his translation of Euripides' Ion, and then promptly went off to work for a leading advertising agency, where after sitting around lying fallow for about six months he leapt to sudden fame and fortune by coining the slogan 'For Mash eat Smash' for a new line in instant spuds. All of which goes to show that being a whizz at Greek verse at an ancient university will put you at the cutting edge of consumer culture in less time than it takes to boil a real potato. When the Bank of England, British Gas and HSBC send their top executives to learn the Whirling Dervish Dance so as to find inner peace and increase their business acumen, when the American Indian Medicine Wheel is used to take pension fund managers on an existential journey to discover their spiritual, emotional and creative selves, or Lao Tzu's *Art of War* serves as the basis for a best selling handbook on sales technique, then it is not surprising to find that the image of a community of scholars grubbing away in some obscure archive to make intellectual mountains out of textual molehills, should have a certain sentimental appeal for academics.

So, before we dismiss the idea of the university as having something to do with a community of scholarly practice as a cynical cover story, perhaps we should try to understand how this notion plays in the wider political context. Is it possible to see the university as the site of an old fashioned Marxist contradiction, between the (increasingly socialised) forces and (ever more individualised) relations of knowledge production? Can the 'crisis of the university' be traced to a growing tension between, on the one hand, the creation of a mass higher education system, charged with the training up of collective knowledge workers and on the other, the persistence of highly localised and hierarchical structures of academic self governance, competitive scholarship and symbolic narcissism, associated with the formation of an independent intelligentsia? Or are there important contradictions within this contradiction which cannot be dismissed as 'secondary' just because they do not fit into the Marxist schema? Not to mention a whole lot of other mediations going on?

THE GRAMMARS OF UN/KNOWING

One way of tracking the genealogy of intellectual work and its current crisis is to specify the shifting codes which connect particular ways of knowing objects to certain kinds of 'knowing subjects' within defined communities of practice. How the world is known through, for example, physics, biology or anthropology constructs iterative webs of story telling about procedures (alias methodologies) that intimately shape the identities of those who work within these frameworks. This process is not just bio- but ethno- and historio-graphically specific; in other words it bears not only on the trajectory of individual lines of thought, but on particular cultures of enquiry, on the history of disciplines, and on knowledge's Other Scenes.

So for example we could begin by distinguishing the founding place of the scholar, ensconced in his or her study in terms of the pursuit of a hermeneutics of vocation as derived ultimately from the mediaeval scholastics. This is a research strategy governed by a quasi-spiritual quest for truths contained within a corpus of texts. The practice of reading here becomes a special form of apprenticeship to inherited wisdoms. The drive is not to produce new ideas, but to interrogate old ones, to bring them alive and reinterpret them in the light of contemporary circumstance. Historically we have the model of the Talmudic or Koranic scholar. More recently we have seen the emergence of a secular equivalent: the poststructuralist who pores over once sacred texts in order to 'deconstruct' their mysteries, either by reading between the lines or by challenging their canonical status. Yet despite the fact that the power of divination has been decisively transferred from text to reader, and thence from the process of authorship to the context of reception, the focus of innovation is still on interpretative strategy as such. From this vantage point nothing new ever happens outside the text and its representation.

In contrast, the romantic movement and its successor avant gardes privilege the vocation of the writer or intellectual as the site of a direct, textually unmediated, encounter between creative individual and phenomenal world. The existential quest for truth may be turned inwards to a transcendental self invented as a medium of genial inspiration; or it may be extraverted towards the Other as site or source of exotic curiosity. In either case what the encounter produces is a shock of the new - new ideas, new cultural texts that challenge the inherited corpus, and forms of engagement with the real in which the desire to know no longer depends for its satisfaction on iterative methods of reading.

Today, readers will not need reminding, the sense of scholarly apprenticeship and creative vocation is mired in the decidedly more profane drives of career. The disciplines of reading are increasingly subsumed under the pursuit of discipleship, the formation of rival schools of interpretation centred not just on canonical texts but on iconic authors. Under this code the main way to make your way up the ladder is to align yourself with a particular clique centred around a 'big name' brand and to demonstrate that you have mastered its distinctive style and ethos. Initiation and ingratiation here become merged in a single rite of passage, typically these days in the coming out of your first publication in a peer reviewed journal. Of course where peers review, rivalry is never far away. From a psychoanalytic viewpoint intellectual gang formation is an all too familiar story: oedipal dynamics hitherto embedded in patriarchal orders of knowledge being displaced into a struggle between rival pretenders over the intellectual succession. The disciples square up against the followers of rival 'names' only then to fall out amongst themselves over the 'true interpretation of the founders' work, the whole process of ambivalence being overdetermined by the emotional need for each new generation to assert its privileged access to the zeitgeist by rubbishing the achievements of the 'old guard'.

At a personal rather than institutional level, the tension between vocation and career, or apprenticeship and inheritance can still constitute a major moral dilemma: whether it is nobler in the mind to hold to the difficult path of independent craftsmanship or creative endeavour and run the risk of falling out of favour with the intellectual fashion houses; or whether it is more sensible to make your fortune by outgunning or outrunning your fellow bratpackers, and by opposing, join them, that is the question on which many a memoir of the 'self made' writer turns.

But however well this works as a dramatic device the terms of the dilemma itself are rapidly becoming obsolete. In Academe the abolition of tenure, and the introduction of short-term teaching and research contracts is dismantling the career structure founded on collegiate loyalty or reputation. The advent of the 'scholar entrepreneur' as a role model for young aspirants is one sign of these new times. The aim of holding down any academic post now becomes to accumulate as much intellectual capital as one can in order to move on and transfer it to another more prestigious and better paying institution as quickly as possible. Equally the subsuming of what used to be called the fine, or high arts within today's creative industries has tended to assimilate even the most anarchic aesthetic impulse to the profit motives of the small business enterprise. Neither an avant garde nor a bohemian subculture is required to keep this party going, only the continuing interest of the media. And now that almost every established writer has an agent, and with a proliferation of residencies, 'creativity teaching' and prizes to compete for, each piece of work, whatever its personal source of inspiration is likely to be part of a considered career move.

So the question becomes is it possible for wannabe academics or writers to still pursue a 'career' as a horses for courses race to the top despite the absence of a stable structure? Or do we have to adopt the other (pre and postmodern) sense of the word - careering about from project to project, reinventing ourselves as we go, in grotesque parody of Marx's vision of what the world would be like when people controlled their own destinies?

THE RISE AND FALL OF THE POSTMODERN ACADEMY

In *One Market Under God* Thomas Frank has shown us how the values and even institutions of 1960s counter culture came to power the creative industries of the 1980s; en route the gurus of 'new age' capitalism ushered in a form of pseudo non coercive management based on maximising individual initiative, information networking and peer group pressure to drive up productivity. The 'inner foreman' was hailed as a far more effective goad than the carrot and stick approach favoured by Fordist line managers. The result, as devotees of 'The Office' will know, was a happy clappy workplace culture which hollowed out any real grounds of human solidarity whilst barely repressing a sense of profound alienation operating under its surface bonhomie.

Yet this is only one part of the story. It was the development of that peculiar epistemological panic known as postmodernism amongst the radicalised 'post 68' generation of university students and teachers that has provided the central reference point for debates about the impact of globalisation upon national cultures and economies. The direction which these debates have taken and their impact on intellectual life both inside and outside the Academy turns on a paradox: a movement originating in a largely philosophical critique of the totalising abstractions of Western Reason, and their tyrannical application to other societies and cultures, succeeded in creating an epistemological order premised on a 'flexible' and 'knowing' subjectivity perfectly adapted to the requirements of a fully marketised knowledge economy, an economy which, its advocates argue, has been at the cutting edge of globalisation since the 1980s.

To understand what role the Academy has played, as a crucial point of mediation between the organisation of knowledge and the economy, we have to go back to what it was in the Western university that the 1960s student movement objected to: namely it's role in promoting an elitist version of the national culture as a civilising mission while advocating norms of scientific rationality that turned out, on closer inspection, to be a thinly disguised imperialist agenda. The organisation of these elements into an administered system of knowledge that was at once hierarchical and bureaucratic, ruled over as it was by the infamous 'pedagogic gerontocracy' was a special source of outrage. Yet in fact, saving the oedipal idioms of youth culture, the main thrust of the critique lay quite elsewhere. It turned on the ways the liberal university was being transformed into a modern corporate enterprise, sacrificing its intellectual autonomy to the research needs of the military industrial complex. So what was being attacked at one moment - the persistence of 'Ivory Tower' attitudes - was at another being implicitly supported as a defence against surrender to market forces. As we will see this same ambivalence was to shape much more recent responses to the 'crisis of the university'.

More immediately the impact of the days of rage was to empower the student, not as a revolutionary subject but as a sovereign consumer. From the early 1970s, as higher education began to expand beyond its traditionally narrow class and race banding, student demand increasingly dictated what was taught. Once disciplines were marketised, only those which attracted sufficient student numbers could establish a critical academic mass and hence sustain a quality staff research culture. So what was teachable has ultimately come to determine what is researchable. At the same time only those institutions with sufficient academic prestige to claim honorary 'Humboldt status' (that is to say, community of scholarship trappings plus state of the art library and science labs) could properly compete in the global marketplace for staff and students. The newly upgraded universities were dependent, as they had been before as polytechnics, on recruiting local student intakes and staff who had a special commitment to teach them.

There was another shift in the axis of knowledge power. In the 1960s and 1970s the 'worldly' disciplines of political and economic science, radicalised by the rediscovery of Marxism amongst a younger generation of scholars, displaced 'unworldly' philosophy and mathematics as centres of intellectual excitement and innovation. Yet once their Marxisant moment was over - and it did not last long - politics and economics faculties quickly took a more utilitarian turn, often amalgamating into Business Schools, where links with industry, commerce and government could be pursued unfettered by the toils of ideology critique.

In the late 1970s, in the spaces first opened up and then evacuated by the revival of Marxian political economy, postmodern philosophy developed its critique of knowledge power and the aestheticisation of everyday life. The postmodern turn coincided with the emergence of Cultural Studies as a new academic configuration, and the fate of the two has been closely bound up ever since. 'Po-Mo' enabled Cultural Studies to assert a distinctive identity and to edge out the longer established - and hence ideologically compromised - 'Humboldian' disciplines. French po-mo philosophers became international celebrities almost overnight - reinventing the intellectual as a global/local commentator on the post everything Zeitgeist, whilst philosophy departments either joined the fray or went into rapid meltdown. At the same time Po-Mo connected Cultural Studies to wider developments within the visual arts, literature and the media which were crystallising into a market oriented cultural economy outside the university.

There was another sense in which Cultural Studies provided a bridge between the new knowledge paradigm and global economic imperatives. It was not an inter-disciplinary project in the strict sense in so far as it did not issue from any argument between or within disciplines that studied culture (that is to say, anthropology, history, sociology, linguistics, literature, and psychology). Rather CS opportunistically appropriated (some would say cannibalised) discursive elements from each and all of these intellectual traditions (especially literature and anthropology) and integrated them syncretically into a common syntax focussed around a set of ideological topics or themes. This fitted in well with the priorities of the new academic enterprise culture in so far as topic focussed studies lent themselves to niche marketing. At the same time the radical impetus which Cultural Studies gave to the questioning of the Eurocentric and patriarchal orders of knowledge associated with the Humbold disciplines resonated with the multicultural disposition of the post 1968 student body formed by the widening of access to higher education.

But by the same token the break up of disciplinary knowledge in the arts and humanities created a space for new modularised forms of examinable knowledge in the Higher Education curriculum. The 'hybridity' of CS lent itself admirably to these new formats which in turn harmonised very well with styles of knowledge presentation and information networking being demanded by employers in the new economy.[2]

A colleague of mine once described the modular curriculum as being about students learning less and less about more and more, from teachers who know more and more about less and less. However radical the initial content of Cultural Studies, the form of its academic transmission remained on the conservative side of knowledge power.[3] In Basil Bernstein's terms its hidden curriculum entails a shift from strong to weak classification, whilst its mode of pedagogic delivery moves from weak to strong framing. Modularisation actually shores up the specialised pedagogic devices which enable teachers to instruct and examine students in the competent performance of routine procedures of knowledge impression management: essay writing and portfolio presentation. And then, once you start to vocationalise the modular curriculum you can generate a whole range of hitherto unheard of, academic specialisms offering flexi-degrees in everything from surfing with equestrian studies to hotel management and comparative cuisine.

In principle, of course, postmodernism challenges the foundations of pedagogic authority. A hermeneutics of generalised suspicion regarding the proclaimed truth of texts, once transferred to an educational context, tends to undermine faith in all sources of received wisdom. Logically the pedagogic task becomes to transfer to students the critical skills needed to de-mystify or de-construct the subtext of what they are being taught. Some of the more radical exponents of Po-Mo did in fact try to do just this, albeit in forms of argumentation of such theoretical density as to render them largely unintelligible to their intended student audience!

In practice Cultural Studies helped to institutionalise postmodernism as a corpus of texts to be studied within the Academy, thus neutralising its more subversive pedagogic implications. Along with this textualisation went a disengagement from empirical research. Conceptually the social was dissolved into its various media of collective representation, and methodologically there was a flight from any unmediated encounter with the Other. Once culture was enclosed within itself, either by being disconnected from the social, or by dissolving the social into it, the way was open to retreat from the politics of situated knowledge in favour of growing involvement with the ideoscapes and mediaflows of the global cultural economy. 'Have Cultural theory - Will Travel' became the visiting card of the first fully-fledged intelligentsia to be thrown up by new age capitalism in it's own image. None of this was achieved without a prolonged struggle against the 'old guard' who held on to Gramsci or Raymond Williams as their guiding lights, but the outcome was never in doubt. The textual turn saw off the critics and walled Cultural Studies up in the library, from whence, some of us have not ceased attempting to liberate it.

To summarise the argument so far: postmodernism far from destroying

2. Let us not forget that modularisation was first developed as a way introducing principles of flexible specialisation into the organisation of production in the post Fordist factory.

3. For a discussion of this point see Francis Mulhern *Culture/Metaculture*, Verso, London, 2000.

the authority of the Academy, as some critics warned it might, facilitated its transition from an elite quasi autonomous institution of national learning into a fully fledged consumer enterprise driven by corporate branding and marketing strategies. Cultural Studies played a key role in this process. Often behind the backs of its most passionate advocates it provided a conduit through which Po-Mo ideas could infiltrate and destabilise the Humboldian curriculum. By powerfully legitimating the bricolage degree in a way which paralleled the strategies of knowledge management being adopted by the new economy, and by developing a style of niche marketing that fitted in with the new academic enterprise culture, CS helped to break the mould set by a more rigid division of academic labour and, however unintentionally and indirectly opened up the way for the introduction of new structures of university governance based on administrative and commercial priorities rather than academic ones.

A parallel could be drawn here with the way the creative industries supported a form of economic regeneration that facilitated the transition from the industrial to the post industrial city. The artists and squatters who moved into the decaying infrastructure of the de-industrialised inner city armed with slogans about community renewal proved to be the advance guard for a process of gentrification which turned these same areas into cultural quarters where only a rich cosmopolitan elite could afford to live. In same way postmodern organisation theory, in the name of promoting intellectual synergy has provided a rationale for the introduction of 'flexibility' as a key performance indicator of academic excellence. It is to this new knowledge managerialism we must now turn.

THE CRISIS OF THE NEO-LIBERAL UNIVERSITY

The 'postmodern' turn coincided with the spread of audit culture into every nook and cranny of academic life as the British government attempted to steer the university into positive, rather than negative engagement with its wider economic environment. Under these circumstances academics, postmodernists or not, had little alternative (if they wanted to keep their jobs) but to go along with moves that reinforced their control over the immediate pedagogic process and hence over students, at the expense of surrendering their power to shape the role of the university in the wider society.

The timing and logic of the transition was impeccable. Through the 1990s many commentators pointed out that the more central knowledge was becoming to Western economy and society, the more marginal the university was becoming as a locus for its production and dissemination. Neither the library nor the laboratory need to be based on campus; universities could not compete with museums or on line archives when it came to making knowledge publicly accessible, while think tanks beat them to the draw when it came to winning friends and influencing people in the corridors of power.

Something had to be done, and that something was called, what else, 'modernisation'. The aim in Britain was to resolve the crisis of the university by gearing its different functions much more tightly into specialised niches in the knowledge economy. According to this dispensation the top ranked 'research universities' (that is to say, where there were existing major in-house research facilities supported by a critical mass of internationally rated scholars) will continue to educate the future governing elites of the network society according to the latest inter-disciplinary protocols; meanwhile the task of the less well endowed institutions is to train up routine 'knowledge workers' by means of a thoroughly vocationalised curriculum while undertaking some applied research or as it is now called ' knowledge transfer activity' to help balance the budget.

'Modernisation' introduced standardised measures of academic productivity within a rigidified two tier HE system and en route intensified processes of academic credential inflation. It also brought greater interference in the way universities, and even faculties are run as the 'disciplines' of the market and public accountancy penetrate into the everyday conduct of teaching and research. A few scholarly eccentrics may be tolerated, especially if they are inspirational teachers or bring in research money, but the new movers and shakers are evangelical bureaucrats wielding mission statements and checklists and talking in acronyms. It all makes for interesting campus novels, but means that many universities are increasingly stressful and unpleasant places in which to work.

Under these circumstances it is not surprising that many erstwhile 1960s student radicals, who have now graduated to positions of power within the Academy have viewed these developments with considerable alarm. Especially if they are located in the 'polyversities', as many are, they find themselves arguing for a return to the academic gold standard (alias the RAE) as a means of resisting the dilution of their disciplines, the de-skilling of their teaching and the devaluing of their research knowledge. This defence of the Academy has taken two forms: maintaining increased vigilance over procedural academic knowledge, and its modes of transmission and evaluation; and defending a 'pure' research culture in which peer review and what has been called para-citology - the authorisation of ones own texts by constant referential and often deferential citation of others - become the defining methods of quality control.

This bizarre mixture of monologic pedagogy and compulsive inter-textuality has unfortunately only served to intensify professional anxieties of influence and rivalry; it leads, for example, to the practice of academic cloning whereby each staff caucus strengthens it's niche in the academic market place by only recruiting those who share similar research interests or attitudes; it also tends to produce heavily defended academic subjects hostile to the emergence of any thinking that upsets (de-centres?) the subjects/ positions in which they have such a strong career investment. In other words it results in a culture strongly opposed to any intellectual innovation not of its own making.

It would not be the first, or the last time that political radicals of yesteryear have turned into 'the people we warned our children against becoming', as pension rights assume greater importance in life plans than street cred. Those of us who began with the promise or the threat to become the gravediggers of capitalism have found that we have dug our own graves, behind our own backs, first by abolishing the 'dictatorship of the professoriat' in defence of a more generous vision of educational possibility that was subsequently exploited as a market opportunity and then by struggling to reinstate it as a last maginot line of defence against the gospel of neo-liberal modernisation preached by government ministers, business tycoons and some Vice Chancellors.

This convoluted trajectory is nowhere more poignantly present than in the current predicament of Cultural Studies. The ancient seats of learning were quick to incorporate postmodern perspectives to enliven their humanities departments, but did not give institutional houseroom to CS as a separate department of knowledge. CS departments did sprout and flourish in the polyversities, but here they have suffered from the increasing vocationalising of the curriculum. Media and increasingly multimedia studies is now increasingly replacing CS in terms of student numbers and prestige: designing websites, or making promo music videos is where the action is, not engaging with complex intellectual debates. In my personal view if CS has a future it may well be in developing a critical but also practical engagement with issues such as urban planning, tourism, heritage and the environment. It will certainly not survive for long as a bastion of postmodern theorisation disengaged from the cultural economy.

CURIOUSER AND CURIOUSER

Alongside the developments I have briefly sketched there runs a counter culture, a counter narrative which is worth more of a guided tour than I can manage here. In Europe we might start with the mendicant religious orders of the middle ages, especially the friars whom Gramsci took as his model for the organic intellectual. We might spend some time with the troubadours and wandering scholars, and trace the links between their peregrinations and some of the key itineraries of Renaissance thought. We'd certainly visit Cordoba and listen to the debates between Jewish, Christian and Islamic scholars and scientists for and against Aristotle's and Plato's views on the origins of ideas. Later on we might spend time with the encyclopaedists, or the practitioners of Vico's gaya scienza, and mend our fences with maverick thinkers who refused to patent their own ideas or respect other peoples intellectual property rights. Coming up to the present we could summon up a whole cast of tricksters, cyborgs and other intellectual shape shifters who seek to unsettle the distinctions between high and low culture, or between the discourses of mind, matter and machine.

For all their differences, and they *are* a very motley crew, these figures have a number of common characteristics. One is that they travel light, they carry a version of a laboratory and/or library around in their heads without requiring a great deal of institutional apparatus to sustain their work. Unlike the Professor of Sinology in Elias Canetti's *Auto da Fe* they do not need someone to unpack the books from their heads so they can sleep at nights, Nor are they dependant on expensive equipment to conduct their experiments because the centre of calculation can be the back of an envelope. They take lines of thought for a walk or a song and dance wherever they happen to be - in a jazz group, or a head to head debate, scribbling in their notebooks, or explaining to children why the earth is not the centre of the universe. They form part of a subterranean tradition which links the history of popular curiosity to the counter intuitive procedures of empirical investigation.

The second common feature is an attitude of mind towards the world. It amounts to that anti-systemic system of sceptical engagement with the real that Carlo Ginzburg has called the conjectural method. In his brilliant essay on Freud, Morelli and Sherlock Homes, Ginzberg identifies a set of common semiotic procedures linking the investigative practices of psychoanalysis, pictorial and textual analysis, medical and forensic science, archaeology, ethno-botany, detective stories, and some forms of popular curiosity. In each case an enigmatic and apparently insignificant detail, a footprint, a sudden untoward gesture or throwaway remark, a shard of pottery, a cigarette burn on an armchair, a piece of math or science that does not 'add up', is made to take on a specific and highly overdetermined significance within a wider but still mysterious framework of meaning. This wider picture is at first entirely unknown, but gradually, through the work of piecing together apparently unrelated fragments the hidden pattern emerges, so that they form a coherent narrative which at its best also explains and dissolves the original mystery in a practically useful or aesthetically satisfying way. Curiosity is here provisionally reunited with its object, by a route that is both normative and speculative, strategic and unrepeatable.

Conjectural thinkers need large amounts of 'idle curiosity' and enough time to pursue what might turn out to be totally useless ideas. Nevertheless they pursue a form of inter-disciplinarity that owes nothing to opportunistic syncretism but is strategic to particular purposes of research.

Finally and perhaps most importantly the conjectural method challenges the 'hard' masculinist values of productivity that have come to dominate both library scholarship and laboratory experiment. Instead of measuring the size of your intellect by the length of your CV, or your publications list, it is the precision of the observation, the elegance of the formulation, the quality of engagement with the problem that counts. The muses of both arts and science have always celebrated these 'feminine virtues' associated with the counter intuitive grasp of what is hidden from or goes against the grain of common sense.

Today far from becoming obsolete, freelance intellectuals continue to find niches, however tenuous and untenured, in the market place of ideas. Of course free spirits are all too easily captured by the spirit of free enterprise, and it certainly does not do to romanticise the situation of people who often eke out a living on the margins of Academe. But perhaps there is also a way of employing this impulse of rational curiosity to rather more sustained purpose, to renew intellectual life in the university itself.

RETURN TO THE SECRET GARDEN

What would happen if we put a group of conjectural thinkers together in a latter day Macy Symposium and asked them to reformulate the idea of the university in a way that neither harked back to the Ivory Tower elitism of the old Liberal academy nor espoused the crude commercialism of its neo-liberal successor? What might *this* third way look like?

The group might start by looking at research culture. They might note that customarily populations who live within easy travelling distance of a university campus can expect to find almost every aspect of their personal and social lives come under investigation. Their health and marriage patterns, their eating and reading habits, their sex lives and political opinions all are grist to the academic mill. Their role as informants is simply to provide the raw data which is transformed by students and staff into intellectual capital, accruing to the professional reputation of the researchers and to the public name - and meaning - of the university as a centre of academic excellence. This process is often mystified by research rhetorics which talk about the long term benefits to the wider community, or even to the informants themselves, but such payoffs are neither estimable, nor do they enter into the short term calculations of those who volunteer their services. They do so, in the main, because their role as informants potentially offers a form of legitimate if still peripheral participation in the production of knowledge, a role they have been otherwise denied by the educational system.

So the conclusion might be that if academic research is to do more than treat people as 'lab fodder' then it must build on this starting point and encourage them to play a much bigger part in its design, delivery and dissemination. It might perhaps be better, and more accurate, for example, to describe them as consultants rather than informants, and indeed to consult them about the kinds of research questions to be asked, to inquire into their own conjectures as to the nature of the phenomenon under investigation, and to, at the very least, treat them as active subjects in the co-construction of the research story. In the case of the very old, the very young, the very ill or the very mad, this may not be possible, but such a dialogical approach is more practicable than is often allowed for in the standard text books on research methodology.

The embedding of empirical research in strategies for building the capacity for critical conjecture within the communities served by the university thus becomes one key way of widening access to higher education. Another might be to reform the teaching process so that it transfers research skills to students in a way that enables them to engage more directly in tackling the problems facing these same communities. For example, the Shopfront project run by University for Technology and Science in Sydney, has run a successful government funded scheme which provides training and support for research students who want to ground their PhD studies in intellectual work that is of direct use and benefit to disadvantaged minorities in the city. Through a lengthy process of negotiation a contract is drawn up between the two parties, guaranteeing on one side the need of the student to pursue research without interference and with the full co-operation of the community and on the other the need of the community to have the issues they want raised fully addressed and communicated in a useable form in this work. The students end up with a PhD and a lot of professional experience they would not otherwise have; the community ends up with reports that provide them with some clear guidelines for future action or with environmental and cultural projects that contribute directly to improving the quality of their lives.

Roskilde University in Denmark runs an undergraduate programme which also involves an active problem solving pedagogy, organising the students into interdisciplinary research teams from the word go. Building on these first principles, our think tank might recommend a foundation year in which students from arts, humanities and science backgrounds are mixed together and have a core programme of lectures and seminars in which mathematicians, musicians, architects, linguists, psychologists, medical sociologists and so on, all discuss their own research attitude and its big questions: why is something the way it is and not some other way, how did it get like that, what if anything would have made for a different result and what can I interestingly say about it. The 'it' might be Godel's theorem, or the law of Tort, Mozart's requiem or the leaning tower of Pisa, autism or the Black Death, environmental pollution, or institutional racism. What the something is, is less important, *at this stage*, than the fact that the students are learning the basic, and highly transferable skills, of a conjectural approach.

This might be followed by an intermediate year based in faculty studies, where students learn the elementary structures of scholarly and experimental disciplines, a propaideutics in which the generative grammar of a specific area of knowledge is acquired. Needless to say in this multicultural university faculties would not be organised along the old divisions of nature and culture, mind and body, individual and society that have so bedevilled Western thought. For example one faculty might bring together studies in biology and biography, putting neuroscience, psychoanalysis and narratology into concerted conversation around the development of an ecological model of mind - not just for the intellectual excitement it might generate, but because it might lead to, say, a better understanding of certain memory disorders.

The final year might be spent in small research teams working on a collaborative project led by a senior member of staff, worrying at a specific research question, learning more about both ways of conceptualising issues and empirical procedures, learning how to think across as well as within disciplines, how to write up reports, and present findings to both expert and lay audiences. The questions to be addressed might also be related to specific problems identified as being important to particular communities of concern.

None of this is exactly new. Many of these ideas have been tried and tested and found to work and there are examples of conjectural pedagogics to be found scattered across the HE curriculum. But they are rarely allowed to cohere into a deliberative approach or to permeate the whole curriculum along the lines which Michel Serres suggested in the *Troubadour of Knowledge*. In his book, Serres critiques the current shift from the journey to the destination (alias the performance indicator) as the telos of education, a shift which has transformed the pedagogue from an intellectual guide and mentor to what the current OED entry variously describes as: a preceptor, usually with negative connotations: a dogmatist, or in J.S. Mill's famous term: a member of the pedantocracy. In other words someone who tells but no longer shows.

Serres argues that we need to return to the original Greek meaning of the word pedagogy, in a way that makes teaching and research into a single indissoluble intellectual project. In the original Greek meaning of the term the pedagogue is the one who does the school run, who not only takes the student to and from the place of instruction, but who makes the journey itself into an educational experience: not going in a straight line from A to B, but wandering off the beaten track, challenging assumptions, questioning everything that makes you feel at home even and especially in your own sense of alienation or otherness. Attempting to return pedagogy to its founding moment Serres writes to his imaginary student, his reader, in the following terms:

> Study, work, something will always come of it. And after? For there to be an after, I mean some kind of future that goes beyond a copy, leave the library (and I would have to add the laboratory) - to run in the fresh air. If you remain inside you will never write anything but books made of books (I would add, experiment with others' experiments). That knowledge, excellent in itself, contributes to instruction, but the goal of the other kind is something other than itself. Depart, go out, become many, brave the outside world, split off somewhere else. These are the first foreign things, the varieties of alterity, initial means of being exposed. For there is no learning without exposure, often dangerous, to the other, to foreign things.

This principle deliberately applies to all aspects of intellectual work. If the distinction between public intellectual and private scholar, researcher and teacher is here abandoned, it is not in order to reduce them to the lowest common denominator but rather to assert their highest common factor as bearers of a shared principle of curiosity about the world both inside and outside the mind, that constitutes knowledge's Other Scene.

As students - and especially those eternal students who are researchers - we need to find mentors, whether inside or outside the Academy, who can help us lose and find our way along this path. Here is how one such figure, a senior administrator, was recently described to me:

> He treats the university a bit like a garden. There are all these plants needing water. It may takes some time for him to get round to all of them, but each gets its turn. He's likely to take as much if not more trouble with a prickly cactus which may be stubbornly refusing to flower, as he does with some exotic bloom that he might just think needs a bit of pruning back. He sometimes takes risks, puts hardy annuals next to perennials, a cactus next to violets, he's sometimes a bit remiss about weeding, it doesn't always come off, but you'd be amazed how often it does.

Gardening metaphors are always a bit suspect, given the role they have played historically in naturalising positions of self cultivation on the part of our national elite. Yet there are few places where such a rich ecology of knowledge, drawing on and combining such various arts and sciences, connecting popular culture and professional expertise , can be said to flourish across such a broad range of social sites. And perhaps it is a better model than most for the kind of a university we might all want to work in, somewhere to nurture our best hopes for making the worlds we so variously inhabit more interesting and more shareable with our students, our colleagues and our fellow citizens.

PROSPECTS FOR KNOWLEDGE WORK: CRITICAL ENGAGEMENT OR EXPERT CONSCRIPTION?

Peter Scott

The university, still (just about) the premier knowledge institution, faces an unfamiliar dilemma at the beginning of the twenty-first century. Never more relevant: the development of a knowledge-based and skills-intensive society means that its socio-economic impacts are no longer mediated through other institutions, but are direct; the permeability of class structures and fluidity of social identities have made participation in higher education (and subsequent 'graduateness') key identifiers of individual status and personal esteem. Never less relevant: the very engagement with (and conscription into?) these wider economic and social systems have eroded the autonomy of the university and reduced its critical potential (or, at any rate, its critical pretensions). Moreover, some would argue, these processes of engagement and conscription have had a 'blow-back' effect. The organisational culture of the university, at any rate in its ideal(ised) form, was once characterised by institutional (and, crucially, sub-institutional) autonomy and academic freedom, which has often been summed up - perhaps misleadingly - in the word 'collegiality'. Now it has been radically modified to accommodate these new forces, in the process acquiring new characteristics such as a much higher degree of 'business' accountability (which must be clearly distinguished from cultural responsibility), the growth of 'managed' rather than 'collegial' environments and an erosion of former distinctions between 'pure' and 'applied' knowledge, research and development, education and training. Consequently the university has a different job to do, much more complex (and crucial?) but also much less distinctive (in the sense of being distinguishable from the jobs of other 'knowledge' institutions), and the university has also become a different place, a different kind of organisation.

For those on the Left the emergence of the powerful-but-powerless university poses a cruel dilemma. They - we - must welcome the closer engagement of higher education with wider society because the autonomy of the (traditional) university enabled it to avoid its democratic responsibilities and to nurture a culture of elitism, both social and intellectual. The extension of the higher education 'franchise', whether through a refinement/modernisation of the existing model by founding new universities in the 1960s or through the articulation of alternative models which was (perhaps) one of the intentions behind the establishment of the former polytechnics, has been a key element in the wider democratisation and liberalisation of British society. Yet the society we imagined higher education would engage was, broadly, a social democratic polity which, although not utterly destroyed, has been substantially eroded since 1979. The emphasis in widening participation in higher education has shifted from individual enlightenment and cultural emancipation, which at times was expressed in crypto- or quasi-aesthetic terms (the values of Lawrence and Leavis transmuted through the language of post-war social science), to economic empowerment, designed to combat social exclusion (and dependence) and to develop the skills needed to compete in a global market economy. The result is a profound ambivalence on the Left: on the one hand, a celebration of the social and economic engagement of modern higher education systems; on the other, regret that the organisational (and, more alarmingly, intellectual) bases for critical and cultural engagement are being lost.

My thesis is that, while we must recognise, and respect the reasons for, this ambivalence, the creative potential of mass higher education systems and more distributed knowledge systems will - in the long haul - outweigh their apparent short-term tendencies to privilege largely utilitarian interpretations of the purposes of higher education and to promote an essentially instrumental conception of knowledge. This will happen, not by retreating to older-fashioned 'liberal' accounts of university education nor by attempting vainly to resurrect the 'autonomy' of science but by 'going with the grain' and recognising the deep-down democratic dynamics of mass higher education and new knowledge production systems. Some of the more negative features of the contemporary university - the spread of so-called 'managerialism' and, much more serious, the rise of anti-intellectualism - are likely to be temporary phenomena during a period of transition from élite to mass (or, better, democratic) higher education and from closed (and holistic) to open (and pluralistic) knowledge systems.

CONCEPTIONS OF KNOWLEDGE

Three broad conceptions of knowledge can be identified, although inevitably they have intertwined and overlapped through history. The first is of knowledge as a source of power and status, and the legitimation of that power and status. Such knowledge was originally regarded as - literally - sacred, God-given, not-to-tampered-with and so not knowledge at all in terms of modern science. It was - deliberately - restricted to a small social élite, sometimes to a priestly caste. They were the 'knowledge workers' of pre-modern society. As states and societies grew more complex, and with the spread of literacy, this conception of knowledge had to be modified. First lay aristocracies and later the emergent middle class demanded the right to participate in this primitive 'knowledge economy'. As a result, the identification of access to knowledge with high and/or rising social status was actually increased. The ghost of that identification still haunts more modern conceptions of knowledge. It is apparent in contemporary statistics such as the (depressingly) tight correlations between social class, success in school examinations and choice of university.

The second conception is of knowledge as intervention, as an agent of change. This has been interpreted in a variety of ways. One dates back to the Reformation (and Counter-Reformation), more radical and urgent intellectual revolutions than the Renaissance, suffused with an apparently classical rationalism, which so often has been allowed to overshadow them. A remarkable demonstration of that radical potential was the emergence of the eighteenth-century Scottish Enlightenment out of dour and divided Calvinist Scotland of the century before.[1] But it is also possible to see French Jansenism as a precursor of Enlightenment values. A second example of knowledge-as-intervention, of course, was the transformation of revolutionary Enlightenment at the end of the eighteenth century and beginning of the nineteenth century into revolutionary Romanticism, self-knowledge and self-realisation through art, from Goethe's *Young Werther* to Freud's *Interpretation of Dreams*. A third example, and perhaps the best known, is the rise of the Left with its massive totem in the person of Marx (mirrored by the equally powerful and significant rise of the Right, conveniently and expediently down-played since the *Götterdämmerung* of Nazism). Both were responses to the challenges posed by the emergence of industrial, secular and mass societies. Both, too, were imbued with earlier Enlightenment and Romantic notions, as the work of seminal figures like Georg Lukács and Walter Benjamin demonstrates. Benjamin's study of the life-world of nineteenth-century Paris is an unsurpassed example of the synthesis of radical and aesthetic ideas.[2]

The third conception is knowledge-as-science, the conception that is now dominant in the modern world (although questioned, of course, by postmodernists). It, too, had close links with the Enlightenment, although its relationship with more aesthetic (if not always wholly Romantic) conceptions of knowledge was always troubled; the debates between Arnold and Huxley in the nineteenth century and Leavis and Snow in the twentieth are only the best known of a series of such encounters which rumble on unresolved. This third conception of knowledge drew its power and influence from two sources. The first was its bold claim to be able to uncover the truth about the natural and, rather less confidently, the social worlds. The second was its, far from unambiguous, links with technology - and, through these links, with the generation of economic wealth and social improvement. These two sources tended to coalesce into notions of expertise and professionalism. The emphasis was placed on 'method', whether particular methodologies of scientific enquiry such as empirical research or more general methodologies for the regulation and reproduction of professional élites. Consequently, but perhaps mistakenly, this third conception of knowledge became emblematic of modernity. Its claims of universalism cloaked its specific origins, geographical and intellectual. Accordingly an arrogance was bred that has yet to be extinguished. Even today the tensions between

1. Charles Camic, *Experience and Enlightenment: Socialization for Cultural Change in Eighteenth-Century Scotland*, Edinburgh, Edinburgh University Press, 1983.

2. Walter Benjamin, *The Arcades Project*, H. Eiland and K. McLaughlin (trans), Cambridge, Mass., Belknap Press, 1999.

the 'West' and the Moslem world is explained by some in terms of the latter's inability or refusal to adopt a 'scientific' outlook - bad history but terribly effective politics.

CONCEPTIONS OF KNOWLEDGE IN THE MODERN UNIVERSITY

All three conceptions of knowledge can be observed in the practice of modern higher education systems and are reflected in contemporary knowledge production systems. Contrary to the expectations of some the links between mass higher education system and 'social' credentialisation are just as tight as they were in the era of élite higher education. Indeed they may be even tighter. As class, ethnic and gender distinctions have been eroded (although far from extinguished) as the primary identifiers of social status, participation in higher education has become a more significant element in 'fixing' status and (relative) position within our more volatile and chaotic contemporary society. To the extent that participation in higher education can be aligned with initiation into (or, at any rate, familiarity with) academic culture(s), the latter may even have become more central to the allocation of status (and even power) positions within society.

Of course, an alternative account is possible. The key advantage conferred by participation in higher education may not be so much the access it offers to academic culture(s) (and so to knowledge-as-power/status) but in its capacity as an ersatz-consumer good. Seen in this perhaps disturbing light a university degree is like an Armani suit, a BMW or a second-home in the Cotswolds, an element within a high-status life-style, an entry-ticket to a bourgeois Zeitgeist. Unlike the first account of the links between higher education and social stratification which emphasises the intrinsic value of access to higher-status academic and professional cultures, this second account concentrates almost exclusively on the externalities of a higher education. But there may be dangers in drawing too sharp a distinction between these two accounts: their consequences are the same - or similar.

The second conception of knowledge-as-intervention is alive, although not perhaps so well. A major driver of the expansion of higher education during the past half-century or more has been pressure from below. As first elementary education and later secondary education become universal and compulsory, the need to make available more places for students in universities and colleges increased. Success bred success. However, the intellectual/ideological dimension was also crucial - both negatively, in the sense that the arguments that 'more means worse', of the high-priests of academic elitism, had to be, if not defeated, at least faced down (which was achieved with the, perhaps unexpected, assistance of the Robbins report in the early 1960s); and also positively, in the sense that there were powerful and persuasive academic and cultural arguments made in support of further expansion. At key moments decisive interventions were made. In the 1950s and 1960s the extra-mural and Workers Education Association tradition was influential in shaping the agenda for the new universities - for example, Asa Briggs, the Leeds historian turned Sussex Vice-Chancellor, straddled both worlds. At the same time, it influenced the new intellectual agendas emerging in the humanities and social sciences, through the agency of people like Richard Hoggart (in cultural studies) and E.P. Thompson (in history). The Open University project was animated by similar forces and values. Even the new polytechnics were hailed - initially - as 'people's universities'. The common thread running through these very different endeavours was the idea of social and cultural transformation, derived from the conception of knowledge-as-intervention.

The third conception of knowledge-as-science, of course, permeates mass higher education and contemporary knowledge production systems. Despite the onslaughts of 'anti-science' (in the form of environmental and ecological doomsters and fundamentalist resisters), and in the insidious effects of postmodernists, positivistically inclined science has survived and thrived. Indeed, to the extent that the ideas of 'knowledge society' and 'globalisation' have encouraged national prestige and geopolitical rivalry to be recast in terms of league-tables of Nobel Prize winners rather than armies and fleets, 'basic' science and 'blue skies' research may even have made a come-back - disguised, of course, in both cases under the seductive but meaningless 'world-class' label. The, rhetorical and actual, emergence of the 'knowledge society' has also strengthened the assumed links between science and technology, which is the other source of the power and prestige of this third conception of knowledge. Technology has ceased to be a sufficiently capacious and comprehensive category; for example, nowadays the humanities are yoked to the 'creative industries' in a disconcertingly utilitarian *schema*. So a third, and even more persuasive, term is now employed - innovation - to describe these allegedly vital connections between knowledge, wealth and social well being. Modern higher education systems are seen as contributing in various ways - through élite research universities and their involvement in 'world-class' science; and through mass institutions which train middle-rank 'knowledge workers' and engage in 'knowledge transfer'.

All three conceptions of knowledge, therefore, continue to co-exist in modern higher education systems, often in alarming intimacy. Their coexistence helps to explain the epi-phenomena that are regarded by some as so troubling. One is the evident 'mission stretch' from which so many higher education institutions now suffer - and its corollary, the (vain) desire to establish new demarcations and divisions of labour among institutions; both, confusingly, labelled 'diversity'. Another is the impact of the 'audit society' on higher education - through research and teaching quality assessments (and institutional audits) and proliferating 'initiatives' and 'strategies' by which universities are beguiled and belaboured. A third, already mentioned, is the drive towards 'managerialism', as institutions both struggle to manage their multiple missions and also to adapt other models of organisational culture. But at the heart of these changes, welcomed or despised, is a transformation of the nature of academic (and, more broadly, intellectual) work which, in turn, can be traced back to these competing but overlapping conceptions of knowledge itself.

THE NEW PRODUCTION OF KNOWLEDGE

The dominant conception of knowledge remains that of 'expert' knowledge which combines the two strands of knowledge-as-truth and knowledge-as-technology/innovation. As such it is seen as self-referential, not in the sense that it is irrelevant or 'ivory-tower' but in the sense that it can only be assessed by other experts (peer review). These 'experts' occupy their own, relatively autonomous, terrain - such as universities and research laboratories (and, possibly, museums and other cultural institutions). 'Expert' knowledge is organised according to a clear taxonomy of disciplines, sub-disciplines and finer-grain specialisms, whether derived from academic affinities or professional structures (or a combination of both). It is also 'objective' or 'neutral', not necessarily in the sense that it is unaffected by its environment (for a start political considerations and funding constraints will always be influential) but in the sense that the generation of knowledge can - and must - be clearly distinguished from its subsequent uses.

However, as was indicated in the introduction to this essay, the very success of this dominant paradigm of knowledge has the potential to undermine it. It is burdened with over-expectations of that success which is becoming more and more difficult to deliver, especially in areas far distant from those in which positivistic science has been used to operate. The 'knowledge society' is both the apotheosis and the nemesis of 'expert' knowledge because all, or most, organisations must now be knowledge-based (and, an even more radical thought, because 'we are all knowledge workers now', or else risk exclusion and disenfranchisement). As a result, new discourses of science and knowledge are emerging.

First, there is a discourse of 'regret' that regards the development of more open, fluid and socially embedded knowledge production systems as inimical to the production of high-quality research (as well, potentially, as a threat to free thought and an open society). The Campaign for Academic Freedom and Democracy has been most articulate, and aggressive, in representing this point of view, which is shared by many scientists and scholars. However, there are two problems with this discourse from the perspective of the Left. First, it ignores the elitism and social inequities embodied, perhaps inevitably, in this assertion of the autonomy/hegemony of science. Secondly, it is far from clear that there is any way back to this status quo ante, even if a way back were desirable. The second is a discourse 'modernisation', emphasising the importance of research within a knowledge society - and consequently the need to align research priorities more closely with social, economic and political goals. For example, successive White

Papers - typically with titles such as *Realising Our Potential* - and European 'Framework' research programmes are examples of this second discourse which is currently dominant. Research Councils have also developed 'themed' programmes which amount to much the same thing.

The third is simply a discourse of empirical investigation, if that is not a contradiction because it seeks to use 'expert' knowledge to understand a knowledge system that is moving beyond traditional notions of expertise. For example, the Institute for Scientific Information (ISI) in Philadelphia has used large-scale data-sets to generate citation indices which, despite their imperfections, have increased our understanding of the dominant nodes of scientific production. Research units such as the Science Policy Research Unit (SPRU) at the University of Sussex have done valuable work on changes in patterns of scientific publication - for example, the trend towards multi-institutional authorship (including many more non-university institutions, notably in the health sector) and the growth of so-called 'grey' literature. Finally, the fourth is a discourse of theoretical speculation. Some examples, such as John Ziman's recent book, have attempted to re-justify the traditional autonomy of science and are perhaps better described as part of the first discourse of 'regret'.[3] Others, such as Henry Etzkowitz's conceptualisation of the science-industry-government relationship as a 'triple helix' have embraced, and sought to explain, a new research paradigm but remain firmly within an empirical (and 'expert') tradition.[4] Others again, such as Katrin Knorr-Cetina's work on the dynamics of disciplinary cultures, have adopted an intermediate position.[5]

Another example of this fourth discourse, and the one on which I would like to concentrate, is the ideas developed in two recent books, *The New Production of Knowledge* and *Re-Thinking Science*.[6] The first book introduced the notion of 'Mode 2' knowledge production - and contrasted with 'Mode 1' research (similar, in many ways, to 'expert' knowledge). The idea of 'Mode 2' knowledge production has been taken up by many people in the science policy community - and equally criticised by many others in the field of science studies. Too readily taken up perhaps, it may be thought, because 'Mode 2' has seemed at times to be more than a slogan than a fully worked-through concept.

However, 'Mode 2' knowledge has a number of characteristics that distinguish it from 'Mode 1' science. The first characteristic is that 'Mode 2' knowledge is generated within the context of application - a different notion from that of 'applied science', because the latter term implies that 'pure' science, generated in theoretical/experimental environments, is then 'applied; any technology 'transferred'; and knowledge subsequently 'managed'. The context of application, in contrast, is an attempt to describe the total environment in which scientific problems arise, methodologies were developed, outcomes disseminated and uses defined. The second characteristic of 'Mode 2' knowledge is its transdisciplinarity. Unlike inter- or multi-disciplinary research, trans-disciplinary work is not necessarily

3. John Ziman, *Real Science: what it is, and what it means*, Cambridge, Cambridge University Press, 2000.

4. Henry Etzkowitz and Loet Leydesdorff (eds), *Universities and the Global Knowledge Economy: a Triple Helix of University-Industry-Government Relations*, London, Pinter, 1997.

5. Karin Knorr-Cetina, *Epistemic Cultures: How the Sciences make Knowledge*, Cambridge Mass., Harvard University Press, 1999.

6. Michael Gibbons, Camille Limoges, Helga Nowotny, Simon Schwartzman, Peter Scott and Martin Trow, *The New Production of Knowledge: The Dynamics of Science and Research in Contemporary Societies*, London, Sage, 1994; Helga Nowotny, Peter Scott and Michael Gibbons, *Re-Thinking Science: Knowledge and the Public in an Age of Uncertainty*, Cambridge, Polity Press, 2001.

derived from pre-existing disciplines nor does it always contribute to the formation of new disciplines. 'Mode 2' knowledge, in this trans-disciplinary form, is embodied in the expertise of individual researchers and research (and project?) teams as much as it is encoded in conventional research products such as journal articles or even patents. Of course, it can be argued that the embodiment of scientific knowledge (and the prestige such knowledge confers) in a cadre of experts has been the historical norm, and its embodiment in research artefacts the exception. Seen in this light 'Mode 2' knowledge can hardly be represented as progressive.

The third characteristic of 'Mode 2' knowledge is the much greater diversity of the sites at which knowledge is now produced and an associated phenomenon, the growing heterogeneity in the types of knowledge production. The first phenomenon, of course, is hardly new. Research communities have always been 'virtual' communities that cross national (and cultural) boundaries. But the orderly hierarchies imposed by these 'old' technologies of interaction are now being eroded by a communicative free-for-all. This shift has been intensified by the second phenomenon, the fact that these research communities now have open frontiers which have allowed many new kinds of 'knowledge' organisation - such as Think-Tanks, management consultants, activist groups such as Greenpeace - to join the research game. The fourth characteristic of 'Mode 2' knowledge is its reflexivity. The research process can no longer be characterised as an 'objective' investigation of the natural (or social) world, or as a cool and reductionist interrogation of categorically defined 'others'. Instead it has become a dialogic process, an intense (and perhaps endless) 'conversation' between research actors and research subjects - to such an extent that the basic vocabulary of research (who, whom, what, how) is in danger of losing its significance.

The fifth characteristic is that novel forms of quality control are emerging. Scientific 'peers' can no longer be reliably identified, because there is no longer a stable taxonomy of codified disciplines from which 'peers' can be drawn - *pace* the Research Assessment Exercise. Nor can reductionist forms of quality control be so easily applied to much more broadly framed research questions because the research 'game' is being joined by more and more players. Finally, unchallengeable criteria of quality may no longer be available. Instead there are multiple definitions of quality, which seriously complicate the processes of discrimination, prioritisation and selectivity on which policy-makers and funding agencies rely. But this final characteristic raises its own danger, of a slide into postmodern relativism.

The initial reaction to these ideas as presented in *The New Production of Knowledge* was that they amounted to little more than a legitimation of existing (and often undesirable) trends towards the politicisation and/or commercialisation of research. A particularly incisive criticism was that no account was taken of the unequal distributions of political power, social status, cultural capital and scientific resources in advanced capitalist societies.

Although the 'social' featured prominently in the book - for example, it was argued that society was now speaking back (and forcefully) to science and that knowledge production was now much more socially distributed - little attempt seemed to have been made to offer an analysis of emerging society; instead it was treated as a given. This was the predominant response, particularly from those who occupied the academic heart-lands. But there were others. For example, the emphases on transdisciplinarity, reflexivity and the overlapping of communities of research and communities of practice appealed to those on the academic periphery. It was also clear that there was both a dominant 'right' (or market) interpretation of 'Mode 2' knowledge and a recessive 'left' (or populist) interpretation.

RE-THINKING SCIENCE

Re-Thinking Science attempted to address some of these criticisms - and in doing so allowed 'Mode 2' knowledge to escape from the applied science/ research commercialisation stereotype. First, the relationships between 'science' and 'society' were articulated more clearly, in order to give substance to the twin notions of 'science speaking to society' and 'society speaking back to science'. In the 1970s these relationships were confidently described in terms of the evolution of industrial society into a more advanced form, postindustrialism in which knowledge accessible to (almost) all would replace physical energy and financial resources rationed to the rich and in which the rough edges of ideological conflict would be smoothed away and knowledge prosper.[7] In the past quarter century this optimistic vision has been progressively superseded by other dark images of future society in which, for example, risks have remorselessly accumulated and new hegemonic 'networks' emerged.[8] Neither account - postindustrial prosperity nor postmodern risk - is satisfactory of itself.

Another way to conceptualise these changes is to argue that the great sub-systems of modernity (state, market, culture - and science itself), once clearly partitioned, are becoming increasingly transgressive; and that this fuzziness helps to create the transaction spaces in which 'Mode 2' knowledge develops (and also, perhaps, makes room for new social movements). There are four key characteristics evident both in society and science. The first is the generation of uncertainty/ies, which reduces the possibility of post-positivistic planning - in both science and society. The second is the trend towards self-organisation, which is intimately related to the growth of reflexivity - again in both domains. The third is the emergence of new forms of 'economic rationality' according to which, as in any 'futures' market, the potential of science was measured by its immanent rather than instrumental value. The fourth is the re-constitution of time/space of which the revolution in information and communication technology was only one aspect; more important was the emergence of new spatial-temporal categories which compromised older ideas of sequencing and distancing, so upsetting

7. Daniel Bell, *The End of Ideology: on the exhaustion of the political ideas of the Fifties* (reissued with *The Resumption of History in the New Century*, 2000), Cambridge, Mass., Harvard University Press, 1960/2000; and Daniel Bell, *The Coming of Post-Industrial Society*, London, Heinemann, 1973.

8. Ulrich Beck, *Risk Society: Towards a New Modernity*, Cambridge, Polity Press, 1992; Manuel Castells, *The Information Age: Economy, Society and Culture*, 3 Vols, Oxford, Blackwell, 1996-99.

traditional relational categories.

Secondly, the assertion in *The New Production of Knowledge* that 'Mode 2' knowledge was produced in a 'context of application' was refined into a more developed argument about different forms of contextualisation, so removing any possible doubt about the mistake of a facile identification between such knowledge and applied research. There are three possible forms of contextualisation. The first is so-called 'weak' contextualisation. Counter-intuitively perhaps national R&D programmes are a good example of 'weak' contextualisation because, to succeed, they must (over?) simplify both social and scientific contexts so diminishing the potentiality of both. The second is 'middle-range' contextualisation, where most 'Mode 2' knowledge production is clustered. Here so-called 'trading zones', transaction spaces and what we labelled 'Mode-2 objects' play a crucial role in determining this form of contextualisation in which local contingencies shape synergy and potential. The third is 'strong' contextualisation where powerful reflexive articulations between science and society are at work. This might take highly specific forms, or relate to the interaction between the world of ideas and much wider social movements such as feminism or environmentalism.

The third way in which a more theoretical account of 'Mode 2' knowledge was developed was to argue that this new knowledge form was not merely a secondary phenomenon, contingent/parasitic on 'Mode 1' science, as some critics had suggested. Three pieces of evidence were offered in support of this claim, which was crucial to the argument in *Re-Thinking Science*. The first is that 'Mode 2', especially in its trans-disciplinary dimension, can make a fundamental contribution to the development not only of new methodologies but also of new concepts and theories; the failure to recognise this contribution probably arises from the fact that it is not encoded in disciplinary frameworks or embodied in familiar research products such as journal articles.

The second piece of evidence is that the epistemological core of science, the values in which it is ultimately rooted, is sometimes a mirage; often it is 'empty' (as, for example, when scientific ideas were absorbed by non-host cultures predominantly as technical artefacts without regard to their original normative significance) or, more usually, crowded with competing epistemologies. The third is that reliable knowledge, the traditional goal of scientific inquiry, is no longer (self?) sufficient in the much open knowledge environments that are now emerging; knowledge also needs to be 'socially robust' because its validity is no longer determined solely, or predominantly, by narrowly circumscribed scientific communities but by much wider communities of engagement comprising knowledge producers, disseminators, traders and users.

These arguments have appealed to different, and contrasting, groups. The first has appealed to 'knowledge workers' outside the academic heartlands because it can be seen as legitimating 'alternative' research methods such as action research. The second argument appeals to postmodernists who, mistakenly perhaps, regard it as endorsing relativism, contingency, ambiguity and other postmodern attributes. The third argument is attractive to those who argue that research priorities should be subordinated to political agendas and market forces, although the same argument can be used to support much more radical, and even subversive, positions.

Finally two new ideas were introduced. The first, related to the fuller explication of contextualisation, is the concept of the *agora*, an archaism deliberately chosen to embrace the political arena and the market place - and to go beyond both. The *agora* is the problem-generating and problem-solving environments in which the contextualisation of knowledge production takes place. It is populated not only by arrays of competing 'experts' and the organisations and institutions through which knowledge is generated and traded but also variously jostling 'publics'. It is not simply a political or commercial arena in which research priorities are identified and funded, or an arena in which research findings are disseminated, traded and used. The *agora* is in its own right a domain of primary knowledge production - through which people enter the research process and where 'Mode 2' knowledge is embodied in people, processes and projects. The role of controversies in realising scientific potential is also played out in the *agora*.

The second new idea is that of the context of application. As has already been said this was taken to be one of the key characteristics of 'Mode 2' knowledge in *The New Production of Knowledge*. But it is no longer sufficient. Indeed, to the extent that the context of application implicitly reinforces notions of hierarchy and linearity and to suggest that positivistic predictions of applicability are still possible, it can be regarded as dangerously misleading. Instead, against a background of inherent uncertainty about the future state of knowledge (and of almost everything else) from which, of course, scientific potential is derived, it is necessary to reach beyond the knowable context of application to the unknowable context of implication. It is necessary to reach out and anticipate reflexively the implications of research - and, more broadly, knowledge work.

***

If these ideas are accepted, the idea of 'expert' knowledge may be undermined - although 'qualified' is perhaps better because its staggering success in solving scientific and technical problems cannot be gainsaid. This has a number of implications, both practical and theoretical. Much of research policy - at all levels (Government, Funding Council, University and - less certainly - Departmental) - appears to be driven by assumptions derived from 'expert' (or 'Mode 1') knowledge. Moreover these assumptions are taken as 'givens'; there is little recognition that they themselves are problematising and problematised. The Research Assessment Exercise is the most notable example, although less formal exercises are conducted according to similar principles on a routine basis at every level of the higher education and research system. Although successive reviews of the RAE have acknowledged the need to pay greater attention to a wider range of more eclectic research practices (for example, interdisciplinary research, practice-based research and 'alternative', or less-standard, methodologies), the outcome has always been to endorse the status quo - which is based on a traditional model of peer review, rooted in clearly defined scientific communities. The erosion of such communities is ignored.

The penumbra of policy assumptions that surround the RAE are equally at odds with the account of knowledge production offered in this essay. One assumption is that judgements made by RAE panels are sufficiently robust to be used as a basis not simply for matching resources to research within overall institutional grants (the original intention of the RAE) but for steering research funding aggressively and selectively. In fact, just as RAE (or research council) panel judgements are being used to ever-increasing policy effect, these judgements are becoming more fallible because of the radical changes in how, where, why and for whom knowledge is being produced. Another assumption is that the missions (and so funding) of higher education institutions can be distinguished in terms of their greater or lesser engagement with research, which in turn is based on the assumption that research and teaching are separate activities. In fact, research and teaching are better seen as overlapping activities along a spectrum of 'knowledge work'. Moreover, in practice 'teaching' (or, rather, student learning) now includes a higher proportion of research-like work - for example, projects and group work - while increasing emphasis is placed on communication, dissemination and other forms of transference/translation in 'research'.

At the beginning of this essay I argued that the university, as the premier knowledge institution, faced a cruel dilemma. Perhaps it could be described as a Mephistophelian bargain, to sign away its soul. The emergence of a 'knowledge society' and the impact of 'globalisation' have placed the university in the front-line - as a producer of human capital and so economic wealth, as a promoter of social well being (but social well being as defined by 'establishments', whether Governments or markets) and as an agent of national prestige (because skills, science, ideology are now the weapons of global competition. But its position in the front-line may have undermined its ability to discharge its wider critical and cultural responsibilities. The university is now directly implicated - so it can no longer be allowed to develop its own intellectual agendas or assert its own scientific priorities (except in a purely 'expert' sense); still less to assert its right to offer more radical critiques.

However, this is perhaps to paint too gloomy a picture. The 'knowledge society' is much more than a technological 'fix', a utopia/dystopia powered by the inexorable rise of information and communication technologies; it also has the potential for radical social change, even cultural revolution. Similarly 'globalisation' is more than round-the-clock round-the-globe financial markets, or global brands; it also empowers global resistances (whether to environmental degradation or free-market capitalism) and reanimates 'alternative' knowledge traditions and cultures (whether through their Creolising interaction with the 'West' or by enabling them to use global technologies to build coalitions of the marginal and dispossessed). If the university engages all aspects of the 'knowledge society', and every aspect of 'globalisation', it may recover some of its room for critical manoeuvre. The important changes in 'knowledge work', outlined in this essay, are also grounds for optimism. There are two ways in which the traditional boundaries of scientific knowledge and intellectual culture can be transcended. One is to allow the market - or, more probably, politics as a surrogate for the market - to enter into the research *agora*. The other is to welcome in other, more democratic, forces. Although it is naïve to ignore existing power structures, and their influence over knowledge agendas, it is important to recognise the fluidities and transgressions characteristic of more open knowledge systems. It is equally important to recognise the synergies between these more open knowledge systems and mass higher education systems, the radical (and emancipatory) implications of which cannot be underestimated.

PUBLIC INTELLECTUALS AND THE PUBLIC DOMAIN

Andrew Gamble

Democracy has never been so widespread as a form of government, but it has also seldom been as sickly as it is at present, particularly in those states where it has been longest established. This malaise of democracy has many aspects, but two are currently receiving particular attention, the decline of participation[1] and the decline of the public.[2] They raise fundamental questions about the nature of intellectual work and the role of public intellectuals.

The decline of participation is indicated by continuing falls in turnout at elections, in membership of political parties, in attendance at public meetings, and in membership of voluntary groups. Some have diagnosed a general retreat from civic engagement, a growth of individualism and consumerism, a decline of social capital and a withering of democracy at its roots.[3] If growing numbers of citizens will not even bother to turn out to vote, the legitimacy of the political process is undermined. The political class becomes both isolated and insulated from the electorate it is supposed to represent, absorbed in a self-destructive set of rituals and games which further undermines the willingness of citizens to participate. Political ignorance and apathy increase, and politics becomes increasingly concerned with celebrity, speculation and scandal.

Closely related to the decline of participation is the decline of the *public*. There has been a marked shrinking of the public domain, in the sense of a weakening of the public ethos and the idea of public service. A public domain is not the same as a public sector, and is not to be measured simply by the services directly controlled and provided by the government, or by the proportion of the national income taxed and spent by the state. The public domain is a political space, overlapping both state and civil society, and sustained by particular institutions among which the universities and the media are particularly important. It is a space where the public interest can be determined through debate and deliberation, a public ethos generated, and a public ethic articulated. Independent, critical intellectual work is essential for it, and those who perform that work are public intellectuals. If the public domain is today in trouble, it is because the kind of intellectual work which public intellectuals have performed in the past is less common than it once was, and increasingly under threat.

The public domain has always been vulnerable to erosion, depending as it does on sustaining a public ethos, a set of norms and values indicating how public affairs should be conducted and how the public interest should be determined. For this the active involvement of public intellectuals is required, who although they may have sharply different perceptions and

1. Charles.Pattie, Patrick Seyd, & Paul Whitely, 'Citizenship and Civic Engagement: Attitudes and Behaviour in Britain', *Political Studies*, 51, 3, 443-468.

2. David Marquand, *Decline of the Public*, Cambridge, Polity, 2004.

3. Robert Putnam, *Bowling Alone: The Collapse and Revival of American Community*, New York, Simon & Shuster, 2000.

ideals, are committed to the idea of the public domain itself, and the essential values for its continuance - such as openness, rationality, diversity, clarity, and tolerance. Where the public domain begins and where it ends, which activities, and institutions, and organisations come within its scope, are not given in advance and will vary between democracies, with their different national political traditions and cultures. But every democracy needs a public domain to function as a democracy. It needs some means of determining what is public and what private, what should be considered by all because it affects the interest of all. This means that the public domain can be defined very narrowly or more broadly. At one extreme it can be conceived as gradually embracing more and more activities, setting the framework for all private exchanges and activities, and influencing the forms of governance throughout society. Its present malaise has many causes, but one of them is the failure of intellectuals to understand the nature of the public domain and their role in sustaining it.

THE ROLE OF PUBLIC INTELLECTUALS

Public intellectuals are hard to categorise precisely, just as the public domain itself has no definite boundaries. One of the simplest conceptions is that of the free floating intelligentsia, a stratum of intellectuals that is not tied to any particular class or interest group. Its relative detachment is the condition for its independence, for its ability to pursue the truth wherever it leads, 'to speak truth to power', to develop its own rules and its own ethos, untrammelled by considerations of policy. Its antecedents lie in Plato's philosopher kings, and its modern formulations by John Stuart Mill and Keynes. The intellectuals become a mandarin elite above politics and above self-interest, whose opinion can be trusted because it is disinterested. There is an anti-democratic tinge to this model, since the mass of citizens are held to be too uneducated and ignorant to decide matters on their own, and need to accept the tutelage of the intellectuals or the professionals, who are much better placed to determine what lies in the public interest than are the citizens themselves.

An alternative model derives from Gramsci, through the way in which he focused on the importance of the institutional, ideological and cultural structure of politics, and therefore the character of the public domain under capitalism. Gramsci's famous essay on intellectuals also offers a very different way of conceiving intellectuals rather than simply as a mandarin elite. Instead he distinguishes between traditional and organic intellectuals, the traditional intellectuals being those strata such as clergy and lawyers formed in the service of the *ancien* regimes of Europe, and whose attitudes and practices are still distinctive and important in many countries. The organic intellectuals by contrast emerged to provide the increasingly specialised functions required by capital, both in the organisation of production, and in the organisation of political rule. This stratum is vital for the smooth operation of the extended state which capital requires, and for organising its hegemony by articulating the common sense understandings necessary for every level of its functioning. Gramsci believed that the organised labour movement in seeking to replace capitalism with socialism had to form its own organic intellectuals and develop a counter-hegemonic project.

With the decline of socialist parties and the cohesion and strength of labour movements the notion of organic working class intellectuals has lost plausibility, but that does not mean that Gramsci's analysis is no longer relevant. Since he wrote there has been a huge increase in the number of organic intellectuals. Many sites, once the preserve of traditional intellectuals such as the universities, have been transformed by the requirements of the economy and the state. There has been an explosion of expertise, with inevitable fragmentation and specialisation. The modern state has become increasingly labyrinthine and complex in its structures, in its networks and in its governance. This more than anything underlies the crisis of the public domain. It has become much harder to determine what the public interest is, to connect decision-making with the citizens, or to imagine alternatives.

The bureaucratic organisation of modern capitalism is not a new theme. It was noted and lamented by Max Weber and Joseph Schumpeter. Herbert Marcuse writing in the 1960s saw the rise of a one dimensional society, brought about by the proliferation of the new organic intellectuals and the decline of the working class as an agent of change.[4] Marcuse was despairing about the possibilities for critical intellectual work in such a society, because the space for opposition had disappeared, and there was no agency by which capitalism could be transformed into a different kind of society. The student movement of the 1960s gave him brief hope that other agents might be found to burst capitalist hegemony, but fundamentally his analysis remained one of resignation and despair. This radical leftism continues to resonate on the left today. Capitalist hegemony is analysed as all-encompassing and one-dimensional. These societies cannot be changed from within, only overthrown from without. If there is no agency to overthrow them then refuge is sought in high-minded fatalism and pessimism.[5] Characteristic of this approach for example is an expanded concept of neo-liberalism, which sees all political parties and governments operating within capitalist systems as neo-liberal, making distinctions between them meaningless.

An alternative approach strongly influenced by Gramsci has been to take democracy, and therefore the notion of a public domain, extremely seriously, and to regard the struggle to define what is the public interest and how it might be implemented not as trivial questions, but as having great significance for any feasible politics of reform and progress.[6] The public domain becomes a sphere of political and ideological contestation, in which attempts to set agendas and define identities and the public interest, assemble coalitions and alliances, and make interventions become all-important.

In this conception the role of public intellectuals is vital. But these are

4. Herbert Marcuse, *One-Dimensional Man*, London, Routledge 1964.

5. Susan Watkins, 'A Weightless Hegemony', *New Left Review* 25 (2004), 5-33; Michael Hardt & Antonio Negri, *Empire*, Cambridge, Mass., Harvard University Press.

6. Ernesto Laclau & Chantal Mouffe *Hegemony and Socialist Strategy: Towards a Radical Democratic Politics*, London, Verso, 1985.

not the free-floating intellectuals of either the traditional liberal or the radical leftist kind. Instead they are organic intellectuals involved at different levels of the great bureaucracies of capital and the state. There may no longer be any organised class interest, but they are still able to become public intellectuals, by attaching themselves to the public domain, articulating a public ethic, and participating in the debates to determine the public interest. The extent to which such intellectuals are willing to become public intellectuals and therefore organic intellectuals for the public domain, rather than simply for their own specialised area of activity, is crucial for the existence of the public domain and for any kind of progressive politics.

The rise of such a stratum of public intellectuals is hampered by a number of factors. The older liberal idea of a free-floating mandarin elite, as well as the radical leftist idea of a detached, oppositional elite, have to be overcome. There need to be adequate outlets and institutions through which public intellectuals can express themselves. And problems inherent in democracy have to be addressed.

THE PROBLEM OF DEMOCRACY

One of the most serious problems corroding modern democracy and with it the idea of a public domain is the increasingly contested nature of authority and expertise. Old forms of authority have been cast down and new ones struggle to establish themselves. This in many ways is a positive development, and far better than the unthinking trust which used to be placed in secretive and narrow elites. A successful public domain needs vigorous argument and critical examination of evidence and of alternatives. But two dangers have constantly to be guarded against. These are complexity and populism, the two fault lines of modern democracy. The first encourages cynicism, the second trivialisation. Both have become characteristic of modern media culture.

The increasing complexity of modern government raises the issue of how democracy can be made meaningful in contemporary conditions. The centralisation of decision-making has made government remote from the people, and the rewards from participation increasingly slim, because the prospect of having any influence on decisions is so small. The effectiveness of representation has been increasingly questioned. The sense of powerlessness which citizens have when confronted by the modern state contributes to a mood of fatalism and cynicism where public policy is concerned. Nothing will ever really change, policy will be shaped by powerful interests behind the scenes and not by any consideration of a wider public interest. This shows itself in the widespread belief that everyone in public life is self-interested, and dishonest about their real motives. So no-one is believed to advocate a course of action because it is right, but only because it will benefit them. Politics is an elaborate charade whereby private interests masquerade as the public interest.

This sense of powerlessness and the cynicism which goes with it has been intensified by continuing pressures towards centralisation. The weakening in Britain for example of so many self-governing institutions, including local authorities, trade unions, universities, and mutuals, as well as the increasing importance of transnational sites of decision-making such as the EU, the WTO, and the IMF, makes democratic deficits seem at times to be near-universal. Lines of accountability have been blurred because of the proliferation of agencies, authorities and levels of governance. Understanding for example how decisions are made in the EU has become largely impenetrable except for specialists on EU governance.

Modern government has become highly technical, involving as it does huge problems of co-ordination and organisation to implement policies. The infrastructural power[7] of the modern state has never been greater, but the nature of that power is very hard to subject to traditional democratic processes of deliberation and consent. In modern government, and indeed in all large organisations, policy appears extremely slow-moving to those outside the networks involved in formulating and implementing it, and also very unresponsive. The timescales are not understood, neither are the difficulties of effective co-ordination. All this fuels popular conceptions that politicians and other public officials are self-serving, liable to be corrupt, dishonest or incompetent, often all three.

7. Michael Mann, *The Sources of Social Power*, Cambridge, CUP, 1986.

This cynicism about the motives of public officials has become pervasive and deeply corrosive of any sense of an autonomous public domain. Cynicism and scepticism come to frame responses to most political events. This takes root first of all among a section of intellectuals, particularly those in the media, but comes to be reflected in the general attitudes of the population. Such general attitudes of hostility and suspicion towards the state were common before universal suffrage and the rise of mass political parties, and took time to dissipate, in some instances never completely. But now such attitudes appear to have been re-ignited. What is new is the central role of the media in generating scepticism and cynicism about the state and all public authorities, and encouraging conspiracy theories for everything that occurs.

The second fault line in democracy is populism. As complexity increases, and cynicism and scepticism spread, so large numbers of voters become more prone to populist appeals and instant solutions. Here again the media is ready to assist. The simplifying of issues such as asylum or health care or the MMR vaccine produces a public discourse which is shaped by scares, prejudices, fears and ignorance rather than reasoned argument. Sections of the media now specialise in attacking and discrediting the decisions of experts, and the cumulative effect is the discrediting of authority in general, and a steady collapse of trust. Into this vacuum populism spreads.

This attitude of distrusting all sources of authority has been justified by some intellectuals as the only responsible position.[8] No form of knowledge is to be privileged over any other, or should be. There are simply no grounds

8. Paul Feyerabend, *Science in a Free Society*, London, Verso, 1978.

for preferring one set of beliefs over any other. The extreme relativism of some forms of contemporary thought here combine to challenge the notion that there can be objectivity or rationality in the discussion of public affairs. Such views have been an important corrective to arguments based on fundamentalist reasoning, which puts certain ideas beyond criticism. But it is hard to imagine any kind of public domain without some forms of authority and a significant level of trust in intermediate institutions. If the authority of key groups like politicians, scientists, doctors and judges collapses, then the making of public policy is no longer mediated through any process of deliberation. Instead an attempt is made to install direct popular mandates or at least to oblige politicians to shift policy directly to match popular sentiment as orchestrated by the media. Outbursts of populist feeling on key issues, such as the petrol tax protests in Britain in the Autumn of 2000, and lobbies such as the campaign for Sarah's Law (designed to reveal the identity and whereabouts of individuals on the paedophile register) have been increasing. Underlying them is the feeling that 'governments don't listen' and that the only way to make them listen is to take direct action. The logical direction of such a democracy would be government by referenda or more likely by tabloid, bypassing representative institutions and forcing instant compliance with the popular will. This would be government by the *Daily Mail*.

THE MEDIA

The media play a key role in all of this. They are one of the intermediate institutions that is indispensable to a viable and flourishing public domain; at the same time they are a major factor in the erosion of the public domain. The media dislike complexity and encourage populism. Journalists are essential for organising and sustaining the public domain, but under competitive pressures, there has been a steady slide in journalistic standards. The constant blurring of comment and news, the slanting of headlines, the exaggeration of stories, speculation masquerading as fact, the selection of material according to editorial agendas, the vendettas and campaigns - these used to be true of the tabloids but they have now spread to all newspapers, and from there to television and radio. What is noticeable about modern media is the way they print speculative stories, many of which turn out to have no basis, but they rarely if ever correct them, or admit fault. Their motto is never explain, never apologise. At the same time they demand much higher standards of probity and consistency from public officials than they are prepared to impose on themselves. The attitude of many contemporary journalists is captured by the remark of Rod Liddle, the former editor of the BBC's Today Programme: 'Andrew Gilligan gets great stories and some of them are even true'.[9]

The British media is seriously out of control, the least trusted of any media in Europe, yet for the most part unaware that it has anything to

9. Quoted by Martin Kettle, 'The threat to the media is real. It comes from within', *Guardian*, 3/02/04.

reproach itself for. The relentless anti-government and anti-authority agenda which it pursues has been a major factor in the denigration of politicians and politics and the collapse of trust. Leading broadcasters such as John Humphreys and Jeremy Paxman display an extraordinary arrogance and self-regard, behaving as unelected tribunes of the people, arrogating to themselves the right to sit in judgement on elected politicians and summoning them to account for their misdeeds. The constant sneering at politicians and other public servants, the constant questioning of their motives, the constant coverage only of stories that highlight shortcomings in government have helped create the deeply cynical culture which we now inhabit. Nothing that comes from official sources is believed any more. Opinion surveys demonstrate, for example, that most citizens rate the public services they encounter quite highly, but because of the relentless negativity of the media, they believe the state of the same services nationally to be dire, and conclude that their experience cannot be typical, and that they must have been lucky.

A degree of scepticism, and even cynicism, is indispensable for critical intellectual work, but if it becomes unbalanced, it can be deeply corrosive of any sense of a public domain. Substantial numbers of journalists define their role not as public intellectuals with a wider responsibility for the public domain but as soldiers of truth fighting against a corrupt and mendacious political class. Yet journalists are as much part of the political class as politicians, and this journalistic tendency, which at its worst Martin Kettle has labelled 'journalistic fascism',[10] is that no-one in authority is to be trusted or believed. If such campaigns were ultimately to succeed the end point would be some kind of authoritarianism, because every intermediate structure that supports the public domain would have been dismantled, to make way for the undiluted expression of the popular will.

10. Ibid.

Can anything be done? The crisis in our media is a crisis of public intellectuals and the public domain. What is needed is a change of culture so that the public domain and those who operate in it are given more respect, and reporting becomes not less critical but more balanced and more accurate. The consequences of continually treating government as though it were not democratic, and that all politicians are fools and knaves, is that it will create the basis for real authoritarian politics. Journalists have a huge responsibility for the health of democratic politics. They create and sustain the narratives through which the citizens obtain political information and their understanding of what is going on, and the basis on which they form their judgements.[11] This is not a neutral process, yet the ideology which many journalists still subscribe to seems to assume that news is objective, out there, merely waiting to be collected, not requiring interpretation.[12] If the Gilligan affair did anything it should have removed that misapprehension. The best journalists are pillars of the public domain, because their reporting or their opinions are designed to open up discussion and argument, rather than close them down, and they practice respect and

11. Jeffrey Friedman, 'Public Opinion: Bringing the Media Back In', *Critical Review*, 15, 3-4 (2003), 239-260.

12. Peter Beharell et al, *Bad News*, London, Routledge, 1976.

tolerance even when they are sharply criticising the behaviour or the opinions of others in the public domain. The current obsession of much of the media with questions of process, who said what to whom and when, and with the absolute consistency of individual politicians, governments and parties, trivialises politics, erodes trust, and neglects substance. Unless we can find a way to reverse this process, resignation and fatalism will take further hold, and the very idea that there might be a public interest and disinterested public service will be destroyed.

UNIVERSITIES

Another key site for public intellectuals and the public domain is the universities. What is common to both universities and the media is that members of both need to recognise that they should operate as public intellectuals with a responsibility to maintain the framework and the values of an open and pluralist public domain. Universities are different from the media however in many ways. In the past they were one of the main sites for formation of traditional intellectuals and that continues to some extent in the older universities. But the big expansion of universities means that they have moved in forty years from educating less than five per cent of the age group to educating over forty per cent. With this have come major changes in funding, organisation, and monitoring. As student numbers have increased so unit costs have been reduced and student/staff ratios have climbed. Universities have been obliged to place much greater emphasis upon training and upon the life skills acquired by courses of study, rather than the substantive content of their degrees. All courses have been obliged to show their relevance to the world of work.

In this way universities have become the principal training ground for the organic intellectuals needed throughout the state and civil society. The monitoring of their performance through external reviews of quality have been greatly increased, and at the same time, the performance of their other main function, the advance of knowledge through original research and scholarship has also been subject to intensive review through the Research Assessment Exercise, which has been taking place every few years since 1989.

The effect of the RAE on university research has been considerable. It has greatly reinforced trends which already existed to make each discipline increasingly specialised and self-enclosed. It has made university academics more productive, by forcing them either to publish research or to leave the profession. It has made the universities much more competitive and has substantially changed the culture in many universities where teaching was given a higher priority than research. The additional financial incentives given to high research rankings sent out unmistakeable signals to university managements and to university lecturers. As a result the quantity of research has substantially increased.

Whether the quality has also increased is much debated within universities and within different disciplines. Certainly the nature of the output has often altered. It has become very much more difficult for University academics to be public intellectuals because the demands of the RAE take precedence, and each subject is assessed by a panel which decides what is to count as the best research in that particular discipline. Although the panels have varied considerably in the criteria they use, all have effectively become gatekeepers deciding which research is valuable and which not, and most have chosen to define the criteria in increasingly narrow ways. The Economics panel for instance considers the best research in economics to be work that is published in a list of top journals, one version of which is the so-called Diamond list, named after the economist who devised it. Research published in other journals or in books is mostly ignored in reaching the evaluations. This hands to the editors of the leading refereed journals a huge role in shaping the careers of all economists. Research to be published has to conform to what is considered good research by the editors of these journals and the peer reviewers they select.

The outcome is very high quality research of a particular kind. But it is of a particular kind. In the natural sciences publications through refereed journals is the route by which research results are publicised and incremental progress in knowledge occurs. The application of this model to social science where progress in knowledge is not incremental in the same way has had some bizarre results. Research tends to become ever more abstract, teasing out the implications of theoretical paradigms which are so narrowly drawn in the first place that the results have little practical relevance or application. What tends to be driven out are critical and eclectic approaches, policy-driven approaches, and in particular analyses which are written in a language few outside a small circle of specialists can understand.

The choice of many of the social sciences to make themselves as like the natural sciences as possible has meant that they have gained greatly in expertise but at the expense of limiting their usefulness to an understanding of the social world. As a result the social sciences which should be such an important resource for the public domain have become less rather than more relevant as the RAE has taken hold. Academic journals bulge with articles that are never read, and the overproduction of research for the research community has become a major industry. Universities have always tended to be self-absorbed places, and in the research sense they have become more so. It will be harder in future for new generations of academics to choose to devote time to become public intellectuals and engage with the public domain, rather than concentrating on building their careers within the closed, self-referential networks of their professional discipline. The Research Councils have tried to counter this to some extent by insisting that research be endorsed by user groups, but this has introduced a new pressure, that of the requirements of external sponsors. The twin pressures of the RAE and external sponsors threaten to squeeze out research not sanctioned by the agendas and methodologies approved by the gatekeepers of the discipline.

Universities have become highly successful in turning out the expert organic intellectuals which society demands, but it is now less good than it was in producing the public intellectuals that can sustain and develop the public domain. In the past the universities' record was patchy and there were times, particularly in the nineteenth century when most of the creative minds and public intellectuals worked outside the universities. But for much of the twentieth century the guarantee of academic freedom to work on whatever subjects the academic chose did make the universities a vital source of public intellectuals.

This is now under threat, and intellectual work of the kind that once was possible in the University may not be so for much longer. This is not because of any central ruling, but simply because academics themselves have adjusted their behaviour in relation to the perverse incentives they face. As a result some of the most original intellectual work in the social sciences now takes place outside the universities in thinktanks or by freelance thinkers and is published in non-refereed journals. Thinktanks such as IPPR, Demos, the Fabians, the IEA, and the Social Market Foundation, have often taken the lead in shaping public debates, creating a new space in which public policy actors and academics and journalists can meet to discuss issues of common concern. This is a very positive development for the public domain, but the resources available to the thinktanks are tiny compared to universities. Given their size, and the number of intellectuals working within them, universities ought to be able to make a much bigger contribution to the public domain, producing research which is relevant and understandable, and acting as both check and resource for the media.

Instead since the 1980s universities have found themselves the victims of one of the last great experiments in central planning, with a regime of performance targets and incentives which have pulled them out of shape. Universities have become more controlled by the state, and have been internally restructured to make their management more like other large bureaucratic organisations than self-governing communities of scholars. While this has helped the universities deliver what the state requires in terms of graduates, it has been at the expense of the older idea of the university as a major source of critical ideas for the future progress of society, and as a key source of energy and innovation for the public domain and the wider civil society.

***

The current failings of the media and the universities are by no means the only reasons for the malaise of the public domain and of democracy. But in so far as the problem in each is the problem of the emergence of sufficient public intellectuals with a commitment to sustain the public domain and to contribute to the delineation of the public interest, then they are certainly one of the reasons. Democracy is never a finished system, and it can wither as easily as it can grow. It has to be sustained by committed action to preserve a public domain ruled by the values of tolerance, pluralism and rationality. Public intellectuals will seldom agree with one another, and it would be undesirable that they should. But what is needed in every generation is for academics and journalists to commit themselves to be public intellectuals, participants in the public domain, with all the obligations and standards which that involves. The public domain is about much more than the state. It is also about civil society, and the definitions of the public interest that will rule there. If intellectuals do not come forward, or if they become simply oppositionists, or if they seek to undermine the public domain rather than sustain it, the public domain will continue to shrink until democracy itself is eventually imperilled.

The role of public intellectual is a hard one, and there are many different styles, some of them specific to particular times, but some of them relevant to all times. Two recent examples of the latter in Britain are Bernard Crick and Stuart Hall. Crick belongs to that tradition which once flourished in Britain of institutional entrepreneurs. He was never content to be confined within the academy, but has always sought to engage with the wider public, and not just through ideas and debate, but also through the creation of lasting institutions which create a public culture and a public ethos. Crick was responsible for setting up the Politics Association to provide a forum for teachers of politics in schools and colleges; he was a long-serving editor of *The Political Quarterly* with its distinctive mission of providing a bridge between specialist knowledge and opinion-makers in good plain English and bringing together the worlds and concerns of government, journalism, and the universities. After his major biography of Orwell he established the Orwell Memorial Trust which funds public lectures, and is one of the joint sponsors of the Orwell Prize, for political journalism and political writing. This prize now in its twelfth year has become firmly established, and pays tribute to the rich tradition of political journalism and political writing that exists in Britain. Winners of the prize for journalism have included Vanora Bennett, Brian Sewell, Yasmin Alibhai Brown, David Aaronovitch, David McKittrick, Robert Fisk, Polly Toynbee and Paul Foot; while the winners for political books have included Robert Cooper, Francis Wheen, Miranda Carter, Michael Ignatieff, Brian Cathcart, Patricia Hollis, Fergal Keane, and Anatol Lieven.

The thread which binds all of Crick's diverse interests and activities together has been citizenship. He has been a passionate believer in the necessity for political education, and in creating the institutions that will widen the opportunities for it. David Blunkett appointed him in 1997 to chair the advisory group on the teaching of citizenship and democracy in schools and later to be Adviser on Active Citizenship to the Home Office. This allowed him to fulfil his long-standing belief that citizenship should be included in the national curriculum as an essential requirement for a democratic society. Crick argued for the teaching of politics not to be just about the nuts and bolts of how government works, but about how to participate in politics, how to argue and debate and become active. He seeks to replace a subject culture with a citizen culture, to recognise the multicultural character of the British state while developing the languages and practice of a common citizenship, and to persuade the political class to stop talking to itself and to engage with citizens. Crick's stance as a public intellectual echoes Orwell in fighting against those tendencies in modern media and politics which reduce citizens to an 'empty mob' or a 'hate-filled mob', or these days, a cynical mob.

Coming from a very different intellectual tradition and political formation, Stuart Hall shares with Bernard Crick a concern with citizenship, and with how to widen and deepen political communication and political education. Hall's involvement in developing Cultural Studies at Birmingham, and his subsequent work with the Open University are practical examples of how to reach out to new audiences and to address new problems, which had found no place in the traditional academic curriculum. Hall's understanding of politics focuses on identity and the nature of power, exploring the way in which identities are constructed, represented, and negotiated, which allows different projects to emerge, and different possibilities to be identified. Ideological struggle and debate are not external reflections on politics, but the heart of politics itself, because they determine the nature of political reality and political possibility.

Hall's famous account of Thatcherism as authoritarian populism, and his acute sense of how the political terrain was being re-made in the 1980s was complemented by his sharp critique of the Left for its immobility and inflexibility in the face of this new threat. Still trapped in the orthodoxies that had defined it in the past, the Labour movement was increasingly out of touch, and an easy target for Thatcherism. Hall's essays on Thatcherism and on Labour were never simply intellectual exercises but political interventions which helped reshape debate on the Left. Part of Hall's strength was his intuitive understanding of what made Thatcherism so effective as a new form of politics, its ability to express its political objectives in the form of both populist commonsense as well as economic doctrine and political philosophy, and to communicate through images and symbols of Britishness which resonated with the electorate. This ability to connect politics with people's lives and use it to express their hopes and desires was for him the core of Thatcherism's success and its ability to mobilise its own support and marginalize the opposition. He often despaired of the ability of the Left to develop a similar politics, and respond to the global changes in capitalism and culture. But he shows in his own work what such a politics should be like.

Public intellectuals are often active participants in politics in the sense that they seek to advance political education of citizens, by articulating choices, framing questions, and offering alternatives. They address themselves to the public, not to coteries of experts, or office holders. They are essential builders of the public domain, and their presence is vital if larger numbers of people are to become involved in politics. At times the project of a public domain appears hopeless, so great are the forces seeking to undermine it, and maintain ignorance, fear and hate as the dominant political responses of citizens. But the need for the public domain does not diminish, which is why in every generation new public intellectuals come forward to assist in the task of building and defining it. The public domain is always a work in progress, and we have to be clear-sighted about the many obstacles in its path, as well as the institutions that are needed to help form public intellectuals and widen political participation.

Talking up Skill and Skilling up Talk: Some Observations on Work in the 'Knowledge Economy'

Deborah Cameron

PROLOGUE: EDUCATION, EDUCATION, EDUCATION

I am writing these words in the week when a prolonged and intense debate on the future of British higher education reached a dramatic climax on the floor of the House of Commons. The Labour government's proposals to fund an expanded university system by allowing institutions in England to charge students variable 'top-up' fees were carried, in a House where the government's majority is 161, by a mere five votes.

Virtually all opposition to the Higher Education Bill centred on the impact its provisions would have on poorer students. Would they be forced to opt for the cheapest courses rather than those best suited to their talents and ambitions? Would the prospect of graduating with enormous debts deter them from applying to university at all? Supporters of the legislation, however, portrayed these concerns as peripheral to the real issue. Over and over again, we heard that the new measures were necessary to secure the nation's future economic prosperity. The government had set a target of 50 per cent participation in HE among 18 to 30-year-olds by 2010, for unless it educated more and more people to a higher and higher level, how could Britain stay internationally competitive? Young people understood that to succeed in today's hi-tech, high-skills economy they needed high-level qualifications; that was why they were applying to university in such unprecedented numbers. Supporters of the government's proposals demanded of their opponents: which of these eager applicants are you going to turn away? On what grounds do you deem it acceptable to frustrate young people's ambitions by refusing to satisfy their thirst for knowledge?

Except for the most unreconstructedly elitist and patrician (the former Chief Inspector of Schools Chris Woodhead, for example), people to whom this question was periodically addressed gave evasive and vacuous answers. The idea that access to higher education should be widened, that degree courses should be for the many and not just the few, has attained the status of received wisdom, and it is hard to dispute it without appearing snobbish, reactionary or simply out of date. What lies behind it is not, however, a desire to democratise the 'life of the mind', but a set of ideas about the changing nature of work. In the globalised economy of the twenty-first century, the kind of unskilled or low-skilled manual labour that once occupied a majority of workers everywhere has become concentrated in those parts of the world where labour and materials are cheapest; if economically advanced societies are to continue to prosper they must specialise in what is known in the jargon as 'knowledge work', work that involves the use of complex new technologies, calls on the worker's mental rather than physical capacities, and accordingly requires workers to be highly skilled and educated. Equipping the workforce with ever-increasing levels of knowledge and skill is thus the key to economic competitiveness in a hi-tech, globalised, post-industrial world.

This kind of thinking informs the current British government's policy not only on higher education but on education in general. It drives, for instance, the very strong skills agenda that is now entrenched in the national curriculum for schools (exemplified by the centralised and prescriptive national literacy and numeracy strategies), and in post-compulsory education through the new 'key skills' qualification. It also drives the government's commitment to 'lifelong learning', whereby everyone is encouraged to upgrade their knowledge, skills and qualifications by undertaking regular education and training throughout their working life. I mention these educational initiatives, initiatives that do not concern specifically *higher* education, in order to underline the point that the expansion of the British university system is part of a larger project, whose goal has nothing to do with producing more 'intellectuals'. 'Knowledge work' should not be confused with 'intellectual work': though both terms are defined by contrast with manual or physical labour, they belong to quite different discourses. That is one reason why conservative elitist criticisms of the British government's higher education policy have had so little impact. When Chris Woodhead explained his objection to the government's 50 per cent HE participation target by asserting that the serious study of an academic discipline was axiomatically a minority pursuit, which most 18-year-olds had neither the desire nor the qualifications to engage in, he was mobilising a traditional view of higher education as a form of intellectual development, which might incidentally serve to prepare its recipients for certain elite kinds of work other than actually being an academic, but whose rationale in most cases was not fundamentally vocational. But this view no longer prevails (even if nostalgic traces of it still linger) among the policymakers and other experts Woodhead was addressing. In the rhetoric used not only by the government, but also by business and industry lobbies, education at all levels *is* fundamentally concerned with the production of a workforce prepared to meet the challenges of today's rapidly-changing, hyper-competitive economic environment (not my clichés, theirs). It is intellectual development which is now regarded as the incidental by-product, while knowledge/ skill is represented as an economic commodity, to be invested in as a means of increasing the competitive advantage of the individual, the organisation s/he works for and the nation in which s/he lives.

Of course I am not suggesting that the commodification of knowledge is itself a new departure. Knowledge has always been - among other things

1. Pierre Bourdieu, *Language and Symbolic Power*, John B. Thompson (ed), Gino Raymond and Matthew Adamson (trans), Cambridge, Polity, 1991.

- an economic commodity which its possessors, including traditional 'intellectuals', could trade for other kinds of capital, and this is even more true of educational qualifications like degrees, as Pierre Bourdieu long ago pointed out.[1] What is new, arguably, is the meaning of 'knowledge' in phrases like 'knowledge work', and the extent of that meaning's influence on educational policy and practice. This essay is about the representation of 'knowledge work' and the reality of some of the work that is encompassed by that term. It is also, though more indirectly or incidentally, about the (considerable) difference between the new category of 'knowledge work' and more traditional conceptions of 'intellectual work'.

WHAT IS 'KNOWLEDGE WORK'?

It is difficult to think of any human occupation whose performance does not depend on some kind of knowledge. The knowledge required to make a living as, say, a subsistence farmer in Papua New Guinea or a market trader in West Africa is both extensive and complex, but people engaged in these age-old occupations are not generally described as 'knowledge workers'. 'Knowledge work' cannot, therefore, be simply a label for any kind of work requiring any kind of knowledge. It is a historically and culturally specific discursive construct produced within a particular configuration of institutional sites, utterances and practices, which Gee, Hull and Lankshear have dubbed 'the new work order'.[2]

2. Paul Gee, Glynda Hull, Colin Lankshear, *The New Work Order*, St Leonards, NSW, Allen & Unwin, 1996.

The new work order has a number of key characteristics. One is the dominance in it of 'post-industrial' forms of work: the service sector is larger and more important economically than the manufacturing sector, and manufacturing itself is transformed by new technologies. Reliance on technology, particularly information and communication technologies (ICTs) is another key characteristic. Work regimes and practices are (re)organised to fit the logic of the technologies that allow work to be done faster and cheaper (an obvious example of this is the massive relocation of customer service work to call centres over the past 20 years, which has dramatically changed the way many kinds of business are transacted). A third key characteristic is the adoption of new managerial approaches which emphasise the 'empowerment' of workers, giving them more responsibility and soliciting their active involvement in managing their own performance using vehicles such as appraisal, coaching, training, target setting, bonus incentive schemes, total quality management programmes, etc. These typically exist within a wider disciplinary regime which may not be experienced by workers as 'empowering', since it also tends to involve increased job insecurity, 'flexible' working (that is to say variable shifts and/or overtime) and more intrusive surveillance (also facilitated by new technology - call centres are again a good example).

One of the earliest and most influential meditations on what I, following Gee et al., am calling 'the new work order' was a book called *The Work of Nations*, written by a former Labour Secretary in the Clinton administration, Robert Reich.[3] Reich asserted that the old division of workers into manual and non-manual categories was being superseded by a new distinction between 'symbolic analysts'- an elite group whose work involves understanding and manipulating symbolic systems, be they words, numbers, images, graphics or computer code - and people engaged in service provision, either as 'in-person servers' (in other words dealing directly with customers or clients) or in less visible 'back-office' functions like data processing. Both groups would fall into the 'non-manual' category, but as Reich pointed out, their positions are very different. Whereas service providers carry out routine functions according to someone else's instructions, are to a high degree interchangeable and easily replaced, symbolic analysts trade on the knowledge and ideas contained in, or capable of being generated by, their own minds. Their value lies in what they know rather than simply in what they do, and it is that knowledge employers pay a high premium to attract and then retain. For that reason, symbolic analysts would seem to be the most obvious candidates for the label 'knowledge workers', and indeed, some uses of the latter term resemble quite closely Reich's notion of the symbolic analyst.

3. Robert Reich, *The Work of Nations*, New York, Knopf, 1991.

But in many discussions of 'knowledge work', the definition (though often vague) seems to stretch to encompass some of the less elite workers that Reich's schema would place in the service provider category. Whereas Reich drew attention to the premium put on knowledge in *one part* of the new work order, some commentators have apparently generalised this observation to the order as a whole, suggesting that anyone whose work falls within the parameters of that order - for instance because they work in the service sector, dealing with symbols rather than tangible objects and using ICTs - is part of the 'knowledge economy'. It is, for example, not uncommon to hear politicians or business leaders invoking the growth of Britain's call centre industry (at least before it started to be outsourced to India) as an illustration of the need for a more educated and skilled labour force. Undoubtedly, the call centre industry is a hi-tech service industry which deals in symbols (words and bits); but as I will shortly seek to demonstrate by describing their work regime, the suggestion that operators have to deploy high levels of knowledge or skill in order to perform their functions is extremely misleading.

Before I turn to the specifics of call centre work, though, there is one more strand in the discourse of the new work order and the 'knowledge economy' it supposedly supports that needs to be unravelled. This is what I will call the rhetoric of 'upskilling', and I can best explain what I mean by that using an illustrative example. What follows is an extract from the person specification for a position in an NHS hospital: it states that qualified applicants must:

♦ Demonstrate sound interpersonal relationships and an awareness of the individual client's psychological and emotional needs.

♦ Understand the need for effective verbal and nonverbal communication.

♦ Support clients and relatives in the care environment by demonstrating empathy and understanding.

The advertised vacancy was not, as one might be tempted to guess, for a counsellor, social worker or psychologist: it was for a hospital cleaner.

The specification just quoted attracted criticism in the mid-1990s as an instance of the 'politically correct' impulse to dignify even the most menial positions by describing them in absurdly elevated terms. In my view, however, what it really illustrates is a more general discursive and rhetorical shift in the way experts think and talk about all kinds of work. That shift exemplifies what Anthony Giddens describes as a late-modern incursion of 'expert systems' into areas of activity that used to be part of the 'lifeworld'.[4] Routine or taken-for-granted social activities come to be systematised and subjected to prescriptive regulation based on expert understandings of what they involve and how they should be done. Giddens's example is 'parenting', an increasingly pervasive and influential expert discourse on the care and upbringing of children. Traditionally, this activity was not learnt through expert instruction, but through observation, experience and advice given by elders, especially by mothers to daughters. Today by contrast there are few parents who do not turn at least occasionally to the expert wisdom contained in books, magazines, radio and TV programmes, or take seriously the guidance offered by health visitors and other professionals charged with overseeing the welfare of children. Parents who are judged not to meet a certain expert-defined standard may be required, in Britain now, to attend parenting classes. In sum, the activity of caring for children has been 'upskilled': represented as a complex and difficult (rather than 'natural' and straightforward) task which requires special knowledge and skill to perform adequately. The knowledge in question is not, moreover, just everyday informal knowledge, but codified knowledge acquired through instruction.

The same tendency towards upskilling is seen in the hospital cleaner person specification, where a cluster of personal qualities that might once have been vaguely referred to in an all-purpose 'lifeworld' formula like, 'must enjoy working with people' are solemnly broken down into discrete 'skills' and rendered in the expert language of psychology. In the context of a cleaning job, this is readily perceived as excessive. But in many other jobs which are not much more complicated, the representation of quite ordinary activities as complex tasks demanding special knowledge and skill is less often questioned. A case in point, which I will consider in detail below, is the recurrent assertion that service workers need high-level 'communication skills'. 'Communication' is another example of the incursion of expert systems into ordinary lifeworld concerns. What is being upskilled in this

4. Antony Giddens, *Modernity and Self-Identity: Self and Society in the Late Modern Age*, Cambridge, Polity, 1991.

case is *talk*: this is not (usually) some highly specialised and particularly consequential kind of talk, such as counselling a distressed client or negotiating a peace treaty, but just the routine everyday interaction one has with one's family, friends, co-workers and customers. Training in communication skills, including instruction in a body of meta-knowledge about the nature and dynamics of communication, has become pervasive in contemporary workplaces. In my research I have come across, for instance, domestic appliance salespeople being instructed in the intricacies of Eric Berne's transactional analysis and assistants in residential care homes studying Abraham Maslow's 'hierarchy of needs' - and countless workers in supermarkets, leisure facilities and call centres acquiring a smattering of the theory of assertiveness or the basics of Neurolinguistic Programming.

I will return to this particular case of upskilling below, but here the point I want to make is more general: that the rhetoric of upskilling plays an important role in the broader discourse of knowledge work and the knowledge economy. According to that discourse, virtually all work available to western workers in the new global economy is getting more and more skilled, more demanding of workers' ability to acquire and deploy expert knowledge; consequently there is no place in the labour market any more for the unskilled, untrained and poorly educated. There is a sense in which the trend to upskilling actually makes this assertion true. If even quite low-level employees are thought to require formal instruction in such matters as how to talk to customers/clients/patients, if this is considered to be a highly skilled form of behaviour which needs to be supported by a body of codified knowledge, and if acquiring the knowledge and skills through training becomes an obligation imposed on the workers by their employer, then these employees do, in a sense, become 'knowledge workers'. Arguably, though, the sense in which they become knowledge workers is a very trivial and superficial one. And if we actually look at what is involved in many kinds of contemporary service work we will soon have cause to ask whether the rhetorical upskilling of these jobs masks a real deskilling of the workers who do them.

CALL CENTRES: LIFE IN THE COMMUNICATION FACTORY

In the late 1990s I became interested in the upskilling of 'communication' that was visible in popular culture (such as in the success of self-help books on how to talk to others like *Men are from Mars, Women are from Venus*[5]), in education (for example the new emphasis on oral communication as a 'key skill') and in new capitalist service workplaces. In the research I undertook for a book about contemporary 'communication culture', I investigated a number of different kinds of service workplaces, but my most concentrated fieldwork was done in call centres.[6] I chose them partly because they had acquired the status of prototypical representatives of the new work order, but also because of their dependence on spoken language.

5. John Gray, *Men are from Mars, Women are from Venus*, New York, HarperCollins, 1992.

6. Deborah Cameron, *Good To Talk? Living and Working in a Communication Culture*, London, Sage, 2000.

In call centres, talk is at one and the same time 'upskilled', in the sense discussed above, and thoroughly deskilled through what is often called 'Taylorisation', after the early twentieth-century time-and-motion expert F.W. Taylor, who proclaimed that for any production process there was 'one right way', the fastest and most efficient method by which to achieve a particular goal. The approach Taylor took to activities such as shovelling pig-iron (work out how it is best done and then train all workers in the correct method, using surveillance to ensure that they follow it consistently) is applied in the call centre to the apparently qualitatively different activity of interacting verbally with customers. Call centres, in short, have as much in common with industrial factories as they do with the offices that they would seem more nearly to resemble.

The job of a call centre operator involves two main activities performed simultaneously: operators sit in front of a computer screen and keyboard wearing a telephone headset. As they interact with customers on the phone, they are also retrieving and inputting data using the computer - amending the customer's bank account details, say, or checking on the availability of a ticket the customer wishes to purchase. The sequence and form of the phone interaction is often determined largely by the on-screen prompts the operator has to respond to.

Interactional routines built around computer prompts are only one dimension of the factory-style regimentation of the call centre. Regimentation is probably most apparent in the way call-handling is organised, on a 'time is money' principle. Incoming calls are in most cases fed to operators by an automated call distribution system which ensures they receive a constant stream of calls, with minimal downtime in between. Typically there are more lines available for customers to call on than operators available to deal with their calls: thus customers will often be held in a queue and operators will rarely be idle. Illuminated displays visible from every workstation provide an at-a-glance summary of how many calls are in progress and how many are waiting. Supervisors can access additional data telling them which operators are taking calls, how long they have been engaged on a call and what their average processing time has been on that shift. There are time-targets for handling particular types of calls: for example, in two call centres in my own sample operators were told that a standard directory assistance call should take no more than thirty-two seconds, and that a rail reservation transaction should take no more than four minutes. In addition to drawing criticism from supervisors, failure to meet these targets may result in the loss of bonus payments.

But at the same time as they are trying to maximise efficiency, defined as handling the largest volume of calls in the shortest time, operators are subject to a further set of performance criteria having to do with the *manner* in which they handle calls. They must endeavour to provide not just efficient but also friendly and personalised service. The directory assistance centre in my sample says in its operating manual that each customer should be made to feel 'that you have been waiting for that particular call all day'. Even in a thirty-two second transaction whose entire content and sequence is determined by the prompts that appear on the operator's computer screen (What town? What address? What name? etc.), the interaction should seem to the customer natural and 'personal', not rushed and formulaic. To make this still more challenging, many or most call centres require operators to provide what one in my sample called a 'consistent experience of the brand', meaning that all operators must perform the same transaction in essentially the same manner. As is well known, many centres require operators to perform a pre-written script. Even those that do not use scripting generally prescribe the basic moves that comprise a 'standard' transaction, and both types also present operators with a list of rules concerning aspects of speech that are not amenable to scripting, such as voice pitch, quality and tone, speed of speaking, the use of minimal responses (indicators of attentiveness like 'mm', 'yeah') and smiling. Like the time targets, the rules for speaking are enforced through surveillance. Systems are set up so that supervisors can monitor calls without operators knowing. Most centres record at least some calls (as they announce to customers, 'for purposes of training and quality assurance') to be replayed later for critical discussion by the operator and a supervisor or manager. And it is not unusual for centres to employ so-called 'mystery callers', people who pose as customers but are really checking up and reporting back on the operator's call-handling skills.

Call centre work as I observed it, as operators spoke of it in interviews and as managers described its demands when I asked what they looked for when recruiting staff, does not match the rhetoric about a hi-tech 'knowledge economy' requiring highly educated, skilled and knowledgeable workers. Rather it tends to bear out what Gee, Hull and Lankshear say about service work generally: that its main requirements are moderate levels of literacy and numeracy, the ability to take instruction, and 'a pleasant demeanour'.[7] Other scholars have unpacked the notion of 'demeanour', pointing out that contemporary service work involves both 'emotional labour'- managing one's own and others' feelings[8] - and what has been called 'aesthetic labour', a kind of expressive performance with sensory appeal for the customer.[9] These scholars rightly emphasise the *embodied*, rather than purely mental, character of modern service work. Though it does not demand physical strength, it does require bodily discipline. In call centres, where operators are not physically co-present with customers, they must use their *voices* in ways that produce the effect of an embodied person (not a machine, but a flesh-and-blood entity with personality and feelings) on the other end of the line. Posture and facial expression are often regulated because of their effects on vocal performance. The incidence of dysphonia (damage to the vocal apparatus) among operators is attributable not only to long hours of continuous call-handling, inefficient equipment and poor workplace acoustics, but also to the strain imposed when your voice becomes a surrogate for your whole embodied presence.

7. Paul Gee, Glynda Hull, Colin Lankshear, *The New Work Order*, op. cit.

8. Arlie Hochschild, *The Managed Heart: the Commercialization of Human Feeling*, Berkeley, CA, University of California Press, 1983.

9. Anne Witz, Chris Warhurst, Dennis Nickson, and Anne-Marie Cullen, '"Human hardware?" Aesthetic labour, the labour of aesthetics and the aesthetics of organization', paper presented at the 'Work, Employment and Society' Conference, Cambridge, 1998.

Call centre managers talking about their recruitment processes tend to place emphasis on 'demeanour', but they clearly do not regard the vocal/ emotional expressiveness they are looking for as a skill, something grounded in knowledge or acquired through training. They see it rather as an aspect of certain individuals' personalities, and endeavour to recruit people for whom it is simply 'natural'. (Unsurprisingly, many believe that the desired qualities are most likely to be found among young women.) Although most call centre managers I interviewed 'talked the talk' about communication skills and the importance of training workers in them, they also expressed, without apparently noticing the contradiction, the belief that good operators were born rather than made, and that many of the most valuable so-called 'communication skills' could not be taught or 'trained into people'.

The widely-held view that a good operator is just someone 'naturally' endowed with the right personal qualities is not the only problem for the argument that call centre workers need complex communication skills. It can also be argued that the regulation of talk in call centres using scripting, styling and surveillance actually *de*-skills workers, obliging them to suppress large parts of what linguists call their 'communicative competence' - the complicated (though generally tacit) knowledge that enables competent language-users to choose what kind of language will best achieve their communicative purpose in a particular context. The ability to make well-judged choices is fundamental to any kind of truly skilled performance: a 'skilled' craftsperson, for instance, is not someone who can follow a set of instructions to produce a technically competent result, but someone who does not need instructions; someone who (explicitly or implicitly) understands the underlying principles of what they are doing sufficiently well to judge what methods will work best in a given case. This kind of skill is completely negated in call centre regimes that prescribe the content, form and manner of every act performed by the worker, or in training courses and 'counselling' sessions that merely groom the surface form of language rather than examining the principles that govern its use. These forms of linguistic regulation and training are about 'styling' workers, not 'skilling' them. .

My research in service workplaces led me to conclude that the upskilling of talk at work under the rubric of 'communication skills' is mainly a means for managers to exert stricter control over the talk produced by service workers. The result is not 'better', more skilful talk - indeed in some cases it is the opposite - but talk that fits the logic of what George Ritzer has dubbed 'McDonaldisation'.[10] Like Taylorisation, whose modern descendant it is, McDonaldisation seeks to maximise efficiency by reducing every process to a set of exhaustively-specified, predictable routines. As Ritzer notes, one key aim of McDonaldisation in workplaces is to *reduce* employers' dependence on the knowledge and skills of their staff - to ensure that an acceptable outcome can be achieved by even the dimmest, idlest and least motivated worker.

10. George Ritzer, *The McDonaldization of Society: An Investigation into the Changing Character of Contemporary Social Life*, (revised edn), Thousand Oaks, CA., Pine Forge Press, 1996.

Of course I am not suggesting that call centre work is undemanding, still less that the people who do it are lacking in intellectual ability. On the contrary, what depressed me during my fieldwork was seeing so many bright and well-educated people (a fair proportion graduates or students working towards a degree) engaged in tedious and repetitive work within a regime that denied them any opportunity to exercise initiative or creativity. This is ironic, since qualities like initiative and creativity are constantly invoked in rhetoric about the need for a more educated population to do the 'knowledge work' of the twenty-first century. Even if this work does not draw directly and specifically on knowledge acquired at school or university, the argument goes, it requires the more general aptitudes and dispositions developed by extensive education and training. Such rhetoric in my view is at odds with anything it is possible to observe in the service workplaces - including such hi-tech cases as call centres - which now employ a large proportion of the labour force in economically advanced societies.

**

The routinisation of work that is so marked in call centres is by no means confined to them, or indeed to the service-provider category of workers: the case could be made that it is far more pervasive. Consider school and university teaching, jobs that might merit the label 'intellectual work', and which unquestionably require specialised knowledge and extensive education. Most experienced practitioners would probably agree that over the past ten or fifteen years they have found themselves progressively ceding autonomy and control over key professional decisions (for instance what to teach, how to teach, how to assess) to centralised external agencies such as the Qualifications and Curriculum Authority, Ofsted, the Higher Education Funding Council and the Quality Assurance Agency, and the Institute for Learning and Teaching in HE. Though the control exerted by these agencies over teachers is looser than the control exerted over call centre operators, there are similarities, such as the use of targets to manage teachers' activities and measure their professional effectiveness, and the role of surveillance (inspection and auditing) in ensuring compliance with externally-defined norms. One might also mention the time teachers now spend producing highly formulaic documents, like QAA-mandated programme specifications for university courses, or reports on school pupils which are dominated by the phraseology of the national curriculum attainment targets and levels. As a result of these trends, teachers are increasingly becoming vehicles for the 'delivery' of outcomes they did not choose and targets they did not set, using methods and approaches prescribed by someone else. In medicine, too, which unlike teaching is generally placed among the highest-status professions, one could tell a similar story. US doctors regularly complain that the standardised protocols of insurance companies now determine what treatment will be given to individual patients, while NHS doctors in Britain are constrained by endless targets, as well as the guidance issued by bodies such as the National Institute for Clinical Excellence.

In the new world of work, one might argue, real decision-making power is increasingly in the hands of a *management* elite, while even workers who are 'elite' in other respects find their autonomy reduced and their functions routinised. This is the logic of the new capitalism, and the kind of political and public sector managerialism that goes along with it. Perhaps, then, it is no wonder that the rhetoric used by our political and corporate masters to 'talk up' education and skills both exaggerates the intellectual demands of much contemporary work and decries the traditional view of education as the pursuit of knowledge for its own sake. Both these tendencies need to be questioned: the challenge is to find a position from which to do it that cannot be dismissed as simply nostalgic and elitist.

IDLENESS FOR ALL

Scott McCracken

Intellectual work today stands in an antagonistic relationship to the larger culture of work now dominant in the Anglo-American capitalism. This demands that intellectual work as 'knowledge work' legitimates itself by criteria of efficiency, productivity and global competitiveness.[1] In the face of such demands, I want to suggest that we need to think about the opposite of work, or at least the opposite of work as it is currently conceived. The model I will suggest for such a thinking-through is provided by Walter Benjamin's concept of idleness in *The Arcades Project*, specifically the short section on *Müßiggang*, Convolute **m**, although that model is informed by a long radical tradition.[2]

'Do nothing!' hardly seems a call to arms for the modern intellectual. Action is the watchword of the modern institution and universities are not immune. 'Actions' have to be attached to every minute. Action plans proliferate. Time is filled with meetings that produce more actions, with targets that produce goals to be achieved, outcomes to be met, outputs to be counted. Academic life is part of a larger culture of work that values visible products and perpetual motion. At some point in the 1990s the phrase 'the 24/7 society' crossed the Atlantic and was embraced by a nation increasingly enamoured of the work-culture of the US. One of the many policies borrowed by New Labour from the New Democrats was 'workfare': schemes which try to get the unemployed, particularly women - and especially single mothers - 'back' to work through a mixture of incentives (for instance, tax credits) and disincentives (that is to say withdrawal of benefits). Cutting benefit for single mothers was one of the 1997 governments first acts, as symbolic as it was real, a concrete sign that Blairism was not a masquerade behind which old Labour would return to power. Marx would have recognised the origins of New Labour's glorification of work from the Gotha programme, which he criticised as follows:

> The bourgeois have very good grounds for falsely ascribing *supernatural creative power* to labour, since precisely from the fact that labour depends on nature, it follows that the man who possesses no other property than his labour power must, in all conditions of society and culture, be the slave of other men who have made themselves owners of the material conditions of labour.[3]

If the idle and property-less poor were to be dragged back into the productive economy, for the middle class, New Labour's partial commitment to gender equality means the right of both partners in heterosexual relationships to

1. See Deborah Cameron's distinction between 'intellectual work' and 'knowledge work' in this issue.

2. *The Arcades Project* is composed of sheafs or 'convolutes' of notes and citations ordered by upper case letters A-Z (A is 'Arcades'; B is 'Fashion') and then lower case letters a-r (with some gaps). The work was unfinished at Benjamin's death. Citations below refer to the numbered paragraphs within each convolute, which are ordered [A1,1], [A1,1a] etc. See Peter Buse, Ken Hirschkop, Scott McCracken, Bertrand Taithe, *The Arcades Project: an unguided tour*, Manchester UP, forthcoming 2005.

3. Karl Marx, 'Notes to the [Gotha] Programme of the German Worker's Party, cited in Walter Benjamin, *The Arcades Project*, Cambridge MA., Belknap Press, 1999, [X5, 1]. Also cited in 'Modernism', Section III of 'The Paris of Second Empire in Baudelaire', in Walter Benjamin, *Charles Baudelaire: A Lyric Poet in the Era of High Capitalism*, London, Verso, 1983, p71. Also in Benjamin's 'On the Concept of History', in *Illuminations*, New York, Schocken, 1969, p259.

participate fully in the world of work. Sitting (for now) in a property the value of which has tripled in the New Labour era, money rich and time poor, with disposable incomes their parents could not have dreamed of, paying for less children born later in life (once both careers have been established), the middle-class couple become employers themselves, recruiting an army of low-paid workers: cleaners, gardeners, childminders, nannies, *au pairs*, and tutors - if they still risk state education. Increasingly though, the middle class does not have the time to commit to the lengthy negotiations that have allowed them to get the best deal out of the post-1945 settlement. Opting out is accepted by New Labour's modernisers as inevitable, its institutionalisation the basis for the continuing 'reforms' of the despised 'one-size-fits-all' public services that were the basis of collective provision. University top-up fees are just one part of a process that seeks to introduce a market into all areas of public life, so that all forms of intellectual work can be priced.

This modernising project does not just create inequalities in itself, it responds to an income structure that had been growing more unequal since the Thatcherite 1980s, a tendency which the two Blair/Brown governments has not mitigated. Despite all the changes in the tax and benefit system designed to help the working poor, the rich are getting richer more quickly than the poor get less poor.[4]

4. Faisal Islam, 'Our Robin Hood's Uphill Struggle', The *Observer*, 14/03/04, <http://observer.guardian.co.uk/business/story/0,6903,1168739,00.html>.

But what are the new rich doing with their money? Not, it would appear, devoting themselves to a life of leisure. They are working harder than ever, employing more people to pick up after them and spending the excess on a range of private services designed to relieve the stress of overwork or just the effects of excess itself. Leisure time is dedicated to self-improvement, self-indulgence or repairing the damage: the private gym; Pilates; Yoga; meditation; the delicatessen; the gourmet restaurant; the café bar; aromatherapy; acupuncture; the osteopath; the therapist. The idea that we might all work less or that we might rethink the structure of the labour market is not part of the political agenda in Britain or the US. The *Independent*'s defiant response to the latest panic about the British propensity to take a 'sickie', was unusual in challenging a culture that views not working with, at best, suspicion and, at worst, macho derision. Why don't we all, its editorial suggested, work less?[5]

5. The *Independent*, Editorial, 'Long Hours, sick days, and the British workplace', 24/05/04.

It is this general climate rather than 'dumbing down' that has given intellectual work its crisis of legitimation. Pure research, thinking for its own sake, being what used to be called a 'freethinker', are not just unfashionable, but unaccountable in the sense that they cannot be entered into an audit sheet. There was a brief moment in the 1960s when play (in a reprise of earlier liberal education theories) was once again considered an important part of early education and university became a fully-funded opportunity to remove the necessity of work for at least three years. Now anti-utilitarian distractions have been expunged from the national curriculum. Financial pressures deprive most students of the space to think.

Teachers are bound by set targets and tests. Academics are under pressure in a severely underfunded system. There are countervailing, but weak resistances, to the new climate. The influence of European social democracy in the shape of work directives has mitigated some of the worst aspects of the British culture of work; but it is only necessary to read the long list of reasons why an employer need not permit an employee to have flexible working hours to see how far the odds are stacked against the employee. These can be one or more of the following:

 burden of additional costs;
 detrimental effect on ability to meet customer demand;
 inability to reorganise work among existing staff;
 inability to recruit additional staff;
 detrimental impact on quality;
 detrimental impact on performance;
 insufficiency of work during periods the employee proposes to work;
 planned structural changes.

With collective bargaining under attack and in decline, the ability of labour to press for less working hours has been weakened. If we add to this the loss of the traditional privileges accorded to elite higher education institutions, the time for speculative thought is further reduced. The professionalism (some would say proletarianisation) of academia (as opposed to an earlier Oxbridge style amateurism[6]), defunding, market pressures[7] and, in Britain, the Research Assessment Exercise (RAE) have all conspired to cramp intellectual work and to limit its scope: for example the role of academics as public intellectuals intervening in politics, the community or the media.

In this context, idleness is an endangered activity. All British academics have just been asked to participate in a 'transparency' exercise to show that no moment of their time is idle; that they are continuously involved in productive work. So what arguments can be deployed against the new work culture? In a forensic critique of New Labour's policy for Higher Education, Stefan Collini concludes: 'that there are some kinds of intellectual enquiry that are goods in themselves, that need to be pursued at the highest level, and that will almost certainly continue to require a certain amount of public support'.[8] But try making that argument to your budget manager or the Faculty accountant and see how far you get. Yet there is an urgent need to think through an alternative to the current situation.

What follows is a move to the abstract and the theoretical, and therefore even less likely to convince the bean counters. But Benjamin's concept of idleness offers three areas which are of some help. First, idleness can be productive, akin to Keats' diligent indolence as both not-work and an alternative form of creative activity. Second, idleness as a form of anti-work, becomes useful rather than instrumental in the sense of use described by William Morris in his distinction between 'useful work' and 'useless toil'.[9]

6. See Eric Hobsbawm, *Interesting Times: a twentieth-century life*, London, Allen Lane, 2002, pp103-6.

7. See Derek Bok, *Universities in the Marketplace: the commercialisation of Higher Education*, Princeton University Press, 2003.

8. Stefan Collini, 'HiEdBiz', *London Review of Books*, 25, 21 (6 Nov 2003), <http://www.lrb.co.uk/v25/n21/coll01_.html>.

9. William Morris, 'Useful Work Versus Useless Toil', in A.L. Morton (ed), *The Political Writings*, London, Lawrence and Wishart, 1973, pp86-109.

Third, the recognition that in all societies, excepting perhaps the semi-mythical realm of Benjamin's reconstructed primitive communism, the space and time to think has depended upon a brutal division of labour. There is no going back to an elite system of education that does not require a new form of exclusion.

A NOTE ON TRANSLATION

10. I am grateful to Elizabeth Harvey for her help and guidance on the translation of Müßiggang. She also directed me to the motto of the University of Liverpool: 'Haec otia fovent studia''(These periods of idleness encourage study).

11. Sigmund Freud, 'The Uncanny', in *Pelican Freud Library* Vol. 14, J. Strachey (trans), Harmondsworth, Penguin, 1985, p341; the German *müssen*, comparable to the English 'must', only achieves a sense of compulsion in Middle High German, before that it is closer *können* (can) or *dürfen* (to permit or allow).

Benjamin's chosen term for the concept he explores in Convolute **m** of *The Arcades Project* is *Müßiggang*,[10] although the convolute also includes the more pejorative 'das Indolenz' or 'l'indolence', and 'Faulheit' (which is closer to laziness) and the French 'l'oisiveté'. *Müßiggang* is a literary term derived from *Muße*, 'leisure', and *Gang*, 'walk, course or passage'. It might be translated literally as 'idle walk', the mode in which Benjamin's urban characters, for example, the flâneur, saunter through the arcades and the appropriate pace for thumbing through the *Passagen-Werk* itself. A related word is *Müßigkeit*, meaning 'futility' or 'pointlessness'. Paradoxically, *das Muße* stems from the same etymological root as *das Muß*, meaning necessity, an origin which, suggests the kind of linguistic ambivalence discussed by Freud in relation to words such as *heimlich*, both 'homely', 'intimate', 'familiar', and 'secret', 'secretive', 'kept from sight'.[11] *Muße* incorporates a sense of its opposite, the necessity of work. While Benjamin never comments explicitly on this root, Convolute **m** is exemplary in its form as an attempt to represent a complex of political, philosophical and aesthetic problems for which the concept of *Müßiggang* stands as the starting point for critical and creative thinking.

ALL WORK AND NO PLAY MAKES JACK A DULL BOY

Idleness is proverbial: in English 'the devil makes work for idle hands'; in German 'Müßiggang ist alle Laster Anfang' (Idleness is the beginning of all sins). By its nature it does not lend itself to the continuity or sequence that Benjamin sees as a requirement of *Erfahrung* (long, considered or reflective experience) [m2a, 4]. It is epigrammatic. Its mode has all the pleasures of uncertainty. Yet this does not mean that it is unproductive. Idleness, Benjamin suggests, is both not-work and anti-work: it involves a resistance to the Calvinist work ethic [m3a, 1] and to Taylorisation [M10,1]. But idleness might also be its opposite, the possibility of a different kind of work, which would not be work as bourgeois society, or indeed the German Social Democrats, understood it. Idleness is premonitory of unalienated work, which only becomes a possibility, according to Marx - again in the 'Critique of the Gotha Programme':

> In a higher phase of communist society, after the enslaving subordination of the individual to the division of labour, and therewith also the antithesis

between mental and physical labour, has vanished; after labour has become not only a means of life but life's prime want ... [X5, 3].[12]

This is the kind of distinction William Morris made when he wrote: 'the ideal of the future does not point to a lessening of men's energy by the reduction of labour to a minimum, but rather to the reduction of *pain in labour* to a minimum'.[13] The theme of replacing alienated labour with pleasurable, satisfying work is part of a tradition in popular and socialist writing that runs from the medieval idea of Cockagne through Charles Fourier, Karl Marx and George Orwell, to Herbert Marcuse. It includes E.P. Thompson's work on the temporality of pre-capitalist forms of work-time and his analysis of the time discipline that is integral to industrialisation.[14] More recently the work of André Gorz and eco-socialist politics have refused to accept a bourgeois work ethic as the norm. Convolute **m** should in relation to that tradition of socialist critique, one which, with the notable exception of the Green movement, has almost been silenced in public debate in Britain, but which remains part of political debate in Europe, notably in France where Lionel Jospin's government introduced a statutory thirty-five hour week.

MODES OF IDLENESS

As an exemplar of intellectual work, Convolute **m** takes a long view (that of 'long experience' or *Erfahrung*), a view that requires time and leisure. Behind the collage of excerpts which gives it its form, lies a historicist account that the Convolute both recognises and then supersedes. A Marxian narrative of development takes the reader through three modes of production, for which Benjamin finds corresponding modes of idleness. In the first section of the Convolute [m1], excerpts on ancient, feudal and capitalist modes of idleness stand in sequence at paragraphs [m1,1], [m1,2] and [m1, 3]. Outside the sequence stand two alternative modes of idleness, primitive and post-capitalist, which call the historicist account into question. Unlike the first three, these two are not directly accessible. Primitive idleness is only available through its residues in the present. Future idleness can only be anticipated through the traces of possibility that exist in the present or what Benjamin elsewhere calls *Jetztzeit*, now-time. Both these modes explode the antitheses of work and not-work and cannot be bound by a determinate class history.

IDLENESS AS FORM

The structure of Convolute **m**, is not and cannot be in a final and complete shape because such a form would be incompatible with idleness, the definition of which involves *Unabschließbarkeit* 'unfinishability', which is also, for Benjamin, one of the characteristics of intellectual work [m2a1]. But **m** is, in terms of *The Arcades Project* as a whole, exemplary in its structure in

12. Translation used, Eugene Kamenka (ed), *The Portable Karl Marx* Harmondsworth, Penguin, 1983, p541.

13. William Morris, 'Review of Edward Bellamy's *Looking Backward*', *The Political Writings*, London, Lawrence and Wishart, 1984, p252.

14. E.P. Thompson, *Customs in Common*, London, Merlin, 1991.

that it attempts to bring the concept of idleness to consciousness through its form. Each section rewrites the preceding sections often by a form of repetition that subtly changes its meaning. Thus, although short in comparison to other convolutes, it cannot be rushed. It calls for an idle pace and a high degree of distraction. The discrete, juxtaposed paragraphs gesture to other parts of the Arcades Project and to other parts of Benjamin's work. It can be read alongside **M**, 'The Flâneur', **J**, 'Baudelaire', and **X**, 'Marx'. It has correspondences with, at least, **H**, 'The Collector', **I**, 'The Interior, The Trace', **O**, 'Prostitution, Gambling' and **a**, 'Social Movements'. If this seems to propose that every part of the Arcades Project needs to be read in relation to other part, that suggests too systematic a conception of the text, which requires a sauntering pace and an idle sensibility to allow the correspondences to emerge. The idler has relationships with Benjamin's other urban types: the gambler, the flâneur, the collector and the brooder and the student, but these types are not distinct. Gamblers, flâneurs and students are all idle, but idlers have tendencies towards gambling, flânerie and studiousness.

Idleness is both a temporality and a sensibility. As a temporality it can be imposed by modernity as 'enforced idleness', but as a sensibility, it might be cultivated in opposition to modernity's most deadening forms. Benjamin quotes Rousseau: 'The idleness [l'oisiveté] of society is deadly because it is obligatory; the idleness of solitude is delightful because it is free and voluntary' [m4,1].

The effect of the Convolute's structure offers a discrete example of one of the aims of the Arcades Project as a whole: to convey the relationship between a determinate and a dialectical approach to history or what might be called enforced work and productive intellectual work. The accounts of different modes of idleness, ripped from their literary and historical context then placed in the collage of the Convolute, are chosen and positioned in such as way as to tease out their contradictions. The first excerpt begins with the ancient world, which is cited, apparently favourably, as a counterexample to the protestant work ethic:[15]

15. Oddly Weber is not mentioned anywhere in *The Arcades Project*.

> Noteworthy conjunction: in ancient Greece, practical labour is branded and proscribed. Although essentially left in the hands of slaves, it is condemned not least because it betrays a base aspiration for earthly goods (riches). [m1,1]

The ideal of intellectual work, 'studious leisure', is valued by the Greeks, an ideal that looks back to primitive idleness and forward to a future of unalienated work. But Benjamin's commentary on his source, Pierre-Maxime Schuhl, brings to light the central contradiction: ancient idleness is bought at the expense of a class of slaves. There is, in effect, no going back to a golden age of intellectual work. Its legitimation must take into account the division of labour on which it depends.

In the second excerpt, on feudal idleness, both the active and the contemplative life are bound to the wheel of fortune; but, while both lives are subject to it, idleness permits a greater freedom, bound, 'immobile' to the centre of the wheel rather than to its outer edge. The intellectual life already permits a separation from the realm of necessity. But under capitalism, as observed by Saint-Beuve and Marx, the class of 'connoisseurs and amateurs' - who, in *The Arcades Project*, always appear as relics of an earlier time - has 'practically disappeared' [m1,3]. In bourgeois society, according to Marx, industry is victorious over 'heroic laziness [Faulheit]' [m1a1]. In a scenario (familiar now even to the formerly leisured professions like academia), idleness ceases to be a privilege and only exists as a form of resistance.

IDLENESS UNDER CAPITALISM

The intervention of Marx, marks a new section in the Convolute, [m1a], and the introduction of a concept of redemptive idleness, a concept found, like so many of Benjamin's critical terms, in the work of Charles Baudelaire. Baudelaire, reinventor of a notion of the heroic for modernity, seeks to salvage idleness for the nineteenth century: 'In the figure of the Dandy, Baudelaire seeks to find some use for idleness, just as leisure once had some use' [m1a,2]. Just as Benjamin finds a dialectical conception of modernity in Baudelaire's lyric poetry, he finds a dialectical relationship between idleness and 'toil' in the process of creative work he undertakes:

> Baudelaire knows the '*indolence naturelle des inspirés*'; Musset - so he says - never understood how much work it takes 'to let a work of art emerge from a daydream' … Barrès claimed that he could recognize 'in every little word of Baudelaire a trace of the toil that helped him achieve great things'.[16]

16. Benjamin, *Charles Baudelaire*, op cit., p66.

In Part III of 'The Paris of the Second Empire in Baudelaire', Benjamin cites 'Le Soleil' as sole example of a poem where the poet is shown at his 'labours':

> Je vais m'exercer seul à ma fantasque escrime
> Flairant dans tous les coins les hasards de la rime
> Trébuchant sur les mots comme sur les pavés
> Heurtant parfois des vers depuis longtemps rêvés
>
> (I go practising my fantastic fencing all alone, scenting a chance rhyme in every corner, stumbling against words as against cobblestones, sometimes striking on verses I had long dreamt of.)[17]

17. Ibid., p67.

For Benjamin, Baudelaire, as heroic idler of the modern age, becomes an example of the intellectual as guerilla, fighting to reconfigure modernity in the face of the imposition of a new regime of work. The relationship between the outlaw intellectual and commodity culture is summed up in the following paragraph of Convolute **m**, which consists solely of the epigrammatic 'Erfahrung is the outcome of work; Erlebnis is the phantasmagoria of the idler', a sentence that condenses the Convolute down to a single phrase, but which, for that reason, needs some unpacking.

Like the proverbs cited above, the epigram appears at first to oppose a positive with a negative: work, leading to full and connected experience (*Erfahrung*) is positive; idleness, leading to the distracted and fragmented experience (*Erlebnis*) that characterises a phantasmagoric modernity, is negative. But the sentence reverses the expected moral opposition. *Erlebnis* is the phantasmagoria experienced by the idler, the idler does not produce it him or herself. Shock experience, paradoxically, is produced by work or, more precisely, alienated labour, as well as being the fragmented experience of the city under capitalism: 'The shock experience which the passerby has in the crowd corresponds to what the worker "experiences" at his machine'.[18] Whereas the worker is, at least for the duration of the working day, bound to the machine, the phantasmagoria of the city of consumption presents the urban idler with the possibility of a new kind of work, although that very possibility is, for the time being at least, dependent on the worker's bondage. Two divergent outcomes are possible: Baudelaire's model of creative idleness or a 'new field of force in the form of planning' [m1a,4]. Against the latter is juxtaposed the idea of 'total *Erlebnis*' for which the correlate is total war [m1a,5].

THE TRACE

The alternative to total *Erlebnis*, which Benjamin suggests involves an empathy with exchange value, is a form of idleness appropriate to historical enquiry - the pursuit of the *Spur* or trace.[19] The introduction of the trace opens a new section of the Convolute, [m2], which now completes the break with a historicist narrative. The idea of the trace, offers the possibility of breaking out of the degraded experience of modernity. The traces of the past might be found in the present, while the configurations of the future might be found in the hidden aspects of modernity. Ironically, the very distractedness (*Zerstreuung*) induced by *Erlebnis*, might also create the right mode to hunt and collect the traces of past and future. The hunter, as both primitive and modern figure, must cultivate a kind of distracted attention:

> Whoever follows traces must not only pay attention; above all, he must have given heed already to a great many things. (The hunter must know about the hoof of the animal whose trail he is on; he must know the hour when that animal goes to drink; he must know the course of the river to which it turns, and the location of the ford by which he himself

18. Ibid., p133.

19. *Die Spur* means both trace and spore in German.

can get across.) In this way there comes into play the peculiar configuration by dint of which *Erfahrung* appears translated into the language of *Erlebnis*. [m2,1]

The figure of the hunter now appears as one who practised the earliest mode of idleness, one which was, at the same time, unalienated work:[20]

> *Erfahrungen* can, in fact, prove invaluable to one who follows a trace - but *Erfahrungen* of a particular sort. The hunt is the one type of work in which they function intrinsically. And the hunt is, as work, very primitive.

Tracing the residues of the hunt in the present - and not unusually with Benjamin the method is the same as the hoped for outcome - allows the possibility of future configurations of unalienated work:

> The *Erfahrungen* of one who attends to the trace result only very remotely from any work activity, or are cut off from such a procedure altogether. (Not for nothing do we speak of 'fortune hunting.') They have no sequence and no system. They are a product of chance, and have about them the essential interminability that distinguishes the preferred obligations of the idler.

In the modern world, the hunter is replaced by the student. Study, properly conceived, represents for Benjamin the form of resistant intellectual work appropriate to his times and, I would suggest, ours. He connects the primitive hunter with the modern student as harbinger of the future: 'The fundamentally unfinished collection of things worth knowing, whose utility depends upon chance, has its prototype in study'.[21] 'The text is a forest in which the reader is hunter. Rustling in the underbrush - the idea, the skittish prey, the citation - another piece "in the bag"'[m2a1]. Benjamin's conception of an ideal life of study goes back to an early essay written during his participation in the German student movement, 'The Life of Students', where intellectual work is seen as antithetical to professionalism or a vocation: 'scholarship, far from leading inexorably to a profession, may in fact preclude it. For it does not permit you to abandon it; in a way, it places the student under an obligation to become a teacher, but never to embrace the official professions of doctor, lawyer, or university professor'.[22] In opposition to the bourgeois profession, idleness has a relationship to a form of privileged decadence, where the spaces of decadence, for example the bachelor's studio, are connected to sexual libertinism or experimentation: 'the *studio* became a sort of pendant to the *boudoir*' [m2,3].

Individual creativity, that which makes intellectual work possible, however, is at odds with the general idleness that pervades commodity culture and which is visible in journalism, the mass entertainment and the alienated experience of routine work. [m2a] introduces the modern conditions that

20. There is, of course, a major problem with this vision of primitive communism in that, in its desire to seek an image of unalienated labour, it fails to see the gendered division of labour simply because it does not include women. This failure of vision has implications for Benjamin's conception of the urban savage, the flâneur, although his masculinist perspective is not always as easy to categorise as some accounts have suggested.

21. The unfinishability [*Unabschließbarkeit*] of unalienated labour does raise a question about the unfinished status of *The Arcades Project* itself. Did its method make it unfinishable?

22. Benjamin, 'The Life of Students', in M. Bullock and M.W. Jennings (eds), *Selected Writings Vol. 1: 1913-1926*, Belknapp Press, Cambridge MA., 1996, p38.

require idleness as a 'form of work preparedness', specifically, 'the news service and nightlife' [m2a,2]. These are socially enforced forms of idleness. Reportage and the feuilleton reflect *Erlebnis*. In response, the individual idleness of the poet is anti-work as defined by the Calvinist ethic: 'Idleness seeks to avoid any sort of tie to the idler's line of work, and ultimately to the labour process in general. That distinguishes it from leisure.' [m3,1]. In the face of the enforced 'atrophy of experience' imposed by commodity production and the phantasmagoria of the modern city the urban idler has to resort to guerrilla tactics. As Benjamin remarks in Convolute M, 'The Flâneur': 'the idleness of the flâneur is a demonstration against the division of labour' [M5,8].

Section [m4] of the Convolute begins the dialectical synthesis where socially enforced idleness is countered by its knowing appreciation: 'Idleness can be considered an early form of distraction or amusement. It consists in the readiness to savour, on one's own, an arbitrary succession of sensations'. Significantly, this is distinguished by Benjamin from mass culture: 'But as soon as the production process began to draw large masses of people into the field, those who "had the time" [*frei hatten*] came to feel a need to distinguish themselves en masse from labourers' [m4,1]. Modern idlers attempt a kind of partial transcendence - imitating the gods - that temporarily overcomes the shock experience of modernity: 'The idler's *imitatio dei*: as flâneur, he is omnipresent; as gambler, he is omnipotent; and as student, he is omniscient.' [m4,3]. These are both real and ideal types. Their ambitions are for transcendence, their reality is a partial success in combating its opposite, empathy, which synchronises itself with shock experience without challenging it. Their individual idleness, 'in a bourgeois society that knows no leisure, is the precondition of artistic production', a prefiguring of unalienated work not otherwise available under capitalism: 'idleness is the very thing that stamps that production with the traits that make its relation to the production process so drastic.' [m4a4].

The final section of **m**, completes the dialectic by bringing modern idleness back into relation with the historical traces that allow it to achieve its full meaning and to gesture to its potential. The limitations of the modern idler's perspective are described in terms of Hegel's 'bad infinity', a false transcendence; but there is an open-endedness, an unfinishedness, to idleness than means that it cannot be curtailed by a Hegelian dialectic:

> The student 'never stops learning'; the gambler 'never has enough'; for the flâneur 'there is always something more to see'. Idleness has in view an unlimited duration, which fundamentally distinguishes it from simple sensuous pleasure of whatever variety. [m5,1]

The Convolute ends, incompletely, in the synthesis that brings together the hunter and the idler as one: 'The spontaneity common to the student, to the gambler; to the flâneur is perhaps that of the hunter - which is to say, that of the oldest type of work, which may be intertwined closest of all with idleness. [m5,2]. It mops up with four citations that allude to the historical sense that is needed to make that connection: Flaubert on the melancholic mind set that is needed to imagine the historical past; Baudelaire on the flâneur as modern savage; Spengler on the urban poor as nomads and the modern intellectual as *'intellectual nomad … wholly microcosmic, wholly homeless, as free intellectually as hunter and herdsman were free sensually'* [m5,6].[23] The utopian synthesis is that outlined by Benjamin in the Exposé of 1935:

> In the dream in which each epoch entertains images of its successor, the latter appears wedded to elements of prehistory - that is, to elements of a classless society. And the experiences of such a society - as stored in the collective unconscious of the collective - engender through interpenetration with what is new, the utopia that has left its trace in a thousand configurations of life, from enduring edifices to passing fashions.[24]

***

What do Benjamin's historical promiscuity and experiments with thought in modernist form do for the current debate about intellectual work? Does his profoundly utopian vision make him impractical in a negative as a well as positive sense for current debates about intellectual work or can he take us further than Collini's liberal 'good in itself'?

It is not difficult to object to the oppressive work ethic that has now become more deeply embedded than in the nineteenth century, seeping into the private and intimate spheres through mobile phones, remote voicemail and, once everyone's darling, now a weed escaped from the groves of academe - email. It is more difficult to think one's way out of it. The work culture - I prefer regime - in which we now exist is addictive. It offers self-esteem only through more work. One of the original attractions of intellectual work, and of education itself, was as a way out of drudgery. Intellectual work and its dissemination through speaking, writing and teaching (in Benjamin's sense of teaching, when it means opening up the world that the 'researcher' has discovered for him or herself and wants to introduce to others, rather than the dull repetition of formulas created by a disciplinary or professional field) was meant to be fulfilling. But hitherto this way out has been only for the few and it is that traditional position of privilege that leaves intellectual work so vulnerable to instrumentalist measures of its worth (or, more usually, to paraphrase Wilde, its price). The irony is that the inclusion of more people in higher education is leading not so much to the knowledge economy, where everyone gets a share of privileged time, but to an economy of knowledge. Universities become knowledge factories, parcelling up information in byte-sized chunks to deliver to students as

23. The idea of the modern savage is expanded at length in Convolute M, 'The Flâneur'. See [M11a,5-M14,3] and *passim*.

24. *The Arcades Project*, op. cit., pp4-5.

25. Madeleine Bunting, *Willing Slaves: How the Overwork Culture is Ruling Our Lives*, London, Harper Collins, 2004.

they pass by on the conveyor belt. The nature of work too has changed. As Madeleine Bunting has argued, following Gorz, the new work regime requires the reification of personality and emotions where earlier forms of industrial work had a deadening effect.[25] The answer then must extend beyond the academy and into questions about the nature of work itself. A proper critique can only come from a different way of looking at the world, a way such as that offered by the politics of eco-socialism. As Kate Soper and Martin Ryle have put it:

> Even in the wealthiest societies, almost everyone's life is dominated by the combined impact of the capitalist mission to enhance profits by cutting jobs and of the puritan insistence that work is the condition of pleasure, a 'moral' insistence which in our kind of society is an all too material fact ... [26]

26. Martin Ryle and Kate Soper, *To Relish the Sublime: Culture and Self-Realization in Postmodern Times*, London, Verso, 2002, p183.

Under this regime, idleness is a form of resistance:

> ... Unmet needs for more free time, greater autonomy, more space for self-chosen activity, constitute a counter-systemic potential, a pressure against the bars of the 'iron cage'.[27]

27. Ibid., p184.

Changing individual priorities is one limited way to assert a different value system, working part-time (for those who can rather those who must), for example, to do more useful work and less useless toil. There is also scope for the resistance tactics advocated by de Certeau, particularly taking time out of the daily routine for moments of idleness and forms of creative truancy.[28] Some of the best work gets done, like Conrad's best novels, while avoiding the big project. But these are guerrilla tactics. The current work regime is based on an inequality of income that loosens commitment to collective provision and reproduces itself in its addiction to constant work and the commodities it can buy. There will always be people, like Benjamin himself, who have a precarious existence outside the academy and produce startling work. Some free thinking will be produced illicitly in the spaces funded for specialist knowledge. But intellectual work for more than the few will only flourish if we all work less.

28. See Michel de Certeau, *The Practice of Everyday Life*, Berkeley, University of California Press, 1984.

Benjamin's concept of idleness offers little comfort for nostalgic and conservative thinkers. But its preserves a utopianism in the belief that intellectual work, despite the most unpromising of environments, can presage a collective engagement in fulfilling work. That collective engagement in thought and action is the necessary precondition of what intellectual work might be. Until then we have to fight for the time to do the thinking (and the dreaming) that might free us from the situation we are in. Our slogan should be: Idleness for all!

Marx to the Rescue! Queer Theory and the Crisis of Prestige

Stephen Shapiro

Surveying the rapid institutionalisation of Cultural Studies near his life's end, Raymond Williams urged us not to suppress the actual social history of collective projects and context of occasional political interventions that motivated a set of concerns later nominated as Cultural Studies.[1] If the cost of securing Cultural Studies' status by establishing it as a recognisable discipline meant that its history of emergence would be collapsed into a narrative of foundational academic monographs and internalised behavioural protocols, then this, for Williams, was a price too high. Once Cultural Studies becomes unlinked from the socio-political dynamics that informed its contours, then it appears as little more than an intellectual fetish, a blockage that compounds the problem rather than enabling a solution.

Something of the same could be said about Queer Studies today. It is commonly felt that Queer Theory is less an ongoing event, than a periodisable moment, a relatively defunct agenda that can be safely syllabised and packaged for digestion through a shrink-wrapped assortment of contained debates (essentialism versus social construction, the politics of outing, transgendering, etc.). The recent 'economic turn' in gender and sexuality studies, exemplified in the exchange between Nancy Fraser and Judith Butler, has the refreshing benefit of creating space for a long over-looked set of questions about the relation of class to sexuality.[2] It may also revitalise the field by drawing attention to constitutive absences in Queer Theory's arguments and disciplinary composition.

Nearly every sentence of Foucault's condensed *History of Sexuality: Volume I* has been scrutinised as a means of establishing major debates. But a decades long willed unknowing has settled over his explicit statement that, 'We must return, therefore, to formulations that have long been disparaged; we must say that there is a bourgeois sexuality, and that there are class sexualities. Or rather, that sexuality is originally, historically bourgeois, and that, in its successive shifts and transpositions, it induces specific class effects'.[3] Foucault argued that a subjectivity of interiorised personhood arose as a political tactic wherein the nascent bourgeoisie conceptualised the category of essentialised desire to confront aristocratic status based on blood-lineage. Once the bourgeoisie had surpassed the *ancien regime*, they utilised sexual regulation as a device to contain the lower classes. Consequently, Foucault saw modern sexual liberationist claims as making two fundamental mistakes. Firstly, they anachronistically assume that early modern (regal) modes of

1. Raymond Williams, 'The Future of Cultural Studies', in *The Politics of Modernism: Against the New Conformists*, London, Verso, 1989, pp151-62.

2. Judith Butler, 'Merely Cultural', *New Left Review*, 227 (1998), 33-44; Nancy Fraser, 'Heterosexism, Misrecognition and Capitalism: A Response to Judith Butler', *New Left Review*, 228 (1998), 140-149. For a more concise later statement of Fraser's position see her 'Rethinking Recognition', *New Left Review*, 3, (2000), 107-120. On the economic turn see Mandy Merck (ed), *Cultures and Economies*, special issue of *new formations*, 52 (Spring 2004).

3. Michel Foucault, *The History of Sexuality*, Vol. 1, New York, Vintage Books, 1978, p127.

repressive power remain as the dominant mode of power relations in modern (bourgeois) societies. Secondly, given the historical deployment of sexuality by the middle-class, no agenda of erotic empowerment can exist outside of Marx's critique of capitalism. In a 1977 exchange, when Bernard-Henri Levy asks what might be a 'positive' explanation for sexual unhappiness, Foucault replies: 'I will make a presumptuous comparison. What did Marx do when in his analysis of capital he came across the problem of the workers' misery? He refused the customary explanation which regarded this misery as the effect of a naturally rare cause or of a concerted theft. And he said substantially: given what capitalist production is, in its fundamental laws, it cannot help but cause misery. Capitalism's *raison d'être* is not to starve the workers but it cannot develop without starving them. Marx replaced the denunciation of theft by the analysis of production. Other things being equal, this is approximately what I wanted to say. It is not a matter of denying sexual misery, nor is it however one of explaining it negatively by a repression. The entire problem is to grasp the positive mechanism which, producing sexuality in this or that fashion, results in misery'.[4]

Foucault implies that any discussion of sexuality in general simply reinscribes bourgeois domination as normative. Erotic empowerment campaigns must, therefore, resist the discipline of classificatory knowledge (*savoir*) by constructing strategies and tactics that 'lead to directly political struggles, whose aim [is] not simply to extract concession from the state or to rescind some intolerable measure, but to change the government and the very structure of power'.[5] Because Anglophone Queer Theory largely participated in the post-1960s retreat from class as a conceptual category, its oddly de-politicised reading of Foucault created a basic contradiction that has short-circuited its prolonged efficacy. With this in mind, I want to make two inter-related arguments about the recent economic turn in sexuality studies, as a metonym for a series of related progressive investigations. Firstly, we need a narrative of social movements that more accurately recognises the role of middle-class agendas within empowerment claims. Secondly, that recent debates about the co-implication of sexuality with modes of political economy often seem more compelled by a belated attempt to regain prestige in the high academic arena than with a continuing engagement with the challenges of enacting post-bourgeois experience. This ungenerous, and perhaps overly Manichean, reading may be unfounded, but the burden of proof lies with the intellectuals' ability to rearticulate theory with popular campaigns.

Butler's own exemplary intervention, in 'Merely Cultural', mainly addresses Nancy Fraser's arguments about the definition of social injustice, but the essay's introduction makes it clear that one motive for this round in her ongoing confrontation with Fraser involves a compensatory response to Alan Sokol's implicit shaming of poststructuralist culturalism and implicitly Queer Theory as a closely aligned field within this tendency.[6] Butler defines Sokol's *Social Text* parody piece to be a case of prestige-envy,

4. Michel Foucault, 'Power and Sex: An Interview with Michel Foucault', *Telos*, 32, (1977), 152-161. Exemplifying Anglophone resistance to contextualising Foucault with Marx, this interview was not included within the canonising *The Essential Works of Foucault 1954-1984*, 3 Vols, New Press, 1997-2000.

5. Michel Foucault, *Discipline and Punish: The Birth of the Prison*, London, Penguin, 1977, p273.

6. Alan D. Sokol, 'Transgressing the Boundaries: Towards a Transformative Hermeneutics of Quantum Gravity', *Social Text*, 46-7 (Spring/Summer, 1996), 217-52.

an attempt to 'acquire and appropriate' the 'cultural fame … popularity and media success' of anti-foundational, cultural theory critics.[7] Fraser rightly recognises how she has been pressed into service as a surrogate target by Butler, but she then graciously moves on to argue the merits of the critique against her case. Rather than closely analyse the various insights or insufficiencies of Butler and Fraser's exchange, I want instead to use the encounter as a point of departure to explore the slightly different question about the linkage between prestige deflation and the return to Marx by way of a periodising tale about canonical Queer Theory's rise and fall. The point is not to disparage the much needed return to Marx, but to understand what actual dynamics led to the gesture, in order to gain a more accurate sense of where we might need to go from there.

My evidentiary focus mainly concentrates on US cultural and academic history for strategic reasons. US experience needs to be relativised within the larger world-system, but its post World War Two hegemony has made its local events seem as common sensical as global ones. One effect of US dominance has been that even its marginalised groups receive its aura to become themselves normative examples. Global and American lesbian and gay politics often synchronise and inform each other, but an internationalised queer history that displaces Stonewall as a marker point, even in the pre-Stonewall reclamatory histories, seems anomalous. The incredibly developed and self-confident lesbian and gay life-world of the 1920s Germanophone West has yet to be fully appreciated because the Allied victories meant that the received history of modernity and modernism was routed through Paris rather than Berlin. The US preoccupation with its own nativist lesbian and gay studies remains dominant not because it represents a more advanced non-heteronormative society, but that the dominant critical field assumes it to be so.[8]

Most academic debates replicate the provincial confines of US nationalist parameters because the overwhelming number of Anglophone scholars work within US institutions of higher education. Quantitative differences become qualitative ones as the professional institutions of merit and publication are not only dominated by US based academics, but also that the protocols of valuation, body of references, and topics that are considered of research interest are often culturally particular to the US. Recent attempts to restructure Western academies as machines of knowledge production typically reinscribe dependency theory claims, as the US model is taken to be the only pathway for scholastic development.[9] Queer Theory needs to be analysed as predominately American because the terms of its arguments routinely only make sense within the limits of US juridicality and entitlement provisions, and the institutions of its discursive dissemination have been hegemonised by US credentialisation assumptions. Consequently, one has to engage on the playing field not of one's choice.

Narratives of Queer Studies commonly locate its rise with the floating tides of high Theory from the 1980s to the last years of the past century.

7. Butler, op. cit., p35.

8. For exemplary interventions against the trend, see: Dennis Altman, *Global Sex*, Chicago, University of Chicago Press, 2001 and Arnaldo Cruz and Manalansan, Martin F. (eds), *Queer Globalizations: Citizenship and the Afterlife of Colonialism*, New York, New York University Press, 2002.

9. Nowhere is the imperial normativity of the US academy more institutionalised than in the British Research Assessment Exercise's declaration of colonial inferiority to US judgments. The RAE's devaluation of research of national, rather than international, importance assumes that recognition by the US-led academy defines excellence. Conversely, no US-based scholar would worry if her or his work is only of significance to other US-based scholars.

10. Rictor Norton, *The Myth of the Modern Homosexual: Queer History and the Search for Cultural Unity*, London, Cassell Academic, 1998.

The explanation certainly makes sense when Rictor Norton's proviso about a lack of originality in many of Queer Theory's textual readings and historical markers is taken into account.[10] Norton notes that much of the same-sex sexuality contextualising of figures and documents had initially been done either by low status, non-institutionalised researchers ('independent scholars') or university professionals highly marginalised within the hierarchy of academic institutions and publishing. If the queer turn is simply Lesbian and Gay Studies with Theory's legitimacy on top, then the current absence of the recent past's theoretical ferment would do much to explain the consequent stasis in Queer Studies and desire to mine Marxist-inflected themes as a rich vein of critical theory that has not yet been fully exploited.

While mapping Queer Studies in relation to the popularisation of Derrida, Foucault, and others has a certain resonance, this idealist history of ideas mistakes effect for cause by assuming that social movements are led by concepts rather than the interest in new methods and terminologies responding to a group's need to enunciate ongoing transformations through neologisms. New critical codes arise because existing ones, themselves forged by the exigencies of prior moments, are inadequate to characterise the particularity of new formations. A better chart of Queer Theory's actual trajectory would foreground the academy's articulation to the constitutive competition for prestige within social movements between reformist and anti-systemic strategies.

Regardless of their specific agenda, all modern empowerment social movements are formed by the competition among activists for formal and informal constituencies. The contest is over prestige as the cultural aura that magnetise a faction's ability to garner tacit acceptance of its leadership, command institutional resources for its maintenance, and attract the next wave of human personnel by those willing to continue the tendency's projects beyond the active life of its current agents. Prestige is also the collective form of charisma and is distinct from status and class although the three can often overlap or be variously configured. Prestige is the cultural capital that groups use to generate competitive advantage through the cyclical rate and mass of human subordination. While two secretaries in separate corporations might have the same status, that is to say place in social stratification, as 'white collar workers', a secretary for a 'hip' new media company will have higher prestige value than one working for a boring old industry manufacturer. The media company's magnetism means that it will find it easier to attract applicants willing to accept lower wages in return for the non-economic benefits of higher prestige. Readers will recognize my evocation of Weber's trinity of class, status, and party. The substitution of prestige for party is not meant to evade the former institutional locus, but to suggest a more Gramscian-influenced labour theory of prestige.[11]

More recently, Bourdieu has used the co-ordinates of status and prestige to define his theory of the cultural field. Yet by assuming that a faction's prestige comes from its ability to define itself autonomously, Bourdieu overly

11. H.H. Gerth and C. Wright Mills (eds), *From Max Weber: Essays in Sociology*, New York, Oxford University Press, 1946, pp180-195.

emphasises a synchronic structure that generates value from its internal configuration. Cultural capital, however, is different from cultural status, and Bourdieu's model repeats the mercantilist hoarder's confusion of massed value with profit. A miser's cache of gold may fantasmically grant him autonomy from the need to generate value, but it has little utility as capital since specie is not circulated with an eye to squeezing profit from the exploitation of human labour-power. A faction's prestige does not solely emerge, as Bourdieu claims, from collegial comparisons, which, like the marketplace, only trade in the fetishised equivalent of price signifiers, but do not produce the actual value that is generated by human activity. The cultural field mediates a group's prestige, but its actual source belongs to the relative sacrifices of human agents who trade allegiance to the group in return for modes of life security. Factions gain prestige according to their ability to attract a surplus of dedication from the extramural mass of non-salaried members, fellow travellers, and a lay public willing to be led. Leavisite Practical/New Criticism became important less for its ability to produce satisfying close readings of its textual matter, than for its ability to establish a framework that brought non-university teachers into alliance with and under the guidance of the academy. Academic factions successfully promote themselves as they accrue prestige in their relation to non-academic reformist and anti-reformist tendencies and its effect on the generation of prospective academic members.

The reformist impulse believes that the structure of existing civil society institutions is essentially the ideal one. If these institutions fail to grant their benefits to certain groups, the task at hand is to remove the gap between foundational principles and current practice. The reformist struggle is a therapeutic one that strives to repair a momentary, but not constitutive, exclusion from inclusion, an exclusion that is argued as impairing the overall utility of the institution's efficiency. Examples of reformist projects are suffrage campaigns to extend the right to vote, affirmative action safeguards for employment, education, and housing opportunities, and entitlement campaigns for social welfare provisions. The ideal is liberal equality, the preferred political tactic is to speak truth to power, and the goal is to gain incorporation within pluralist consensus by getting 'a place at the [institutional] table'. The slogan 'must try harder' defines the limit of the reformist agenda, which accepts the inevitability of its own obsolescence after what it considers as regrettable, but momentary, aberrations are resolved.

In Nancy Fraser's terms, the reformist project of identity politics is often concerned less with egalitarian redistribution than what she calls a politics of recognition. An agenda of recognition looks primarily to address the problem of injurious abjection caused by a displacement from the gaze of social acceptance (to be 'misrecognised'). Reformist-recognition politics demand an end to cultural devaluation, but do not feel that the repair of misrecognition also requires a structural redistribution of collective resources.

An example of the limits to recognition appears with Butler's 1996 response to Fraser as it includes a list of heteronormative asymmetries that excludes lesbian and gays from 'state-sanctioned notions of the family (which is, according to both tax and property law, an economic unit) ... citizenship ... freedom of speech and freedom of assembly ... [and inability to] make emergency medical decisions about one's dying lover, to receive the property of one's dying lover, to receive from the hospital the body of one's dead lover'.[12] These are vital demands, but none questions how juridically guaranteed property and inheritance rights structure the economic disparities produced by capitalism's privatisation of social resources or how the ideal of citizenship tacitly accepts the lower status of a nation's denizens (non-vested immigrants, undocumented residents, asylum seekers, etc.).

Reformers' use of misrecognition as a term for disempowerment further confuses the problem. Pace Foucault, modern disciplinary society disempowers by surveillant recognition, where the normative position is un-marked, un-remarkable, and un-recognised, hence misrecognised. The source of the misdirection belongs to Althusser's conflation of Lacanian *mésconnaissance*, as an immanent effect of the Imaginary, with the bourgeois construction of separate spheres. The Lacanian matrix assumes that power relations are without origin, ahistorical, and inescapable. The Marxist critique has no specific position on power relations in general. Its project regards a historically specific mode of power relations: capitalism. Even if one grants the unconscious to be a formation outside of history, the equation of an eternal psychogenetic category with a periodisable one of civil society cannot but undermine Marx's basic historiographic axioms.

Furthermore, as Wendy Brown argues, contemporary recognition politics increasingly tends to redefine the need for civil rights in terms of the desire for consumer privilege. As the universalising struggle for electoral enfranchisement becomes submerged to the particularistic right of the ethnic professional to avoid mass transportation and purchase a taxi ride at will, the trauma of de-citizening historical domination ('social death') is recodified as the resentment for being alienated from bourgeois status, the constitution of which is not itself put under critique.[13] On the other hand, Fraser's brittle binarisation of recognition versus redistribution itself excludes how a politics of visibility ('coming out') may not look for official recognition. Visibility seeks to encourage other isolated subjects within a new collectivity and make the transition from a subject's consciousness 'of itself' as a class to one that is 'for' itself.

The anti-systemic (radical, revolutionary) impulse seeks to achieve this extra step and therefore condemns existing institutions and modes of social regulation as constitutively structured for the purposes of exclusion and maintenance of asymmetric hierarchies. Rather than primarily seeking to negotiate with the current matrix of administration or expand the elasticity of its provisions, the anti-reformist imagination ultimately desires its explosion and replacement by institutions that operate through wholly

12. Butler, op. cit., p41.

13. Wendy Brown, 'Wounded Attachments', in *States of Injury*, Princeton, Princeton University Press, 1995, pp52-76.

different logics or, for some, no institutions at all. Transformation, not reformation, is the slogan here. In academic and ACT UPper Maxine Wolfe's phrase, 'Our job is not to be invited to coffee or to schmooze at a cocktail party. Our job is to make change happen as fast as possible and direct action works for that'.[14]

Because reformism and radicalism, like the terms public and private, have a complicated spectrum of meanings, two clarifications are necessary. Reform agendas are not inconsequential to anti-systemic agents, but these activists struggle for civil rights as a penultimate, not terminal goal. As Marx says, '*Political* emancipation is certainly a big step forward. It may not be the last form of general human emancipation, but it is the last form of human emancipation *within* the prevailing scheme of things'.[15] Charlotte Brunch incisively describes how radicals may demand reform without being reformist. She defines reform as 'a proposed change that alters the conditions of life in a particular arena ... Reform*ism*, on the other hand, has come to mean a particular ideological position ... [that] women's liberation can be achieved by a series of changes that bring us equality within the existing social, economic, and political order of the United States. Reformism assumes that the interests of women are not in fundamental conflict within the American system ... by contrast, a radical analysis sees American society rooted in patriarchy, capitalism, and white supremacy and therefore in fundamental conflict with the interests of women; freedom for oppressed groups ultimately does not come through reforms or equality in those systems, but through a total restructuring of the ideology and institutions of the society'.[16]

A second problem has been the confusion in recent Cultural Studies about Gramsci's distinction between a 'war of movement' and a 'war of position'. These terms refer to Gramsci's redaction of a Comintern debate involving communist strategy. Ought the party encourage the Luxemburg line of mass strike (war of movement) or the one of building the party's institutional stability (war of position)? Both stances are anti-systemic ones about revolutionary tactics; neither is reformist since both Luxemburg and Gramsci equally reject social democrats' reformism.

While reformers and anti-reformers may temporarily share goals, they differ in terms of their horizon of change. In the pursuit of their goals, reformers and anti-reformers continually compete for relative prestige among their perceived audiences, which variously decide what strategy appears to be the more successful one at any moment. As a general phenomenon, though, reformers often maintain dominance for longer periods of time and with a broader base. Anti-reformist movements often remain residual, partly because the more complex task of confronting existing institutions while also trying to establish durable counter-institutions often seems to be losing the contest. Consequently anti-systemic factors usually come to the forefront only when reformers have failed in a major undertaking that results in their ensuing legitimation crisis.

14. Maxine Wolfe, 'After Ten Years: The Realities of the Crisis, Direct Action, and Setting the Agenda', 1997, <http://www.actupny.org/%2010thanniversary/wolfespeech.html>

15. Karl Marx, 'On the Jewish Question', in *Early Writings*, New York, Vintage, 1975, p221.

16. Charlotte Bunch, 'The Reform Tool Kit', in *Passionate Politics: Feminist Theory in Action: Essays 1968-1986*, New York, St Martins Press, 1988, pp103-117.

In this light, Queer Studies' rise results less from the autonomous ability of critical theory about linguistic discursivity to carry forward a Kuhnian paradigm change in the field of sexuality, than its ability to benefit from the collapse of lesbian and gay reformist projects in the mid-1980s. After World War Two, lesbian and gay homophile organisations, like the Mattachine Society and the Daughters of Bilitis (DOB) sought an assimilationist, integrationist agenda. New York members of Mattachine confronted Jim Crow-like legislation that prohibited serving alcohol to male homosexuals by going to bars dressed in conservative suit and tie, announcing their sexual orientation, and asking (!) to be served. The DOB's name echoed nativist reactionary associations, like the Daughters of the American Revolution, as if ostensibly staking a claim for lesbian inclusion within the nationalist imaginary. Homophobic Cold War hysteria was impervious to reformers' rationality and homophile projects failed spectacularly to make durable change. Both organisations were short-lived and localised in their effects.

Throughout the 1960s, a spectrum series of anti-systemic movements emerged that used the safety of an economic boom to establish a counter-hegemonic common sense involving resistance to US-led mass-market consumerism, imperialism (Vietnam), racism, and sexual Puritanism. Though loosely, if not incoherently structured, the combined weight of these campaigns facilitated the passage to the 1969 Stonewall Riot, which bypassed the language of civil rights and tactics of civil disobedience for the more disruptive rhetoric of liberation and methods of urban insurgency. Because homophile integrationists had consistently failed to secure inclusion within the 'Great Society', lesbian and gay subjects looked to those factions rhetorically aligning themselves with guerrilla decolonisation movements (such as the Gay Liberation Front), political engagement through confrontational tactics of public spectacle (the GLF's direct action 'zaps' of unexpected face-to-face encounters with surprised officials); and a counter-public of community newspapers and broadsheets that rejected dominant terminology to propose neologistic self-descriptors ('gay' rather than 'homosexual'; 'out of the closet' rather than 'in the life').

The eventual containment of the 1960s horizon of possibilities, especially after 1973-74, led to splintering, isolationist micro-politics, on the one hand, and the return to the ideal of reform, on the other, with the long march through institutions. While the latter has often been discredited from the perspective of the 1980s, a more objective consideration would note the comparative greater success during this period of the reformist wing in securing its goals and attracting personnel. The phase between the mid-1970s and the early/mid-1980s saw both the construction of lesbian and gay institutions and a more open entry for discrete individuals within mainstream organisations. Certain lesbians and gays who would not insist on structural changes in social behaviour increasingly managed to achieve and maintain professional posts, leverage a modicum of political power in some urban regimes (for example, Harvey Milk in San Francisco), economic advantage through geographies of residential property ownership, and moderate recognition in mass popular culture. The general trend of tacit inclusion in this period, even given pockets of resistance, encouraged reformers in the feasibility of a softly, softly approach that increasingly blurred the difference between a heteronormative culture and a transgressive 'homosexual' one in favour of the former, such as with the rise of the butch gym-body male that rejects a 'feminised' refusal by certain men to participate in the will to musculature.

In the US context, two events within the cultural wars led by 1980s neoconservatism foreclosed the incrementalism of the post-1960s passage: *Bowers v. Hardwick* and AIDS. When Michael Hardwick was arrested for transgressing Georgia's anti-sodomy laws in his bedroom, he contested the charge in the Supreme Court as a violation of his right to privacy. The Supreme Court's 1986 decision against Hardwick denied lesbians and gays constitutional protection and dealt a stunning blow to assimilationist groups who had committed themselves to a slow but sure process of official recognition. *Bowers v. Hardwick* conclusively drew a line in the sand beyond which enfranchisement campaigns could not advance. Yet even the court ruling might have simply shifted the focus away from the federal level back to state and local campaigns were it not for AIDS.

As Peter Cohen shows, the compact of white, gay male inclusion within middle-class privilege, based on their refusal to insist forcefully on civil rights so long as they received consumer access, shuddered to a halt with the AIDS crisis. As the disease's dermal markings outed gay men, it reinscribed difference by publicising their unremarked inclusion within the US's managerial and professional status structures.[17] AIDS cut the heart of reformist desires as it demanded the one thing that middle-class men could not either buy or nuance - a cure. Given the absence of a free-market solution, HIV positive men were thrust back onto whatever limited protection that constitutionality provided, and this is where *Bowers v. Hardwick's* exclusions hurt.

The conjuncture of federally-guaranteed homophobia and a health crisis exacerbated by the absence of state medical provision and protection against corporate greed caused a legitimation crisis for pre-existing lesbian and gay integrationist lobby organisations, like the National Lesbian and Gay Task Force (NLGTF), who were immobilised by events. Increasingly unable to retain the allegiance of their membership and authority as community leaders, these reforming groups suffered a large-scale loss of prestige. The reformers' disestablishment created the opportunity for a return to radical disruptiveness typified by ACT UP (the AIDS Coalition to Unleash Power) and its initial break-the-rules attitude. The incapacity of reformers to maintain prestige was exploited by rebellious factions who then garnered the support of many individuals who would have never become politically active, let alone directly confrontational.

The truism about ACT UP is that the AIDS crisis facilitated a new coalition

17. Peter F. Cohen, *Love and Anger: Essays on AIDS, Activism, and Politics*, Binghampton, NY, The Haworth Press, 1998.

between middle-class white gay men, who had expertise with media, real estate, and financial networks, and often lower-class ranked lesbians, who provided the practical experience and popular memory of long-term grass-roots activism. This gendered division of labour was present, but it also overly simplifies the role of other 'problem' groups who were able to come to prominence after a long period of being shut out by reformers' desires to present lesbian and gays in a wholesome light, such as women who felt that a mode of lesbian separatism had itself become censorious of same-sex sex and those men who did not easily accept a liberal consumerist lifestyle or corporatised behaviour: unmusculated 'East Villagers'; sissies; and the, at that point, long demonised proponents of camp and drag.

Jonathan Demme's 1993 *Philadelphia* neatly captures this moment's conjunctural turn. Andrew Beckett (Tom Hanks), an Ivy League graduate working for a white-shoe corporate law firm, has achieved a comfortable life filled with all the apparatus of an idealised upper middle-class life: unreserved support of his homosexuality and acceptance of his lover by his suburban family; easily accessible medical care of the most sophisticated kind available; and a dedicated partner who never has to doubt that he will receive control of their designer loft or face challenge to Beckett's probate will. The only blemish on this gay success story is the surface KS lesion that initiates Beckett's wrongful dismissal. Abandoned by his status colleagues, Beckett falls into a coalition with disrespectful characters, a move toward anti-reformism witnessed by the first ever representation of an ACT UP demonstration within a Hollywood film.

ACT UP's ability to magnetise a new coalition of disparate interests catapulted the rise of Queer Theory more than Jacques Derrida's interrogation of the sign. As AIDS street activism reinvigorated an anti-reformist alliance of different gender, class, and, to a lesser degree, racial elements, it energised intellectual work by bridging the gap between institutional isolation and broader public relevance. Activism's cachet in creating a new alliance was read back into academic prose in ways that helped to elevate critics into celebrities as readers defined their work as transparently amplifying ongoing concerns. Anyone who has recently tried teaching Eve Sedgwick to contemporary students will know the tremendous contextualisation required to deliver the received sense of her 1980s interpretative claims that are often difficult to locate precisely in the actual printed argument.

As Queer Theory appeared to bridge the chasm that separates the US academy from any contact, let alone impact, with a broader public, it quickly gained newfound status within the university. The sudden transformation of an often fragmented group of scholars working on lesbian and gay themes into a recognisable field turned what had long been a career liability for scholars into a means of securing publication contracts, conference plenaries, degree programmes, and upper hierarchy academic posts. Prestige also accumulated. More so than other Anglophone academies, the highly privatised US university system, relatively free from otiose ministerial interventions, depends on a consumer model. The American humanities academy often gauges merit based on the popularity of academic trends within the undergraduate and graduate populations as much as it does among other professors. On the other hand, because the university also functions as a key site in the US for an individual's class assignment or recodification, it paradoxically also acts as a main institutional site for the search for anti-systemic expressions in the absence of other left institutions. In this light, the rise and fall of various modes of literary criticism often follows the cycle where a new school attracts proponents as it seems to house anti-reformist energies. When the inevitable contradictions between its purported claims and requirements of its institutional location become self-evident, the field declines and is replaced by the next intellectual great hope. From the 1980s, student interest in this regard motivated the succession of 'hot' fields in a sequence from African-American studies, semiotics and poststructuralism, New Historicism, Queer Theory, and, more recently, postcolonialism.

The fall of the House of Queer Theory dates from an over-determined moment in the mid-1990s just as Sokol's parody and the Butler-Fraser debate were seeing publication. The crisis of Queer Studies' erosion of prestige results from several inter-connecting factors. Firstly, the rise of third-way politics, led by Clinton, co-opted the anger and resentment fuelled by years of Republican party fundamentalisms and splintered the anti-reformist coalition as it lent its support to the reformist language of recognition politics. Candidate Clinton's signature 'I feel your pain' promised the therapeutic salve that abjection politics desired. The phrase was first said to PWA and ACT UPper Bob Rafsky who had interrupted a speech by Clinton in order to call attention to the ongoing crisis.[18] By drawing the emotional focus onto himself and away from a visibly KS lesioned Rafsky, Clinton helped to deflate the air of emergency surrounding AIDS and would replace it with more reform oriented projects, like gays in the military. Rafsky meanwhile would be dead within the year. The political momentum of the late 1980s dissolved as activists remained uncertain if it was tactically wise to attack a regime that initially promised to break from Reaganite policies.

Meanwhile, the 1996 Vancouver International AIDS conference stage-managed the 'end of AIDS' with the arrival of combination therapy drugs that dramatically reduced mortality and prolonged life for the HIV positive. Now that something like a cure could be bought for those with access to these resources, the political agenda returned back to incremental lobby-oriented politics, such as the first efforts to what would later develop into the set-piece for reformers: gay marriage. As combo therapy meant that time for long-term planning and the reconstruction of a private-sphere life was available in ways that had not been the case for more than a decade, the crisis coalition of gender and class interests that ACT UP so brilliantly housed fell apart.

18. Background on the event can be found at <http://www.actupny.org/campaign96/rafsky-clinton.html>

From the late 1990s through the current moment, anti-systemic activists have been unable to recuperate the affinities of the prior period amidst the increased success of reformist projects. A pivotal moment occurred when the Supreme Court's recent *Lawrence v. Texas* overturned *Bowers v. Hardwick*. Like Hardwick, John Lawrence contested his arrest for violating Texas's sodomy laws in his home. This time the Supreme Court granted lesbians and gays privacy rights. After *Lawrence* and similar advances in equality enfranchisement, it is now hard to imagine that Butler's 1996 list of demands will not be achieved by 2006, if not sooner. For conservative reformers like Andrew Sullivan, the act of recognition ought to conclude the lesbian and gay social movement, which, for him, existed only to achieve normativity.[19]

As third-way politics and the changed environment of AIDS in America dismantled the extramural activism that motivated, focused, and established academic discourse, Queer Theory was increasingly left on its own to develop a new agenda. But without the broad public interface, Queer Theory now faced the problem of inauthenticity and stasis that comes home to roost for all disciplinary fields based on popular or mass cultures. When a 'studies' (women's, Black, cultural, etc.) becomes a disciplinary field, it bears the academic institutional burden of organising itself as an originary nexus of conceptual problematics that propels continuing research projects. Yet the social life on which the study was founded neither operates in this fashion nor insists on adjudicating 'debates' in the way demanded by university publishing protocols.[20] As Raymond Williams warned, a cultural studies separated from public engagement had no future at all.

Isolated from the electricity of anti-reformist energies, which were themselves dampened, Queer Theory faced a crisis of lost prestige within the academy in four ways. Firstly, literary and visual studies departments, which saw themselves as the avant-garde of Queer Studies because of their early reception of Francophone theory, began to be overtaken by historical research. While many of the theoretical debates did not progress further, archival research, which requires a longer span of time from initial research to publication, has brought forward a host of methodological questions about the generalisability of evidence that a theoretically informed cultural studies has had less experience considering. For literary and cultural studies the distinction between a statement and a discourse rarely matters, especially since the legacy of New/Practical criticism favours particularity. The field of history has organised its foundational debates more around what qualifies as the threshold of generality. The latter draws history closer to the question of social movements that energises progressive studies in the first instance.

The second decline came with the failure of autonomous Queer Studies departments to materialise. The elite research institutions that would have had the most latitude for establishing these in the face of neoconservatism did not, since the potential student demographic base was not large enough to carry the day. More damagingly, the failure of institutional expansion left the first wave of Queer theorists, who had benefited from the brief open

19. Andrew Sullivan, *Virtually Normal: An Argument About Homosexuality*, New York, Vintage, 1996.

20. Ann Leffler, Dair L. Gillespie and Elinor Lerner, *Academic Feminists and the Women's Movement*, Iowa City, Iowa City Women's Press, 1973. Available online at <http://www.nostatusquo.com/ACLU/Nikki/academic1.html>

window of rapid professional advancement, increasingly being seen by more junior colleagues and graduate students as a privileged intellectual labour aristocracy within a corporatised university that was increasingly revealed as intrinsically dependent on the exploitation of casualised labour contracts. Despite many academics' individual support for graduate and adjunct labour, few institutional reforms occurred. Queer Theory graduate students saw reformist projects succeed elsewhere, but not within the academy itself, which was remarkably resilient against structural change. As the next wave of would-be Queer Studies scholars saw their future employability return to pre-1980s conditions and their current living conditions worsen, as the 1997 collection *Will Teach for Food* demonstrated, many felt alienated from the aura of their scholarly role-models.[21] Graduate students responded by repositioning their research profile in ways that downplayed their intellectual lineage and functionally damaged its potential to attract a third-wave of scholars.

As graduate students turned away from Queer Theory, the first moment of collegiate post-identity politics started to appear in the initial waves of anti-globalisation politics. These first took the form of student campaigns against branded university logo-wear as a product of the new international sweat-shop matrix. As the ever attuned Andrew Ross's 1997 collection *No Sweat* shows, these campaigns became the ACT UP for the 1990s campus.[22] Beyond simply replacing the focus on AIDS, young anti-globalisation activists who had been taught Queer Theory-influenced arguments now felt that their professors were naive about the growth of neo-liberalism and the academy's own uncritical relationship to capitalist commodification. Theoretical claims about performativity and fabulous self-construction seemed to students as if they were little more than puff pieces for retail therapy as a mode of resistance. As a member of this demographic, Naomi Klein argues her age cohort's case in *No Logo*, one of the influential syncretic manifestos of the anti-globalisation movement. Klein accuses the 1980s professoriate for paying so much attention to 'the politics of mirrors and metaphors', that they 'mask[ed] for us the fact that many of our demands for better representation were quickly accommodated by marketers, media makers and pop-culture producers alike'.[23] 'Identity politics weren't fighting the system, or even subverting it. When it came to the vast new industry of corporate branding, they were feeding it'.[24]

The legacy of linguistic discursivity served Queer Theory poorly here. The performative statement, 'I'm out!' works excellently when subjectivity is conceptualised in terms of liberalism's possessive individualism. A statement, like 'We're here, we're queer, get used to it' is substantive, not performative, since the constitution of a collectivity (the 'we') needs to be constructed prior to the speaking subject's announcement. Because performativity elides the history of group mutuality's construction, it appears to function just like the commodity-fetish. It valorises a sphere of intentional, voluntarist action where cultural value seems to come from dialogic exchange rather than the production of social relations formed by material sites of

21. Cary Nelson (ed), *Will Teach for Food: Academic Labor in Crisis*, Minneapolis, University of Minnesota Press, 1997.

22. Andrew Ross (ed), *No Sweat: Fashion, Free Trade, and the Rights of Garment Workers*, London, Verso, 1997. A more recent collection argues for the anti-globalisation movement's links to and substitution of AIDS activism, see: Benjamin Shepard and Ronald Hayduk (eds), *From ACT UP to the WTO: Urban Protest and Community Building in the Era of Globalization*, London, Verso, 2002.

23. Naomi Klein, *No Logo: Taking Aim at the Brand Bullies*, London, Picador, 2002, pp113, 110.

24. Ibid., p113.

coerced subjectivity.

If Queer Theory today appears at a standstill, it is because it has lost prestige and its publics. The non-academic constituency who might have read its work has been moved back by the leadership of reformists to property rights issues, like marriage. The student interest that formerly buoyed the work sees other agendas as occupying the locus of radical energies in ways that do not (yet) fall into the bad consciousness of attempting radical critiques while safeguarding the rigor of an academic field. The unquestioned institutional privilege of Queer Theorists, increasingly seen as estranged from their own public and promoting arguments that connote the principles of liberalism/libertarianism, now means that Queer Theory has to prove its street credibility once more to a post-1989 generation that lacks any felt need to apologise for 'actually existing socialism' and increasingly looks back to 'old left' arguments. Marx to the rescue! The moment for the long-disregarded economic turn in sexuality and gender studies had come.

Perhaps my reading is too sinister or, worse, beside the point. Whatever Queer Theory's initial motives for the economic turn, it remains a much-needed reveille for radicals to begin reconstructing the alliance necessary for the next phase of anti-systemic activism. Before this hard road to renewal can either occur or produce new enactable claims, many longstanding debates, especially those about concretising organic, left institutions, need to be worked through. In this process, many of the implicit assumptions within an earlier phase of Queer Studies may ultimately need re-theorising before we can achieve the incomplete project of a post-bourgeois lifeworld.

THE WORK OF FORGETTING: RAYMOND WILLIAMS AND THE PROBLEM OF EXPERIENCE

Keya Ganguly

Is there never to be an end to petit-bourgeois theorists making long-term adjustments to short-term situations?
(Raymond Williams, *The Politics of Modernism*)

Earlier this year I attended a talk in which the speaker attributed the phrase 'structure of feeling' to a feminist film scholar, Patricia White, in the course of developing her ideas about female spectators of film noir and related discourses of fandom. Pressed to explain her attribution, the speaker would only say that she found the phrase very suggestive for expanding the category of viewing pleasure and for thinking about patterns of consumption surrounding film-going, without evincing any knowledge about the provenance of the phrase or any self-consciousness about how this might matter. Aside from bemoaning the state of the profession and, specifically, that of 'theory' in its poststructuralist dominant (at least within film and literary studies), this incident gives a small indication of the ways that generations of future scholars are being trained to forget what they never knew in the first place: how the present was wrested from the past in the name of eschewing a 'vulgar Marxism' and replacing its shortcomings with a supposedly more complex and critical vocabulary.

The advantage of this new regime of theoretical training, we are told, is that one can now select from various intellectual and political traditions to offer what passes for non-dogmatic theorisations of culture and history. This selective eclecticism is defended on such bases as Michel Foucault's assertion of theory as a 'toolkit', or Jean-François Lyotard's notion that theoretical choices are only 'language games'. Accordingly, it is no longer necessary, even from the vantage point of an interpretive practice that claims to be involved in what is archly - if vaguely - dubbed the 'critique of capitalism', to work through the ideas of Marxist or Left Hegelian critics. Nor is it important to be concerned with the origins of any idea, particularly if it seems to be generated from a quarter that cannot immediately be assimilated into some presently fashionable approach to criticism. Indeed, one need only utter the phrase 'master discourse' or 'the myth of authorial origins' for such concerns to be swept away as lacking in merit. The turn towards *reading* as the most critical act in the act of 'critique' has consequently obviated the need to know about the warring histories of thought which produced the very ideas that allow one to become more complex and critical.[1]

1. For longer arguments about the contemporary tendency of poststructuralist approaches to repress the past, see Neil Lazarus, 'Introduction: Hating Tradition Properly', in his *Nationalism and Cultural Practice in the Postcolonial World*, Cambridge University Press, 1999, pp1-15; and Timothy Brennan, 'Antonio Gramsci and Post-Colonial Theory', *Diaspora*, 10, 2 (Fall 2001), 143-87, as well as 'The Empire's New Clothes', *Critical Inquiry*, 29, 2 (Winter 2003), 337-367. A similar approach to the Left Hegelian tradition has also been pursued over many years by Fredric Jameson; much of his most insightful commentary occurs in *Marxism and Form*, Princeton University Press, 1971.

So it is that coinages both important and ultimately trivial - everything from 'structures of feeling' and 'imagined communities' to 'provincializing Europe', 'subject positions', 'the critique of Enlightenment' as well as the 'critique of capitalism' itself, not to mention the phrase that trumps all else, 'vulgar Marxism' - can be deployed like bulwarks against thinking through the stakes or substance of ideas rendered into sound bytes. In what follows, I would like to chart some contours of the route that Raymond Williams' ideas have travelled, especially within feminist discussions of the status of experience in understanding culture. The phrase 'structure of feeling' functions here as a *mise-en-abîme* precisely of the ways that Williams today stands as the passé, superseded figure of the 'dead white man' in vulgar feminist parlance, whose conceptual arguments can be assimilated into a fashionable representation only once they have been shorn of their parentage and their materialist anchoring. Moreover, if he must be dealt with at all, the contemporary critic must find ways to read Williams that reveal his essentialism - over against which a reflexive feminism's avowed commitment to anti-essentialist readings of culture, history, and experience stand illuminated.

Elizabeth J. Bellamy and Artemis Leontis have argued that 'Experience has become so fully and completely "interpellated" into our consciousness that it often tends to escape notice or consideration'.[2] Their expansive ruminations about the need to construct experience as a discursive category are capped off as follows: 'A focus on "experience" need not be relegated simply to that which is blind to its own discursive constructedness. Rather, a specifically postmodern focus on "experience" *could* [authors' emphasis] potentially become a dynamic way of reintroducing experience to the political field'.[3] The authors accordingly find their way to an unquestioned 'postmodern' emphasis on 'discursive construction' - eliding in the process the epistemological status of discourse itself as well as revealing a presentist assumption about the postmodern. With specific reference to Williams, the authors also make the dubious charge that he fails 'to link the experience of "ordinary people" with the larger realm of the sociocultural'.[4] Thus is Williams, with whom an entire tradition of sociocultural criticism came to be associated, upbraided for his neglect of the sociocultural!

The implication is that Williams must be read not so much 'against the grain' (another formulation which finds favour these days when the desire is to attribute to a thinker arguments that run counter to what he or she may actually have said) but on the terms of a wholly invented one: we might, for lack of a better phrase, call it 'inventing a grain'. Lest this sound merely tendentious, let me add that although I find some of the modes of reading that have the upper hand in cultural criticism today formulaic and predictable, it is still the case that serious work goes into revisions of position and re-readings of thought.[5]

The work of forgetting alluded to in my title is intended to evoke the kind of intellectual work that may, more accurately, be thought of as a *working through* by means of which the accumulated weight of past traditions is dealt

2. Elizabeth J. Bellamy and Artemis Leontis, 'A Genealogy of Experience: From Epistemology to Politics', *The Yale Journal of Criticism*, 6, 1, 163.

3. Ibid., p180.

4. Ibid., p169.

5. In the case of valuable assessments of Williams, for instance, see Colin Sparks, 'Raymond Williams, Culture and Marxism', *International Socialism*, 2, 9, (1980), 131-144. Also see the important memorial issue of *News from Nowhere* entitled, 'Raymond Williams: Third Generation', 6 (February 1989), *passim*.

with in a reckoning that is, on occasion, false (albeit influential). It is to one such false reckoning that I want to turn my attention below. I should also add that what follows is in sympathy with and very much indebted to the account of the importance of Williams's work given by John Higgins in his essay, 'Forgetting Williams' (1995) and the title of my discussion is of course also a play on his.[6] But whereas Higgins attempts to think through the painful productivity of the 'work of mourning' by providing a careful reading of the place of psychoanalysis (particularly in relation to propositions about language and the unconscious) in Williams's writing, my effort is a modest reading of the practical aspects of rememoration; specifically, I want to look at the historical light by which Williams is remembered on the question of experience.

Alongside the complexities of Higgins' implication that acts of remembrance take on the cast of confirming a loss, an implication that frames his reconsideration of the ambivalent tributes paid to Williams after his death, it is also the case that working through the past is more simply about a certain expenditure of labour. This idea of working through is one that complements the Freudian sense that Higgins deploys to refer to the emergence of unconscious impulses and repressed memories through such 'deferred actions' as trauma and mourning. And its usage can be attributed to Theodor Adorno's specification in 'The Meaning of Working through the Past' (first published in German in 1959 and delivered again in 1962 as a lecture on the dangers of suppressing the history of Fascism). Re-issued in a recent English edition of Adorno's writings printed in 1998, Adorno clarifies the idea of working through as discharging the concrete burden of the past - by undertaking the tasks of cleaning up and clearing away the cobwebs that have been left behind.[7] As the translator of this volume, Henry W. Pickford, tells us, Adorno relies here on the commonplace inflection in German of 'working through' (*Aufarbeitung*) to signal that managing the past is not entirely about psychic reworkings (more appropriately designated by the term *Durcharbeitung*, with its psychoanalytic inflection of the 'working out' of an unconscious blockage) but also the mundane, if instrumental, ways of everyday work. The idea of working through, then, depends very much on work itself, given its common sense and practical meaning of dispatching with unnecessary distractions and matters that prevent one from going forward in one's decided course. Working through thus connotes active self-management even as it also conjures up an 'acting out' of self-mastery.

We see this kind of labour expended in theoretical efforts in which the objective, above all, is to relegate an idea or argument to the ordinariness one believes it deserves on the grounds of conceptual, explanatory, or political inadequacy. This is of course in the nature of intellectual discourse itself (with its roots in traditions of disputation within both European and non-Western philosophy), although the downgrading of an author or an idea also has much to do with the imperatives for intellectuals - like other

6. John Higgins, 'Forgetting Williams', in C. Prendergast (ed), *Cultural Materialism: On Raymond Williams*, University of Minnesota Press, 1995, pp117-139.

7. Theodor W. Adorno, *Critical Models: Interventions and Catchwords*, Columbia University Press, 1998, pp89-103; this collection is a translation of *Eingriffe: Neuen kritische Modelle*, Suhrkamp Verlag, 1963. The translator's notes relevant to my discussion appear on pp337-338.

workers under the regime of capital - to distinguish their products in terms of innovation and refinement. Particularly if the present theoretical milieu has to be represented as an improvement over the past, the incentive to assess a set of ideas in ways that devalue (or, by contrast, overvalue) their contribution becomes evident. And, sometimes, such assessments acquire the weight of legitimacy, if only by dint of assertion rather than an actual working through of the idea or position in question. In such instances, the process of working through may very much resemble an acting out - with the net result being the decline in the academic fortunes of past ideas over against the rise in the purported value of present readings.

In a highly acclaimed essay entitled 'The Evidence of Experience' (first published in 1991 in *Critical Inquiry* and reprinted two years later in the influential anthology, *The Lesbian and Gay Studies Reader*), the feminist historian Joan Scott offers a critique of the epistemological weight given to experience within the discourse of history-writing.[8] As a much-needed corrective to the conviction in the minds of historians that experience represents the bedrock of the knowable past (and present), Scott proposes that the authority granted to experience provides a litmus test of whether or not historians have been able to shed their 'foundationalist' assumptions in the wake of 'insights drawn from the sociology of knowledge, structural linguistics, feminist theory, or cultural anthropology ... ' (401). If the reader notices the elision of any mention of the wholly constitutive lessons against metaphysical thinking that these fields themselves derived from the history of Marxist thought (the work of the Young Hegelians including but not limited to Marx himself, Georg Lukács, or the entire Frankfurt School, for example) this may, for the moment, be overlooked in order to grant Scott's main point that '[i]t is not individuals who have experience, but subjects who are constituted through experience. Experience in this definition then becomes not the origin of our explanation, not the authoritative (because seen or felt) evidence that grounds what is known, but rather that which we seek to explain, about which knowledge is produced' (401). Scott further states that to think about experience as constituted rather than *a priori* represents ' ... a historicising that implies critical scrutiny of all explanatory categories usually taken for granted, including the category of "experience"' (401).

In so far as Scott's intervention works to urge contemporary scholars to rethink the 'evidence of experience', it is undoubtedly commendable (especially to the extent that she draws attention to feminist accounts - seeking to replace 'histories' with 'herstories' - for their unproblematic assumptions regarding experience as the source of truth). But her own evidentiary claims about complicating the status of experience depend upon an extremely limited conception of the experiencing subject as well as an equally limited conception of the uses of experience in the writings of critics - such as Williams - whom she takes to task. There is a 'heads-I-win, tails-you-lose' strategy at work in Scott's discussion and it enables the masking of

8. Joan W. Scott, 'The Evidence of Experience', in H. Abelove, M.A. Barale, D.M. Halperin (eds), *The Lesbian and Gay Studies Reader*, Routledge, 1993, pp397-415.

her underlying investments. If, as Scott states, 'the evolution of "experience" appears to solve a problem of explanation for professed anti-empiricists even as it reinstates a foundational ground' (402), what sort of approach to the issue of experience would mark an improvement over such 'foundationalist' appeals? Her answer proceeds by way of quoting from Williams's entry on 'experience' in *Keywords* as follows: '(i) knowledge gathered from past events, whether by conscious observation or by consideration and reflection; and (ii) a particular kind of consciousness, which can in some contexts be distinguished from "reason" or "knowledge"' (402). She represents Williams further: 'Until the early eighteenth century, he says, experience and experiment were closely connected terms, designating how knowledge was arrived at through testing and observation (here the visual metaphor is important)' (402). Scott finally summarises Williams's historical parsing of the term by saying,

> In the various usages described by Williams, 'experience', whether conceived as internal or external, subjective or objective, establishes the prior existence of individuals. When it is defined as internal, it is an expression of an individual's being or consciousness; when external, it is the material on which consciousness acts. Talking about experience in these ways leads us to take the existence of individuals for granted (experience is something people have) rather than to ask how conceptions of selves (of subjects and their identities) are produced (402).

The judgment thus rendered allows Scott to then turn to her main objective: to establish experience as a conceptualisation of the *production of identities*. However, before we take this turn with Scott, we ought to pause before her representation of Williams's account of experience. Quite apart from the fact that Williams wrote about the problem of experience in far more elaborated ways in works that spanned his entire career - from his early book, *The Long Revolution* (1961), through *The Country and the City* (1973) to the posthumously published collection, *The Politics of Modernism* (1989) - a range that makes Scott's abbreviated citation of *Keywords* seem simplistic, militating against the drift of her case for an exemplary complexity, there is the matter of what Williams actually proposes in his entry on experience.[9] Far from taking for granted the 'prior existence of individuals' in describing either the subjective or objective dimensions of experience, Williams in fact suggests a crucial distinction:

> At one extreme, experience (present) is offered as the necessary (immediate and authentic) ground for all (subsequent) reasoning and analysis. At the other extreme, experience (once the present participle not of 'feeling' but of 'trying' or 'testing' something) is seen as the product of social conditions or of systems of belief or of fundamental systems of perception, and thus *not as material for truths but as evidence of conditions or systems which by definition it cannot itself explain*.[10] (emphases added)

9. See Raymond Williams, *Keywords: A Vocabulary of Culture and Society* (revised edition), Oxford University Press, 1983 [1976], pp126-129.

10. Ibid., p128.

The issue here is less that Scott selectively quotes from Williams's description of the development of the idea of experience than that she ascribes to him a position that is demonstrably incorrect; but it is the move that makes possible her corresponding claim that his perspective 'operates within an ideological construction that not only makes individuals the starting point of knowledge, but that also naturalises categories ... treating them as given characteristics of individuals' (402). Contrary to her representation, almost at the beginning of his entry on the term Williams contrasts the way Burke's *Reflections on the Revolution in France* (1790) evokes the sense of experience: 'If I might venture to appeal to what is so much out of fashion in Paris, I mean to experience ... ', with a riposte which makes clear that experience needs to be understood in a more settled and structural manner: 'Someone in Paris might have replied', says Williams, 'that the Revolution itself was an "experience"'. Only after suggesting this initial contrast between experience past and experience present as a problem of *historical* consciousness, which is certainly not about the 'characteristics of individuals', does Williams proceed with the rest of his entry.

Scott's modus operandi is to attribute a personalist and individualist framework of understanding to Williams as well as others - which she can then call into question - in order to proffer the alleged corrective of feminist-theoretical explanations whose emphasis on subject-construction enables 'examining the relationships between [sic] discourse, cognition, and reality, the relevance of the position or situatedness of subjects to the knowledge they produce, and the effects of difference on knowledge' (403). Even in the abridged context of *Keywords* Williams can be shown to have said something similar, albeit using different terms: 'The strength of this appeal [within conceptions of experience] to wholeness, against forms of thought which would exclude certain kinds of consciousness as merely "personal", "subjective" or "emotional" is evident. Yet within the form of appeal ... *the stress on wholeness can become a form of exclusion of other nominated partialities'*

11. Ibid., pp127-8.

(emphases added).[11] My point is to draw attention not only to the way Scott distorts Williams's presentation but also to the fact that her recommendations on behalf of a specific mode of feminist theorising rest on eliding whole sections of the entry that is her sole reference to the many-sided and nuanced discussions of experience in the oeuvre of Williams's work (that he, for one, was never hesitant to re-appraise or be challenged to reconsider). The selectivity by means of which Scott represents Williams is not only in stark contrast to Williams's own more reflective and open scholarly mien, it is in direct proportion to the intellectual effort necessary to demote the insights available from Williams himself.

In this context, Williams's brilliant parsing of the problem of experience in relation to a structure of feeling provides one example of the complexity of his thought, although it is the kind of evidence for which Scott has no use. Nonetheless, it might be worth our while to recall how he discussed the structuring tensions of the experience of Welsh life in the 1979 essay, 'The

Welsh Industrial Novel'.[12] In that particular venue, he made a case for taking the pastoral out of the ambit of a nostalgic and exoticising mode of literary representation into an understanding of the sociological and historical constitution of pastoral elements. In doing so, he self-consciously elevated an emphasis on the socio-economic realities of Welsh life, as opposed to abstract identitarian ones. In fact, he proposed, the harsh actualities of Wales - its mining towns, its blackened landscape, its smoky environments - were more capable of provoking new insights than any sentimental retelling of ancestral stories and identity tales. The Welsh industrial novel emblematises a kind of fiction in which there is no getting away from social relations (which are also economic ones). Williams puts it the following way:

> [I]ndustrial work, and its characteristic places and communities, are not just a new background: a new setting for a story ... The working society - actual work, actual relations, an actual and visibly altered place - is in the industrial novel central: not because, or not necessarily because, the writer is 'more interested in sociology than in people' - which is what a degraded establishment criticism would have us believe - but because in these working communities it is a trivial fantasy to suppose that these general and pressing conditions are for long or even at all separable from the immediate and the personal.[13]

Williams here advocates a perspective in which questions of labour, work, and struggle are fully presupposed in attempts at representing experience *because* rather than *despite* the fact that this experience is produced by the exigencies of work rather than the ethnos of Welshness. Williams's portrayal of Welsh experience neither idealises existential consciousness nor does it reduce experience simply to a matter of brute economism. To the contrary, his explanation maintains the tensions underwriting the production of consciousness in its manifold forms. Even from this brief description, we can see the nuanced way Williams recasts the place of work and labour - from being regarded as the entailments of a vulgar and sociologistic Marxism to the stuff of industrial pastoral and a new mode of reading, without hypostatising subjectivity.

The reigning ideology of the linguistic turn requires that the legacy of materialist and dialectical traditions of thought be vacated in favour of the poststructuralist paradigm with its hypostatisation of subject positions. So, in the end, it is unsurprising that Williams's various dialecticisations of structure and feeling are largely overlooked in contemporary critical approaches. What ought, perhaps, to be a bit more vexing is that in Scott's case such an evacuation occurs on the very pretext of scrutinising explanatory categories in the interests of better historical knowledge. For there is no inherent contradiction between the proposals of many feminist critics and the ideas put forth by Williams; nor is this merely a matter of paying homage (although from the point of view of a sociology of knowledge that may not

12. Raymond Williams, 'The Welsh Industrial Novel' in his *Problems in Materialism and Culture*, London, Verso, 1980, pp213-229.

13. Ibid., p222.

be such a bad thing) but, rather, of accounting for the conditions of one's own protocols of theoretical or historical explanation on the right terms. Contra Foucault, all readings cannot simply be misreadings since they come attached with both politics and procedural consequences. To follow Scott's own logic, the writing of history depends upon the assumptions of historians about ways of knowing the past and a willed forgetting of Williams should be contested on that basis alone.

Let me now turn to some of the concrete advantages that purportedly accrue, in Scott's rendition, to rethinking the evidence of experience from the perspective of poststructuralist feminism. After spending some time questioning the epistemological status of experience in the work of historians other than Williams (chief among her targets are R.G. Collingwood's *The Idea of History* and E.P. Thompson's *The Making of the English Working Class*), Scott gets to the place where she reveals the stakes of her revisionist effort:

> It ought to be possible for historians … to 'make visible the assignment of subject-positions', [quoting Gayatri Chakravorty Spivak] not in the sense of capturing the reality of the objects seen, but of trying to understand the operations of the complex and changing discursive processes by which identities are ascribed, resisted, or embraced, and which processes themselves are unremarked and indeed achieve their effect because they are not noticed (408).

By themselves, the propositions are indeed unremarkable with the exception of one major point of emphasis that becomes clearer when she goes on to state that '[t]reating the emergence of a new identity as a discursive event is not to introduce a new form of linguistic determinism, nor to deprive subjects of agency. It is to refuse a separation between 'experience' and language and to insist instead on *the productivity of discourse*' (409, emphases added). From there it is only a step or two before it must be intoned that '[s]ubjects are constituted discursively and experience is a linguistic event … ' (409). The terminus for all this hand-wringing can then finally be reached with the following proclamation: 'Experience is a subject's history. Language is the site of history's enactment. Historical explanation cannot, therefore, separate the two' (409). The injunction to recognise the conditions of existence that underwrite experience or to think about the discursive construction of subjects is, by itself, salutary since both subjects and objects of history (historians themselves as well as the accounts they produce) are produced in the relay between consciousness and material realities or, as the Frankfurt School thinkers routinely put it, in the adequation of concepts and objects. Of course, as I have already mentioned, the vocabulary of the Frankfurt School is one to which Scott has no recourse either because she is unfamiliar with it (although Williams - whom she criticises for not being sufficiently expansive - was well-versed in this tradition) or, perhaps, because reckoning with the critical theory of the Frankfurt School would necessitate a rather different kind of intellectual labour from the one she performs on behalf of the poststructuralist reading of experience as a linguistic event.[14]

Be that as it may, what is noteworthy for our purposes is Scott's stress on the 'productivity of discourse'; in effect, this is where the worm turns. If it has become *de rigueur* in cultural theory to question the metaphysical and ontologised foundations of traditional modes of knowledge production (including but not limited to historical analysis), the corollary manoeuvre is to then propose the primacy of discourse - 'the productivity of discourse' to which Scott refers. Of course the question is begged as to whether or not 'discourse' is thus rendered into a foundational category of its own but, more pertinently, the issue is what sorts of conceptualisations are made possible - in this case, with regard to the problem of experience? In Scott's account, she allows that '[s]ince discourse is by definition shared, experience is collective as well as individual'. But the entire thrust of her argument works to emphasise a conception of experience that, because of its privileging of 'subject positions', is covertly individualist and identitarian while insisting otherwise: ' ... subjects do have agency. They are not unified, autonomous individuals exercising free will, but rather subjects whose agency is created through situations and statuses conferred on them' (409), a statement in which the use of terms such as 'subject', 'agency', 'situation' and 'status' is as much an avoidance of the category of 'class' as it is about the newly refurbished idea that class is somehow historicized - that is to say, de-essentialized - by referring it to the agencies of 'race, ethnicity, and sexuality' (404).

Aside from evading how such a refurbishment accounts for the inescapable structuring reality of capitalist class relations within any experience of race, gender or sexuality in the modern world (to require this is neither to essentialise class nor to ward off other determinants of experience), Scott's account negates the *collective* nature of social existence - even as she invokes the historical construction of subjectivity - by demoting any talk of 'relations of production' in favour of 'other kinds of diversity' (404). In her argument, the idea of class itself is turned into a matter of 'identity' rather than position, particularly when she refers to the work of her mentor, Thompson (which I cite as another symptom in her efforts to work through the past): 'In Thompson's use of the term, experience is the start of a process that culminates in the realization and articulation of social consciousness, in this case a common identity of class' (404). And later in the same context Scott states, 'When class becomes an overriding identity', other subject-positions are subsumed by it, those of gender, for example (or, in other instances of this kind, of history, race, ethnicity, and sexuality)' (404). We have learned a great deal from feminist critics both within and without the Marxist tradition (for example, Simone de Beauvoir, Alexandra Kollontai, or Rosa Luxemburg - although one is hard-pressed to find references to the latter two in most contemporary feminist criticism) about the importance of gender in the constitution of class relations. So, to this extent, Scott's criticism of Thompson is both in order and unexceptional.

14. Often the writings of the Frankfurt School critics have re-entered the discourse of cultural theory, stripped of many of their investments in political economy and transformed as well into a Nietzschean anti-normativism. See the critique by Herbert Schnädelbach, 'The Cultural Legacy of Critical Theory', *new formations*, 38 (Summer 1999), 64-77, Carsten Siebert and Ian Foster (trans). We can recognize this co-opted form of critical theory's arguments in the recent work of critics such as Judith Butler.

But neither in Thompson's writing, Williams's writing, nor any other Marxist analysis worthy of its name is class taken to be an 'overriding identity', since it is not an 'identity' at all but a 'relation'. Indeed, as Scott herself adduces Thompson on this matter, experience is seen as a 'junction-concept' that mediates, precisely, the relation between class position and historical understanding - or, what Thompson calls the means by which 'structure is transmuted into process, and the subject re-enters into history' (404).

The vulgarisation of Marxism as 'vulgar Marxism' is made possible only by first ascribing to it the reductive notion of class as an identity and then denying (against the facts of the very case cited) that the processual, historical, and even psychological dimensions of consciousness have any place within its framework. The complex conceptual history of a term such as 'determination' - whose role in formulating experiential consciousness provides the basis of much of Thompson's study - can, through this manoeuvre, be devalued with a flourish: 'In Thompson's account class is finally an identity rooted in structural relations that preexist politics' (405).

One of the abiding successes of the contemporary theoretical turn is to have managed to issue the diktat that the analysis of subject-positioning via the categories of identity (with qualifications about their historical construction, performative and strategic essentialism, and so on) must be understood as the hallmark of a truly reflexive critical perspective. While one surely wants to recommend that the category of experience be complicated, its irreducibility can be granted seriously not only if this is seen as 'somehow outside its signification' but also not inside or within signification alone. Here, 'questions about discourse, difference, and subjectivity, as well as about what counts as experience and who gets to make that determination' may, as Scott suggests, all be good ones but they are only very partially addressed by focusing on the 'subjective position of historians' (407). This is the crux of the matter, because although, as Scott (citing Dominick La Capra) proposes, there is a 'transferential relationship between the historian and the past', what is left unsaid is that it is as much about the ways that certain categories have 'achieved their foundational status' as it is about displacing the rather bald truth regarding the crypto-transcendental status of representation itself. Notwithstanding Scott's assertion that to 'grant to "the literary" an integral, even irreducible, status of its own' is not to make '"the literary" foundational' (409), this has a less than convincing ring to it in the face of her conclusion that interrogating the evidence of experience 'entails focusing on processes of identity production, insisting on the discursive nature of 'experience' and on the politics of its construction' (412). By now, if such a position seems completely unobjectionable it is because the work that has gone into its production disguises its own foundational assumptions along with attempting to close the door on past ideas.

The specific sense of working through as a discarding of the past rather than a confrontation with it may describe best the imperative of certain feminist theorists such as Scott to withhold the credit due to the likes of Thompson and Williams (who were very different from each other), but the work of thinking obviously cannot progress via such exclusion, as acknowledged within some feminist quarters. Cora Kaplan, for instance, has suggested that 'Williams's untimely death has allowed those feminists deeply indebted to his writing but somehow reluctant to cite or challenge it in his lifetime out of a combination of politeness and anger to break their silence in essays that read like productive if critical acts of mourning'.[15] If my broader contentions about the nature of working through are at all persuasive, then we have, at least, to consider the possibility that working through the past may involve mourning but it may also represent a way to dispatch with bygones. In my own experience of teaching cultural studies for the past fifteen years, it has become amply if unfortunately evident that for younger generations of feminists the work of Williams is, at best, a footnote - although the anecdote with which I began suggests that he may not even get that credit.

But aside from which theorists are viewed as *au courant* despite their actual datedness, the more pertinent question we must ask is whether feminist anger at Williams's refusal to adopt gender as an axiomatic for understanding culture or marginalisation should now be reconsidered both to the extent that certain feminist assumptions have themselves become exclusionary (as my reading of Scott has tried to demonstrate) and to the degree that class contradictions continue to be deepened and intensified beyond all others across the globe? To say this is certainly not to require a pledge of allegiance to a stipulated Marxism of an older variety but to suggest that what appear to be novel counterpositions are more often than not appropriations of ideas from the past. These ideas can then be posed triumphantly as discoveries by those who never knew the tradition - only that it had to be consigned to ashes. The political and even psychological forces at work in these dismissals under a New Left orthodoxy, often reproducing Cold War attitudes (albeit unconsciously), is worth investigating.

In an important sense, we need to rethink the theoretical consequences of *materialism* in the cultural materialism that Williams espoused, now no longer to be equated with an attention to the textuality of history, the open-endedness of everyday practice, or the quiddity of abstraction itself. Williams in his later writings himself suggested that the culturalist turn in cultural studies needs now to become the object of a different *détournement* - if the critique of capitalism is to be undertaken not out of blind faith in the 'good old' against the 'bad new' (to quote Bertolt Brecht), but in the light of stakes that are much larger than intellectual fashions.[16] The possibilities inhering in Williams's project of cultural materialism, it must be said, have everything to do with re-centring the question of social transformation, with his emphasis on the social and the collective rather than the personal and subject-positional moves ushered in under the guise of the so-called 'new social movements'. That, however, is the topic of a different discussion.[17] Still, we might recall that the pages of this very journal offered an editorial valediction after Williams's

15. Cora Kaplan, '"What We Have Again to Say": Williams, Feminism, and the 1840s' in C. Prendergast (ed), op. cit., p212.

16. See Raymond Williams, 'The Future of Cultural Studies' and 'The Uses of Cultural Theory' in his *The Politics of Modernism: Against the New Conformists*, Verso, 1989, pp151-176.

17. See 'Some Questions Concerning the Theory of Power: Foucault Again' in Jürgen Habermas, *The Philosophical Discourses of Modernity*, The MIT Press, 1987, pp266-293; translation of *Der philosophische Diskurs der Moderne: Zwölf Vorlesungen*, Frankfurt, Suhrkamp Verlag, 1985.

death in 1988 in which the occasion to remember him became the moment for the former editors to uphold the 'fragmented' and 'post-modern' advantages accruing to Homi Bhabha's 'account of an agonistic political fluidity' and Stuart Hall's 'vision of a radical pluralism'. Against these perspectives, Williams was represented as holding fast to a less complex, less supple view of culture because of his stubborn personal attachment to an outdated mode of thought.[18] The questionable idealisation of ineffability and fragmentation notwithstanding, mourning in this form also takes on an aspect of diminishment that Higgins (whom I cited earlier at the top) captures very effectively. In his thorough assessment of the banefulness of the claim not to bury Williams but to mourn him, Higgins states:

18. 'Identities' *new formations*, 5 (Summer 1988), 3-4.

> The terms of this remembering of Williams are at the same time the terms that enable us to forget him, in the sense of decreasing the interest of his work and diminishing its value, worth, and relevance. The process of mourning is completed once Williams's work can be named, can be remembered, and then through that naming and remembering can be seen to belong to the past, can be safely forgotten (119).

Perhaps, we have come to a different place and a different mode of intellectual accounting. To adduce Williams's reservations towards feminism, psychoanalysis, or poststructuralism by characterising his positions in entirely personal terms rather than as substantial theoretical disagreements is, as Higgins reveals, a dubious manoeuvre:

> … [R]epresenting intellectual disagreement as a matter of some personal 'reluctance' and 'resistance' makes impossible any real debate of the central theoretical issues. To remember Williams in this way … amounts to little more than an invitation to forget his work by consigning it to the vaults of memory dusty enough never to be opened again (119).

What is needed now is a newer formation, so to speak, that might give us another opportunity to remind ourselves and future generations of the continuing utility as well as intellectual generosity of Williams or Thompson; the former, we know, was unafraid to be taken on and asked to rethink his positions even by the inheritors of the very journal, *New Left Review*, of which he was once the guiding intelligence.[19]

Needless to say, Williams's own intellectual style was very different from the one that demands allegiance as a matter of theoretical taste and forgetting as a matter of dealing with the incontrovertible aspects of arguments from the past. This openness and clarity is, to adapt the title of one of Williams's last collections, what distinguishes 'what he came to say' from the purportedly radical theorisations of the self-styled '68ist generation of French critics. We could do a lot worse than to celebrate him - once more for structure, but this time with feeling.

19. The contentious and, at times, severely critical tone of interviews constituting the volume, *Politics and Letters*, was received by Williams 'in a spirit at once of independence and solidarity'. The substance and range of topics covered in the interviews were far more extensive than anything we have subsequently become accustomed to reading, even though they were conducted by his compatriots Perry Anderson, Anthony Barnett and Francis Mulhern. That their intellectual sympathies were within the tradition of Western Marxism that Williams in part represented did not necessitate either a cult-like following nor a dismissal of his ideas. See Raymond Williams, *Politics and Letters: Interviews with New Left Review*, London, Verso, 1981 [1979]: citation in Foreword, p9.

CINEMATIC INSOMNIA

Jani Scandura

LOS ANGELES, Oct. 1 - Allen Parkinson, a star-struck entrepreneur who developed an over-the-counter sleep aid and built a wax museum dedicated to Hollywood legends, died on Aug. 19 at his home in Warwick, R.I. He was 83.

New York Times, 2/10/02

Picture Emmanuel Levinas, incarcerated in 1940 in a Nazi work camp, fatigued certainly, unable to sleep, distraught that the man whose thought he most admired, Martin Heidegger - a man whose work he had and would introduce to a generation of French philosophers - had not only *not* taken a stand against Hitler, but had joined the Nazi party. And Levinas, sleepless, cramped in the quarters of the *Stalag*, scribbles his disavowal of Heidegger's ontology - of the problem of being itself. And still, he is hopeful. Hopeful, but tired - he has not yet thought through the ethical philosophy that will, belatedly, make him famous. 'To be weary', he writes, 'is to be weary of being'.[1] He is mournful, embarrassed. Seven years later, he writes an apology in his preface to what will be *De l'existence à l'existant* (*Existence and Existents*) for not mentioning the writings of Sartre, Merleau-Ponty and others, 'those philosophical works published, with so much impact, between 1940 and 1945'.[2]

Picture as well Georges Bataille, in 1940 Paris on the brink of the Nazi invasion, purposely misfiling in the overburdened archives of La Bibliothèque Nationale de France the hundreds of pages of typed fragments, scribbles, musings and French and German citations that make up the manuscript of what will eventually be known as Walter Benjamin's masterwork about the dream city of Paris, the *Passagen-Werk*, or *Arcades Project*, and then digging those pages out of hiding seven years later in the fragility of post-war peace and lugging the bundle to New York for Benjamin's friend and sometime champion, Theodor Adorno, to sift through. In that same year, 1947, Bataille comes across Levinas' *Existence and Existents*, and reviews it favourably for *Critique* before the Levinas book falls into the ether of unread philosophy for the next fifteen years.[3] 'What do I have to do ... here ... and now?' Bataille had asked himself in 1946 and, after reading Levinas, could never ask again. 'Writing, I wanted to touch the depth of these problems. And having given myself this occupation, *I fell asleep*'.[4]

Picture too, in 1952, Theodor Adorno, awake too early in the morning on a return visit to the purgatory of a Hollywood still drunk on the candy of mass culture, remembering anew the oppression of Southern California's dry desert heat and, yes, feeling a twinge of the shame of the survivor as he

1. Emmanuel Levinas, *Existence and Existents*, A. Lingis (trans), Pittsburgh, Duquesne UP, 2001, p24. *De l'existence à l'existant* was originally published in French in 1947.

2. Ibid., pxxvii.

3. Georges Bataille, 'De l'existentialisme au primat de l'economie', *Critique*, 3, 19 (1947), 515-526 and *Critique*, 4, 21 (1948), 126-41. See also Jill Robbins' English translation: 'From Existentialism to the Primacy of Economy', in Jill Robbins, *Altered Readings: Levinas and Literature*, Chicago, University of Chicago Press, 1999, pp154-180.

4. Georges Bataille, 'Method of Meditation', *The Unfinished System of Nonknowledge*, Stuart Kendall (ed), Michelle Kendall and Stuart Kendall (trans), Minneapolis, University of Minnesota Press, 2001, p81.

drinks cup after cup of coffee to ward off fatigue while browsing through the horoscope pages of the *Los Angeles Times* (he is a Virgo). And as he reads the column, day after day, he grows fearful. Perhaps, he suggests, astrology is analogous to the irrationality of the dream state which, carefully severed from the rationality of waking, functions to keep 'the individual "normal" by channelizing and to a certain extent neutralizing some of the individual's more threatening id impulses'.[5] This idea nags at him. And he intuits that the situation is even worse. There is something about newspaper astrology that seems reminiscent of the structure of totalitarian anti-Semitism in which 'the individual [is] "isolated" and at the same time collectivized', and therefore able to participate in mass delusion without becoming psychotic. 'To the individual, astrological belief is not a spontaneous expression of his mental life, not "his own" as much of the dream content is', he finally argues, 'but is as it were, ready-made, carefully prepared and predigested irrationality'.[6] The pre-chewed and mass-produced irrationality of astrology might be said to be as much part and parcel of the 'dream factory' as the movies, especially Hollywood Studio films, which seemed to do away with the distinction between the rational and irrational, fiction and fact, and one might add, eschewed a clear separation between individual conscious experience and collective delusion.

Adorno, admittedly, is a bit of a wet blanket. Then again, who can blame him? It was he who first noted that what we think of as most personal - writing a lyric poem, for instance, reading a horoscope, the affective experience of watching a film - is (not at all paradoxically) the most social of acts.[7] It is appropriate, certainly, that these thoughts occur to him in Hollywood, a place he hates, yet like a bad dream cannot extricate himself from. Hollywood's moniker as 'dream factory' is, of course, not Adorno's invention and is itself a misnomer; Hollywood cinema, especially after the advent of synchronised sound is less 'dream-like' than resistant to dream worlds - outside the continuum of the sleep and wake cycle.

Adorno is himself suspicious of dreams and of those critics and artists such as the Surrealists who were enthralled by psychoanalysis with its penchant for analogy, for the collapsing of dream-work with the work of artistic production.[8] In Adorno's view, those like Walter Benjamin, who was certainly more concerned with sleep than with sleeplessness, identified 'all too complacently with the aggressor'.[9] Yet it is hard to say what would have happened to Benjamin's dream vision if he had succeeded in his escape into Spain. For sleeplessness seems a survivors' tactic, a model of and impetus for artistic and intellectual work that becomes visible only belatedly, *in the wake* and *at the wake* of a modernity gone awry - a modernity that is anxious, hunted, on perpetual red alert and that is, simultaneously, haunted by the reign of Fascist spectacle, by the irrational dream world put to totalitarian use.

***

5. Theodor W. Adorno, 'The Stars Down to Earth: The *Los Angeles Times* Astrology Column', *The Stars Down to Earth and other essays on the irrational in culture*, Stephen Crook (ed), London, Routledge, 1994, p67.

6. Ibid., pp67-78. See also pp158-164.

7. See, for instance, Theodor W. Adorno, 'On Lyric Poetry and Society', in Rolf Tiedemann (ed), Shierry Weber Nicholsen (trans), *Notes to Literature*, Vol 1, New York, Columbia UP, 1991, pp37-54.

8. Theodor W. Adorno, *Aesthetic Theory*, C. Lenhardt (trans), London, Routledge & Kegan Paul, 1984, pp12, 198.

9. Ibid., p309.

Let us return, then, to 1929 Hollywood, before Adorno arrives, before Hitler comes to power, to the moment when it became clear that talking film would reign supreme. Filmmakers and censors were in a tizzy. Avant-garde filmmakers and a new genre of politically-engaged critics feared that talking film might usher in an epoch of banal 'highly cultured dramas'; moralistic Americans and ranking members of the American Catholic Church feared that talking films might not be 'highly cultured' enough.[10] Between 1929 and 1932, the Payne Fund, a philanthropic organisation in Cleveland, in cahoots with the conservative Motion Picture Research Council, financed nearly twenty studies on the health and behavioural effects of movie watching on children.[11] Eight volumes on the studies were published by Macmillan between 1933 and 1935 and covered such topics as *Motion Pictures and Standards of Morality*, *Movies and Conduct*, and *Boys, Movies, and City Streets*. The findings were summarised in a polemical book in 1933, *Our Movie Made Children*, which became a bestseller.[12] The Payne studies, controversial at the time and considered by some to have 'as much scientific value as a recipe for noodle soup', were nonetheless hugely influential and widely accepted, and are even now considered a landmark in social science research as the first empirical investigations of the impact of mass media on individuals.[13]

The most important aspect of the studies, at least in terms of cinema history, however, is the fact that they were inspired by and provided legitimacy for the early 1930s movements that sought to increase government regulation of film content. The moralistic Production Code had been established in Hollywood in 1930 as a means to 'preserve movie purity', but it had been largely ineffective until the Catholic Legion of Decency campaign, galvanised in part by the results of the Payne Studies, launched a campaign to boycott 'immoral' movies.[14] Threatened with government regulation and, more importantly, reduced profits, in July 1934, Will Hayes, president of the industry trade association, the Motion Picture Producers and Distributors of America, created a new censorship office, The Production Code Administration (PCA), with Joe Breen at the helm, whose task it was to scrutinise every script and film image for supposed improprieties before issuing the PCA seal of approval that became necessary for the film to be exhibited in theatres.

Against this backdrop, the sleep study, conducted by three psychologists at Ohio State University who investigated the impact of movie watching on the sleep habits of 170 children living at a state children's home, seems a good deal less provocative than those linking film spectatorship to increased rates of drinking, violence, petty crime, 'race prejudice', and promiscuity. The study was most notable for being a disaster of scientific design. The scientists divided the children into two groups; they took the first group to see movies every evening; the other group saw no films, although occasionally they went on other excursions. The scientists then recorded both groups' movements during the night by wiring their bed springs. Although the data

10. See S.M. Eisenstein, V.I. Pudovkin, and G.V. Alexandrov's 1928 manifesto on sound, 'A Statement', reprinted in E. Weis and J. Belton (eds), *Film Sound: Theory and Practice*, New York, Columbia UP, 1985, pp83-85.

11. For the publication, research, and reception history of the Motion Picture and Youth series financed by the Payne Fund, see G.S. Jowett, I.C. Jarvie, and K.H. Fuller, *Children and the Movies: Media Influence and the Payne Fund Controversy*, Cambridge, Cambridge UP, 1996.

12. Gregory D. Black, *Hollywood Censored: Morality Codes, Catholics, and the Movies*, Cambridge, Cambridge UP, 1994, p152.

13. Ibid., pp151-155. See also Jowett, et al, op. cit. and Arthur Kellogg, 'Minds Made By the Movies', *Survey Graphic*, 22, 5 (1933).

14. For a more detailed history of film censorship and the Hayes office, see Black, op. cit., especially pp21-49.

15. Jowett, et al, op. cit., p70.

16. Ibid., pp24-5, and Jane Addams, *The Spirit of Youth and City Streets*, New York, Macmillan,1909.

17. The term has been frequently used to describe Hollywood since the 1920s. For example, a 1927 documentary about the so-called 'movie colony' was titled *The Hollywood Dream Factory and How it Grew* (Blackhawk Films 1927).

18. Nathanael West, *Miss Lonelyhearts & The Day of the Locust*, New York, New Directions, 1969, pp132. *The Day of the Locust* was completed in 1933.

19. Siegfried Kracauer, *Theory of Film: The Redemption of Physical Reality*, New York, Oxford UP, 1960, pp163. He cites Serge Lebovici, 'Psychoanalyse et cinéma', *Revue internationale de filmologie*, 2, 5, 54.

20. Iris Barry, *Let's go to the Movies*, New York, Payson & Clarke Ltd., 1926, pp30-31. Barry became the founding Curator of the Museum of Modern Art Film Library when it opened in 1935.

21. Kracauer, op. cit., p159.

from the experiments 'showed few patterns', according to the authors of *Children and the Movies: Media Influence and the Payne Fund Controversy*, the Ohio State scientists nonetheless 'categorized non-movie [watching] children who slept soundly through the night as well rested, but ... intimated that movie stimulation could induce a drug-like stupor in film-viewing children. They construed tossing in bed at night as healthy for non-movie children and for moviegoers as the physical manifestation of disturbing, movie-inspired dreams'.[15]

What is most remarkable about the study, then, are not its findings, but the assumptions that led the researchers to associate sleep problems with film spectatorship. The connection they were making between film watching and sleeping was, of course, not theirs alone. From the early days of cinema, the association between film viewing and sleeping, though especially dreaming, had been a central, if at times contested, concern of almost all sociological and aesthetic analyses of film spectatorship. Jane Addams, the director of Chicago's Hull House, for instance, aptly titled her chapter about children's movie watching in her 1909 book, *The Spirit of Youth and City Streets*, 'House of Dreams'.[16] And, long before Adorno arrived in Los Angeles, Hollywood had been represented both as a 'Dream Factory'[17] that manufactured Horatio Alger stories of success and, in Nathanael West's famous words, a dystopian and continually growing 'dream dump'.[18]

Most studies on cinema take for granted that an association between dreaming and film watching can be made. 'Film is a dream ... which makes [one] dream', writes Siegfried Kracauer in his 1960 book, *Theory of Film*, citing an essay on psychoanalysis and cinema by Serge Lebovici.[19] It was, in fact, the supposed dream-like quality of film viewing that distinguished it from the experience of going to the theatre. The Museum of Modern Art's first film curator, Iris Barry, writes in her 1926 book, *Let's Go to the Movies*:

> To go to the pictures is to purchase a dream. To go to the theatre is to buy an experience, and between experience and dream there is a vast difference. That is why when we leave the theatre, we are galvanized into a strange and temporary vigour, why so many people run home and act and strut in their own rooms before the wardrobe mirror. But we come out of the pictures soothed and drugged like sleepers wakened, having half-forgotten our own existence, hardly knowing our own names. The theatre is a tonic, the cinema a sedative.[20]

Kracauer notes that since the 1920s 'devotees of film and its opponents alike have compared the medium to a sort of drug and have drawn attention to its stupefying effects'.[21] Drug-induced intoxication is, after all, a common trope used to mediate the transformation of cinematic characters into metaphorical film spectators who mimic the supposed identification between film audiences and the cinematic diegesis. For example, Dorothy's becoming-spectator in

The Wizard of Oz, when she 'awakens' after being hit on the head to see what Salman Rushdie describes as 'the window [in her room] acting as a cinema-screen', is predicated on a previously-presented association between cinema spectatorship and the drug-like induction into a dream-state.[22] Her delirium has already been performed visually through a montage - a close-up and prism shot of Dorothy that is '*superimposed over shots of the whirling cyclone and the house whirling through space*'. The purpose, the screenplay announces, is to '*suggest the sensations of a person going under gas or ether*'.[23] Rushdie remarks in his reading of the film, 'this device - the knocking-out of Dorothy - is the most radical and in some ways the worst of all the changes wrought in Frank Baum's original conception.[24] (In Baum's story, it is never clear whether or not Oz is a *real* place.) In fact, this device is not radical at all; it is precisely what produces Dorothy as a spectator *and*, simultaneously, anchors the film's allegorical connection to MGM's 'dream factory' and to the history of motion picture production more generally. The New Deal hobo-turned-extra Al Babson's sedative-induced transportation from the film set of Ali Baba to the dream world of ancient Babylon in the 1937 Eddie Cantor film, *Ali Baba Goes to Town*, relies on a similar collapse between intoxication, dreaming, and watching cinema.

It was precisely the nebulous (and seductive) discourse of dreaming that shaped cinema studies that the Payne Fund sought to undermine with the pseudo-empiricism of their 'scientific' investigations. Wide-spread acceptance of the narcotic effects of film spectatorship legitimated the anxieties of those who advocated increased scrutiny on film content (there is *something* suspect about strangers sitting together semi-drugged in the dark), even as this collapse was both alluded to and, at times, undermined in Hollywood cinema. It was, moreover, the supposed drugged, dream-like state induced by film watching that was glorified by Surrealist and Expressionist filmmakers such as Luis Buñuel and Sergei Eisenstein, who were interested in taping into the resources of the unconscious and in the experimentations of the psyche. And it was the transformation in perception engendered by film watching, 'reception in a state of distraction' in Walter Benjamin's words, that scientists, politicians, artists, and critics found interesting - or threatening - depending upon their understandings of the psyche and its relationships to bourgeois and mass cultures.[25] Benjamin, for instance, while intrigued by the potential transformation in perception provoked by cinema, also argues that it transforms the masses into 'absent-minded' and passive critics who have honed modes of perception that might make them more acquiescent to the twin tyrannies of capitalism and Fascism. (For Adorno, of course, Benjamin did not go far enough in his critique.)

Despite these collapses, even classic film theorists are careful to point out that dreaming and film watching are not wholly comparative states. 'The dreamer does not know that he is dreaming; the film spectator knows that he is at the cinema: this is the first principle difference between the situations of film and dream', writes Christian Metz. 'We sometimes speak

22. Salman Rushdie, *The Wizard of Oz*, London, British Film Institute, 1992, p30.

23. Noel Langley, Florence Ryerson, and Edgar Allen Woolf, *The Wizard of Oz: The Screenplay*, Michael Patrick Hearn (ed), New York, Dell, 1989, p50.

24. Rushdie, p30.

25. Walter Benjamin, 'The Work of Art in the Age of Mechanical Reproduction', *Illuminations*, Hannah Arendt (ed), Harry Zohn (trans), New York, Schocken Books, 1969, p240.

26. Christian Metz, *The Imaginary Signifier: Psychoanalysis and Cinema*, Celia Britton, Annwyl Williams, Ben Brewster and Alfred Guzzetti (trans), Bloomington, Indiana UP, 1982, p101.

27. See Kracauer op. cit., especially chapter 9, 'The Spectator', pp157-172.

28. Metz, op. cit., p102.

29. Ibid., pp116-117.

30. Walter Benjamin, *The Arcades Project*, Rolf Tiedemann (ed), Howard Eiland and Kevin McLaughlin (trans), Cambridge, MA, Harvard UP, 1999, p389.

31. Samuel Renshaw, et al, *Children's Sleep*, New York, MacMillan Co, 1933, p208.

32. William S. Walsh, M.D., *Yours For Sleep*, New York, E.P. Dutton, 1920, pp157-158.

33. See, for instance, E.P. Thompson, 'Time, Work-Discipline, and Industrial Capitalism', *Past & Present*, 38, (Dec 1967), 56-97.

34. Filippo Tommaso Marinetti, 'The Founding and Manifesto of Futurism 1909', in Vassiliki Kolocotroni, Jane Goldman, and Olga Taxidou (eds),

of the illusion of reality in one or the other, but true illusion belongs to the dream and to it alone'.[26] Metz, like Kracauer in *Theory of Film*, acknowledges that the experience of watching a film nonetheless can seem to blur the boundaries between the waking and dreaming states.[27] 'The spectator lets himself be carried away - perhaps deceived, for the space of a second - by the anagogic powers belonging to a diegetic film, and he begins to act; but it is precisely this action that awakens him, pulls him back from his brief lapse into a kind of sleep, where the action had its root, and ends up by restoring the distance between the film and him'.[28] In this view, film spectatorship is constituted by a kind of repetitive and enforced awakening, the disruptive and serial dosing and awakening that is a hallmark of day dreaming rather than dream sleep. Because film watching is associated with motor inhibition, Metz surmises, it might best be likened to 'a kind of sleep in miniature, a waking sleep'.[29]

It helps to remember, of course, that dreaming and waking are not oppositional states. 'It is one of the tacit suppositions of psychoanalysis', muses Benjamin in *The Arcades Project*, 'that the clear-cut antithesis of sleeping and waking has no value for determining the empirical form of consciousness of the human being, but instead yields before an unending variety of concrete states of consciousness conditioned by every conceivable level of wakefulness within all possible centres'.[30] Even the Payne sleep study researchers are ambivalent about cinema's supposed sedative effects. They argue that cinema watching induces dreaming - and dreaming means restless sleep. But so too, they point out, do cinema watchers risk *not* falling asleep. Watching motion pictures, the Payne researchers surmise, is more likely to cause night-time restlessness in children than would drinking several cups of coffee before bed. 'Parents who would strongly protest against their children ingesting from 4 to 6 grains of caffein between the hours 6:00 and 9:00 P.M. nevertheless permit attendance at motion pictures whose effects on sleep motility may be as great or greater than that of coffee and possibly more lasting in influence'.[31] In a 1920 self-help book designed to 'help the sleepless sleep' and 'to instruct them on a few principles of right living', William S. Walsh, M.D., advises readers to 'patronize the better [motion picture] theaters' and warns that 'prolonged attendance or frequent attendance at motion picture entertainments may cause eye strain, [a primary cause of insomnia] particularly in those whose eyes are sensitive'.[32]

Modernity's claim on the dream world is well recognised. Yet it is insomnia, even more than dreaming, that is a byproduct of modernity, of a world regimented by caffeine and the clock.[33] Filippo Marinetti heralds insomnia in his 1909 'Manifesto of Futurism' as one of the glories of the machine age: 'We intend to exalt aggressive action, a feverish insomnia, the racer's stride, the mortal leap, the punch and the slap'.[34] From the commercial filmmakers' standpoint, praising insomnia makes a certain sense. If 'film is a dream … which makes one dream', it cannot be a dream that puts [one] to sleep.[35] At least not completely. The sleeping screening room spectator who finds his way into so many films about filmmaking represents as much an anxiety about the risks of producing an art form that people watch while lounging half-asleep in the dark, as any kind of diegetic critique.

There are several ways one can read the presence of insomnia in discourse about Hollywood cinema and in Hollywood cinema itself. On one hand, insomnia seems to imply the temporal irreversibility and ever-increasing production constitutive of progressive modernity for which, Mary Ann Doane argues, cinema is a most potent metaphor.[36] In this sense, insomnia seems to allude to an anxiety about production and about the modern subject's relationship to production. On the other hand, insomnia might be said to allow for a different model of cinematic spectatorship vis-à-vis the subject, one that constitutes a mechanism of survival.

In a fragment on insomnia in his essay, 'Pure Happiness', Georges Bataille laments, 'I need to produce and I can only rest while granting myself the feeling of increased production'.[37] Unlike Marinetti, who in the first blush of the twentieth century, associated insomnia with action, increased production, and the feverish glorification of war, Bataille, writing with the malaise of a survivor, suggests instead that insomnia is associated with anxieties about one's production and about the bind between modernity's impetus for ever-increasing production as a means for 'living', and the problematic that one cannot think/represent living without action. 'To live without acting is unthinkable', he writes. 'In the same way, I can only represent myself as *sleeping*, I can *only* represent myself as *dead*'.[38]

Not surprisingly, then, the relationship between dream-like sleepiness and sleeplessness in Studio-era Hollywood narratives is rarely clear-cut. If Hollywood narratives are populated by cinematic *daydreamers*, such as Faye Greener in *Day of the Locust,* for whom 'all these little stories, these little daydreams of hers, were what gave such extraordinary color and mystery to her movements',[39] or by the sleepy clients of The Brown Derby restaurant, which is described by F. Scott Fitzgerald in *The Love of the Last Tycoon*, as 'a languid restaurant patronized for its food by clients who always look as if they'd like to lie down',[40] Hollywood cinema is, not surprisingly, depicted as being produced by famous insomniacs.[41] *The Love of the Last Tycoon's* Monroe Stahr (like Irving Thalberg after whom he was scripted) was 'born sleepless without a talent for rest or the desire for it'.[42] When his doctor asks him shortly before he dies if he is 'getting any sleep', he replies, 'No - about five hours. If I go to bed early I just lie there'.[43] And prominent among all of John Dos Passos' sleepless moderns in the *USA* trilogy, is Margo, the film starlet-to-be in *The Big Money* who requires an aspirin at bedtime because she is 'too excited to sleep' the night before beginning the film that will be her 'big break'.[44] Yet when she falls into an 'aspirin'-induced sleep, she dreams cinematically of 'finishing the *Everybody's Doing It* number and the pink cave of faces was roaring with applause'.[45]

By contrast, when Homer Simpson, in West's *The Day of the Locust*, first settles in his new home in Los Angeles he is overcome by sleepiness despite

Modernism: An Anthology of Sources and Documents, Chicago, University of Chicago Press, 1999, p251.

35. Cited in Kracauer, *Theory of Film*, p163.

36. See Mary Ann Doane, *The Emergence of Cinematic Time: Modernity, Contingency, the Archive*, Cambridge, MA, Harvard UP, 2002, pp8-20, 206-232.

37. Georges Bataille, 'Pure Happiness', *The Unfinished System of Nonknowledge*, p225.

38. Ibid., p225.

39. West, op. cit., p106.

40. F. Scott Fitzgerald, *The Love of the Last Tycoon*, Matthew J. Bruccoli (ed), New York, Scribner's, 1993, p15. The unfinished novel, edited by Edmund Wilson, was first published posthumously in 1941.

41. West, op. cit., p106.

42. Fitzgerald, op. cit., p15.

43. Ibid., p109.

44. John Dos Passos, *The Big Money*, New York, Penguin, 1969, pp422-423.

45. Ibid., p423.

46. West, op. cit., p82.

the fact that 'he was afraid to stretch out and go to sleep', because 'he was always afraid that he would never get up'.[46] The longer he stays in Hollywood, however, his terror of staying awake overpowers his fear of falling asleep:

> His thoughts frightened him and he bolted into the house, hoping to leave them behind like a hat. He ran into his bedroom and threw himself down on the bed. He was simple enough to believe that people don't think while asleep.
>
> In his troubled state, even this delusion was denied him and he was unable to fall asleep. He closed his eyes and tried to make himself drowsy. The approach to sleep which had once been automatic had somehow become a long, shinning tunnel. Sleep was at the far end of it, a soft bit of shadow in the hard glare. He couldn't run, only crawl toward the black patch. Just as he was about to give up, habit came to his rescue. It collapsed the shinning tunnel and hurled him into the shadow.[47]

47. Ibid., p102.

Certainly, insomnia lacks both the sexiness of sleep and the euphoria of awakening; for this reason, as much as any other, it is often relegated to the world of side effects, remaining, for the most part, nothing more than an unwanted waste product of anxiety. The difficulty with insomnia is, in part, that it is representable only as that which eludes that which is not. 'It is sometimes so difficult to sleep!' writes Bataille. 'I tell myself: I am finally falling asleep. The feeling of falling asleep escapes me. If it escapes me, I am, in effect, falling asleep. But if it subsists … ? I cannot fall asleep and I must tell myself: the feeling that I had deceived me […] I cannot arrive at the experience of "what does not happen", except through "what happens"'.[48]

48. Bataille, 'Pure Happiness', op. cit., p226.

At the least, insomnia might be dismissed as a kind of failure. It was Maurice Merleau-Ponty who understood that sleep was constituted by a kind of play-acting; one succeeds in sleeping only when the apparently real (acting as if one is asleep) and reality itself (being asleep) become indistinguishable. 'I lie down in my bed on my left side, with my knees drawn up; I close my eyes and breathe slowly, putting my plans out of my mind. But the power of my will or consciousness stops there', Merleau-Ponty writes in *Phenomenology of Perception*:

> As the faithful, in the Dionysian mysteries, invoke the god by miming scenes from his life, I call up the visitation of sleep by imitating the breathing and posture of the sleeper. The god is actually there when the faithful can no longer distinguish themselves from the part they are playing, when their body and their consciousness cease to bring in, as an obstacle, their particular opacity, and when they are totally fused in the myth. There is a moment when sleep 'comes', settling on this imitation of itself which I have been offering to it, and I succeed in becoming what I was trying to be: an unseeing and almost unthinking mass, riveted to a point in space and in the world henceforth only through the anonymous alertness of the senses.[49]

49. Maurice Merleau-Ponty, *Phenomenology of Perception*, Colin Smith (trans), London, Routledge, 1998, pp163-164.

Yet the parallel that Merleau-Ponty makes suggests that insomnia actually results less from a failure of performance than from a performance that refuses to relinquish itself. The point here with regard to cinema spectatorship, then, is not that in watching a film performance (acting as if one is sleeping/dreaming) and reality (dreaming itself) become indistinguishable, but that Hollywood cinema presents the dream in order to keep the spectator wakeful - wakeful, yet unable to be awakened.

Insomnia is, in effect, the dream from which one cannot awaken. After all, one has never been asleep. To be kept a-wake is instead to be kept in a perpetual state of mourning - always present at the wake, yet never dying, never dead.[50] For Emmanuel Levinas, writing in captivity in the early 1940s, the '*horror*' of insomnia is that it happens to no one. It is, in short, indeterminate, a 'state without a subject' and a 'state that is impossible to recount'.[51] 'In insomnia one can and one cannot say that there is an 'I' which cannot manage to fall asleep', Levinas writes. 'The impossibility of escaping wakefulness is something 'objective'; independent of my initiative. This impersonality absorbs my consciousness; consciousness is depersonalised. I do not stay awake; "it" stays awake … In the maddening "experience" of the "there is" (*il y a*), one has the impression of a total impossibility of escaping it, of "stopping the music"'.[52] In the French, Sara Guyer notes, Levinas uses the verb, *veiller*, in its double sense - as both wakefulness and watching or witnessing, to describe this phenomenon.[53] One watches, witnesses - despite oneself - and in doing so risks becoming 'some-thing'.[54]

The dread of silence (death/sleep/the unknowable) is supplanted by the *horror* of sound (wakefulness). Insomnia might be said to lead to a kind of synesthesia, in which enforced *watching* is propelled by a bombardment of inescapable *sound*. Watching, one cannot 'stop the music' and thereby becomes an *it*. Not coincidentally, the advent of talking cinema, which solidified Hollywood's cinematic reign, has been described as a kind of cinematic death - and, specifically, a death of film's dream function. 'It's not so much the *absence of voices* that the talking film came to disrupt', Michel Chion writes, as the spectator's 'freedom to imagine them in her own way … We're no longer allowed to *dream the voices* - in fact, to *dream period*'.[55]

For Levinas, though, insomnia constitutes a heightened awareness not so much of death - or even the death drive, but for that dreadful waiting and longing for a sleep/death, that never seems to arrive, indeed can never arrive, and over which one has no control. This state is the *other* of consciousness, of which sleep and awakening are constitutive parts; it is, as I noted, what Levinas calls the 'there is', (*il y a*), which he uses to designate that which resists the personal, or 'being in general'.[56] Consciousness, by contrast, the sense of the self as a subject, as an 'I', of being at home (*chez soi*) is *here*; it is found not in abstract space, but in the phenomenon of localisation and of sleep. To sleep, for Levinas, is not only to find a place, but to lie down and thereby 'limit existence *to a place*, a position'.[57] Sleep -

50. I am indebted to Anca Parvulescu for this formulation.

51. Levinas uses horror to describe the 'rustling' of the '*there is*', which is outside of consciousness and therefore refers neither to dream sleep nor wakefulness. See especially *Existence and Existents*, pp51-64. See also, Sara Guyer, 'Wordsworthian Wakefulness', *The Yale Journal of Criticism*, 16, 1 (2003), 106.

52. Emmanuel Levinas, *Ethics and Infinity: Conversations with Philippe Nemo*, Richard Cohen (trans), Pittsburgh, Duquesne UP, 1985, p49.

53. Guyer, op. cit., p102. See also, Emmanuel Levinas, *Ethics and Infinity*, p49, and *Existence and Existents*, pp61-66.

54. The phrase is C. Fred Alford's in 'Emmanuel Levinas and Iris Murdoch: Ethics as Exit?', *Philosophy and Literature*, 26, 1 (2002), p31.

55. Michel Chion, *The Voice in Cinema*, Claudia Gorbman (trans), New York Columbia UP, 1999, p9.

56. Levinas, *Existence and Existents*, op. cit., pp52-57.

57. Ibid., pp66-67.

58. From the translator, Alphonso Lingis' introduction in ibid., pxix.

59. See especially, Levinas' late lecture, 'In Praise of Insomnia', presented at La Sorbonne on May 7, 1976 in Emmanuel Levinas, *God, Death, and Time*, Bettina Bergo (trans), Stanford, Stanford UP, 2000, pp207-212. Here, Levinas offers a revised definition of insomnia, as 'the Other *within* the Same who does not alienate the Same but who awakens him', that is shaped by his ethical work on the face-to-face. Levinas again makes the important point in this lecture that insomnia cannot be 'defined as a simple negation of the natural phenomenon of sleep', since sleep is always 'on the verge of waking up'.

60. Jonathan Crary, *Suspensions of Perception: Attention, Spectacle, and Modern Culture*, Cambridge, MA, MIT P, 2001, pp48-50.

61. Mark Garrett Cooper, *Love Rules: Silent Hollywood and the Rise of the Managerial Class*, Minneapolis, University of Minnesota Press, 2003, p80; and Michael Tratner, 'Working the Crowd: Movies and Mass Politics', *Criticism*, 45,1, (2003), 53-73.

and dreaming - are not separate from, but forms of existence, not the 'reverse of consciousness, but a mode of being in the world'.[58]

Dreaming then takes *place* in the realm of the subjective and particular, a point to which Freud alludes when he suggests that while general rules may hold for dream symbols, these symbols are culturally prescribed; and dreams only have meaning within the context of an individual's life. We might argue then that 'to lose oneself' in a film is not a condition of dreaming, when one is most fully inside oneself, it is instead to be wakeful. To watch, without 'watching over'. It means to lose one's *place*, one's base or 'condition of being', in Levinas's terms, and thereby to lose oneself as a *subject*. What Levinas does not take into account when he 'praises' insomnia (and, let's face it, why should he) is the kind of double-play Hollywood films often perform.[59]

Pointing out that 'the work of Georg Simmel, Walter Benjamin, Siegfried Kracauer, and Theodor Adorno … presumed that a distracted perception was central to any account of subjectivity within modernity', Jonathan Crary argues perceptively that 'modern distraction was *not* a disruption of stable or "natural" kinds of sustained, value-laden perception that had existed for centuries but was an *effect*, and in many cases a constituent element, of the many attempts to produce attentiveness in human subjects'.[60] Crucial to this point is not that spectators (or critics) confuse the enforced watchfulness of cinematic insomnia *with* distraction or dreaming, but that a viewer's extrication from subjectivity spiralling off into the 'abyss' of non-place, the 'there is' (*il y a*), occurs at precisely the moment she imagines herself most a subject, most individual, most *here*, in *place*, *chez soi*. It is, in fact, the interplay between these two states that makes one's induction into the impersonality of a collective film audience *feel* like an individual subjective experience. What Levinas constitutes as an experience *outside* of being is reconfigured by Hollywood cinema to be *constitutive of* being.

Mark Garrett Cooper and Michael Tratner have recently argued that while most film theory presupposes an individual spectator at risk for over-identification with the film spectacle, post-1910 Hollywood cinema appealed to a '"universal" heterogeneous mass audience' and defined cinema as a '"universal language" that, [apparently] paradoxically, was also supremely American'.[61] A reading of cinematic insomnia, however, suggests that the supposed opposition between the individual spectator-as-subject and the 'non-subjectivity' of the cinematic crowd merely refers to two sides of the same coin, much like awakening and sleep, since both the individual subject and the 'public' are constituted through being. Instead, we might see Hollywood cinema as masking the non-being, the 'there is' of the insomniac, framing it as the supreme moment of being 'at home'.

***

In the preface to his 1947 book, *From Caligari To Hitler: A Psychological History of the German Film*, the first book that he wrote in exile in the United States,

Siegfried Kracauer proposes to expose the deep psychological underpinnings of National Socialism through an analysis of the German films from 1918 to 1933. He adds that he hopes his method can serve as well as a model for research on mass behaviour in the United States. Yet when Kracauer's text gets to the arrival of the talkie - both in Germany and in the United States - his analysis breaks down. Arguing that the visual aspects of a film are more likely to 'penetrate' the unintentional and subconscious components of cinema than do spoken words, Kracauer observes that throughout the Nazi era German cinema relied more heavily on pictorial imagery than did American cinema (and by this he means mainstream Hollywood cinema and newsreels), which he sees as largely dialogue-driven. 'Talkies are as symptomatic of mass attitudes as silent films', he admits, 'although analysis of these attitudes is hampered rather than facilitated by addition of the spoken words'.[62] He then continues his discussion by focusing on the psychological impact of musical scores. My point here is not to indict Kracauer for not fully analysing the social or psychological impact of talking film on the masses, but to emphasise that at this point in his writing his concept of the unconscious and the psychological cannot account for the presence of talking in film. In the face of talking cinema, Kracauer loses his voice.

He has, in a sense, written his analysis too soon. If the sleeplessness that Marinetti lauds might be better characterised as mania and, therefore, not irreconcilable with the tenets of Fascism, insomniac spectatorship might be said to be a premature phenomenon that becomes interpretable only belatedly, in the face of a testimonial culture of witnessing. Before he describes his performative model of falling asleep, Merleau-Ponty asserts that 'loss of voice as a situation may be compared to sleep'.[63] However, the comparison he makes to the loss of voice actually refers not to falling asleep, but to a *failure* to fall asleep, to insomnia, in other words; his analysis draws on the case of a 'girl whose mother has forbidden her to see again the young man with whom she is in love', and who consequently 'cannot sleep, loses her appetite and finally the use of speech'.[64] She 'does not *cease* to speak', Merleau-Ponty remarks, 'she "loses" her voice, as one loses a memory', by which he means that the voice is not actually lost, but rejected.[65] Her loss of speech/sleep is characterised not by a refusal of life, he argues, but a refusal of the future, or taken further, I would suggest, a refusal of historical time and of being itself.

'*It wasn't a dream it was a place*', Dorothy protests at the end of *The Wizard of Oz*. '*A real truly live place! Doesn't anyone believe me?*' Salman Rushdie points out that, 'Many, many people did believe her'; yet, he has missed the full impact of her complaint.[66] If *The Wizard of Oz*, which was released in 1939, allegorises Dorothy's becoming-spectator and her entrée into Hollywood's dream factory, which is brought to fruition with her Emerald City makeover (a scene lifted right out of the 1937 film *A Star Is Born*), the film also is haunted by the spectre of Fascism.[67] The authoritarian Wicked Witch sends

62. Siegfried Kracauer, *From Caligari to Hitler: A Psychological History of the German Film*, Princeton, Princeton UP, 1947, pp205-206.

63. Merleau-Ponty, op. cit., p163.

64. Ibid., p160.

65. Ibid., pp163-164,

66. Rushdie, op. cit., p57.

67. Over the years, the film has been read as an allegory for many, many things - as a national romance, as propaganda for American isolationism, as a two-fold struggle between Wickedness in the East (Stalinism) and the West (Fascism), as a Depression narrative of capitalism. I am not going to quibble about these readings, but wish simply to alert readers to them.

68. Rushdie, op. cit., p42.

69. I refer to Max Horkheimer and Theodor W. Adorno's use of the term in *Dialectic of Enlightenment*, Gunzelin Schmid Noerr (ed), Edmund Jephcott (trans), Stanford, Stanford UP, 2002, pp94-136. The essays, written mostly in Hollywood during the Second World War, were published in Amsterdam in 1947.

winged monkeys off like a fleet of bomber planes from her neo-Gothic castle and, as Rushdie wryly comments, she has kept 'no doubt such trains as there might be, running on time'.[68]

Within this context, we might understand Dorothy's protest as allegorical, not simply because these two facets of the film - the totalitarianism of Fascism and the seductiveness of Hollywood's 'Culture Industry'[69] - are inextricably intertwined, but because Dorothy, like Kracauer, has asked her question too soon. Her plaint is not just the plaint of the spectator, but of the witness. There is no place like home in *The Wizard of Oz*, because 'home', in Levinas' terms *is* sleep. And Dorothy does anything but sleep in Oz. (Yes, the Wicked Witch gives her some respite in a field of red poppies. But the Good Witch Glinda takes care of that.) Like a good spectator, Dorothy is not so much awakened *as kept awake* - to return home where, she is told, she has never left. Dorothy recognises that what she has seen cannot be explained away as a dream, but what she must ask is a question for which she cannot find the words: 'What is it that we *will* have lived through?' Her interruption ('it wasn't a dream, it was a place') and the mollification of her speech by the other characters ('they all laugh') points to what is still uninterpretable in cinema in 1939, the articulation of an anxiety that can be made sense of only retrospectively within the context of a culture of survival and through the insights of witnesses who cannot be awakened, because for too long they have been kept a-wake.

THE BODY OF EVIL

Jacqueline Rose

The wind of faith is blowing to remove evil from the peninsula.
> Osama Bin Laden, statement broadcast on al-Jazeera television, September 2001

Out of the shadows of this evil should emerge lasting good.
> Tony Blair, Labour Party Conference, 2/10/01

The way of the wicked will be defeated, those who profess evil will not prosper.
> Ariel Sharon, cited *Sunday Times*, 10/03/02

Evil, as these quotes suggest, is a moveable feast. It has the strange characteristic of being at once an absolute and something far closer to what linguistics calls a 'shifter'. Pronouns, as we know, famously the pronoun 'I', are purely indexical signs, which refer only to the moment they are spoken. They only work for any one of us because they can be appropriated by everyone else. Hence 'shifter'. Their meaning resides in their capacity to move. There is of course something deeply unsettling about this - after all the pronoun 'I' is the word in which we invest our most fundamental sense of self. Evil has something of the same aura. When people use the word 'evil', it is very unusual to question whether they in fact know what they are talking about. And yet, in the above quotes, 'evil' refers alternately to the United States, to Al-Qaida, and to suicide bombers in Israel/Palestine. Read them out without identifying the sources, as I did at a debate organised by the *London Review of Books* in May 2002: 'The War on Terror - is there an alternative?', and people are hard pressed to say, not only who is being referred to as evil, but more interestingly who is *speaking*. People using the term 'evil' all sound the same.

In considering evil, we should perhaps start by noticing this contradiction. Surest of terms, invariably invoked with the most passionate if at times desperate conviction, evil also spins on its axis, loses its way. It behaves like that part of language which fatally, if invisibly, undermines the certainty of our speech. Evil is also mobile in another sense. Like all words for 'immediately' which gradually degrade into meaning something like 'in a while', 'evil' has a remarkable capacity for extending and diluting itself. The *Oxford English Dictionary* lists as the meanings for 'evil': 'wickedness, moral depravity, sin', then 'whatever is censurable, painful, malicious or disastrous', and finally 'any particular thing that is physically or morally harmful'. Provided it is unwelcome, evil can be *any particular thing*. A void opens waiting to be filled. During his first election campaign (so before

September 11), Bush commented on the enemies of America: 'We're not so sure who they are, but we know they're there'. More recently, Defence Secretary Donald Rumsfeld explained the Pentagon's shift from a 'threat-based strategy' to an offensive 'capabilities-based approach' in terms of the need 'to defend our nation against the unknown' (as Frances Fitzgerald puts it: '[this] means simply that the Pentagon can ask for whatever it wants without having to justify its requests by the existence of even a potential enemy').[1] In this essay, I want to pursue the radical instability, or vacuity, of evil - as distinct from the 'banality of evil' - to take and remake Hannah Arendt's famous phrase.

Since September 11, 2001, evil, as one might say, is in the air. In an interview I conducted with Noam Chomsky for a television film on Israel, he described how Turkey, Israel and the United States are referred to in the Egyptian press as the 'axis of evil': 'plenty of evil', he continued, 'in this case a real axis, not an invented one'. Similarly, as Russian formalist Boris Tomachevsky pointed out in 1925, new literary schools, opposing an older aesthetic, nearly always proclaim themselves, one way or another, more 'realistic' or attuned to reality than the one that went before. The issue here is not who has the greater right to make the claim, but the contested nature of its grounds. Sometimes vocally, more often silently, there is an argument going on whenever 'evil' is proclaimed. Chomsky is in fact making a very simple point. He is suggesting that those who brandish the epithet 'evil' post September 11, notably Bush in his 'axis of evil' speech, ignore the uneven distribution of power (it was not, Bush has repeatedly insisted, America's power that was the target but her freedom). Choosy and yet indiscriminating, evil becomes the supreme and unjust equaliser between men. When you accuse someone of evil, history disappears. In the great and uneven distribution of the world's resources, it becomes strictly irrelevant where or who they are.

In the Report of South Africa's Truth and Reconciliation Commission, the Commissioners point to a striking disparity - the 'magnitude gap' - between the perception of violations of human rights under apartheid by the victims and by the perpetrators of the crime.[2] For the victims, such action either exceeds the range of the comprehensible, enters a realm of mystery, or it is 'deliberately malicious', 'sadistic', 'an end in itself' (Gillian Slovo's account of the amnesty hearings of the man responsible for her mother's death was entitled by the *Guardian*, 'Evil has a Human Face').[3] Either way, the act is beyond the pale; it fails to enter a world in which anyone would choose to recognise him or herself. For the perpetrators the same act is the rational consequence of historic necessity. South Africa was defending itself by all available means from a Communist threat: as Archbishop Desmond Tutu puts it in his introduction 'The supporters of the previous regime have been at great pains to insist that the reason they did many of the unsavoury things that have since come to light was largely because they were fighting an evil and predatory Communism' (1, 13). The

1. All quotes from Martin Kettle, the *Guardian*, 12/09/02.

2. *Truth and Reconciliation Commission of South Africa Report*, 5 volumes, London, Macmillan, hereafter cited parenthetically in text.

3. Gillian Slovo, 'Evil has a human face', *Guardian*, 3/10/1998.

disparity is eloquent of the way evil 'shifts' in another sense - more 'shifty' as one might say. 'I' am never evil; only 'you' are. In this respect the term 'evil' perversely mimics the first person pronoun in reverse. No one wants to wear it; unlike the 'I' which each human subject spends a large part of their life rushing - however ruthlessly - to claim. But it may be too that the South African experience can help us understand one of the reasons why Arendt's 'banality of evil' was such a controversial phrase. If evil, it must be total. No part of the personality must escape. 'Evil' states Elizabeth Costello in J.M.Coetzee's essay/short story on this topic, which will be the focus of much of this essay, 'would not be true evil if it can be exited and entered at will'.[4] Evil accepts no qualifiers. You can't do evil partly (it is never something you 'sort of' do). Reduce the force of evil one iota, and the perpetrator of atrocity has won the argument. His actions just might be reasoned, necessary. Or, simple, banal, they make up the colours of the day. For the victims, the Commissioners comment, the experience was sheer 'horror'; for the perpetrators, more often, 'a very small thing'. 'Perpetrators', they continue dryly, 'tend to have less emotions about their acts' (5, 271-72).

4. Coetzee's essays in the voice of Elizabeth Costello have now been published as *Elizabeth Costello - Eight Lessons* London, Secker and Warburg, 2003, hereafter cited parenthetically in text. The original text has been slightly modified in the published version in which this quotation no longer appears.

What seems to be at stake then is the issue of how much, or rather how little, it is permissible to feel. The worst outrage is for someone to have committed an atrocity without the requisite affect. In Gillian Slovo's memoir *Every Secret Thing*, she describes her encounter with the man who organised the murder of her mother as a moment of mutual dissociation: 'Our meeting,' she writes, 'had been an exercise in dissociation from which I'd emerged in a stupor that had sent me straight into a dreamless afternoon sleep' (267). Craig Williamson is incapable - syntactically incapable - of recognising what he has done. Read the pronouns in this sentence when Slovo presses whether Ruth's death weighed on him:

> 'Yeah,' he said grudgingly, 'I said that you'll never get rid of. You can wish it or regret it or do as much as you like but you can't change it. What's done is done and if you try to analyse why it was done and how it was done and what the strategy and belief behind it was … it's difficult to believe that it could have been done but it was' (268).

The 'I' hardly figures here, nor indeed the crime '*that* you'll never get rid of'. I spend sometime arguing with my students on a course I teach on South African writing, whether that last sentence 'it's difficult to believe that it could have been done but it was' indicates a subject struggling to enter his statement, acknowledging that he is faced with something too dreadful to be thought, or is merely the voice, in Slovo's own words, of 'a huge mountain of a man, all oil, and lies, and half-excuses' (266).

We could perhaps ask, then, whether it is the action that is the worst evil or the perpetrator's refusal to recognise the horror, to identify psychically with his victim, or in simpler language, to 'connect'. One of the wagers of South Africa's Truth Commission was to make victims and perpetrators go the distance and recognise each other across what the Commissioners themselves describe as an almost insurmountable abyss. In the trial of Ruth Ellis who murdered her lover in 1950s Britain (she was the last person to hang in this country) or in the response to social worker Marietta Higgs who had withdrawn from their homes scores of children she suspected of being victims of abuse in midlands Britain in the 1980s, the worst outrage was the lack of emotion both women displayed. Higgs was of course wresting children from a crime many would classify as 'evil', Ellis was technically on the other side. And yet the screaming outrage against these two women, partly one suspects because they were women, put something graphic on display. Anyone brushed with 'evil' must, for *us* to survive *their* encounter, lose or appear to lose control of their minds. 'Evil' is unbearable or it is nothing. Like death, it is something from which you don't return.

Two years ago I attended a conference organised by the Nexus institute in Tilburg entitled 'Evil' part 2 of a series called 'The Quest for Life'. J.M. Coetzee accepted the invitation on condition that he could deliver his paper in fictional form. Returning to the format of his Tanner Lectures of 1998, published as *The Lives of Animals*, now republished as *Elizabeth Costello*, Coetzee chose to use the occasion to revive the character of Elizabeth Costello, feminist, vegetarian and campaigner who chooses to give a prestigious series of literary lectures on the somewhat unexpected topic of animal slaughter (she was invited as the famous author of a 1969 novel about Molly Bloom, the wife of Leopold Bloom, nowadays spoken of in the same breath as *The Golden Notebook* and *The Story of Christa T* as path breaking feminist works). In this instance she has been invited to Amsterdam to address a Conference on evil. Once again Coetzee doubles his character with his own position as speaker (although the immediacy of this is lost in the published version of the text). The story turns on a crisis. Costello has come to speak about a book - Paul West's *The Very Rich Hours of Count von Stauffenberg* - a book whose depiction of evil has deeply repelled her and led her to question the ethical limits of the writer's craft and task, only to discover that Paul West is attending the Conference. For Costello, the issue is precisely how or where to place evil in her mind. Paul West's *The Very Rich Hours of Count von Stauffenberg* tells the story of Hitler and his would-be assassins in the Wehrmacht, above all of their execution which is described in a physical and mental detail which she finds obscene. West goes too far into a realm where she now feels, as a result of the effect on her of reading this book, writers perhaps should not tread: 'in representing the workings of evil, the writer may *unwittingly* make evil seem attractive and thereby do more harm than good' (164, that 'unwittingly', in italics in the text, is a late concession - Costello knows by now that West is in the audience). The story is wonderfully self-defeating, because its central proposition will only work if we enact in relationship to Elizabeth the very form of fictional identification she is now cautioning against. That is to say, it only works if we find ourselves, without let or inhibition, entering Elizabeth's own mind. A mind which includes, not just the horror of reading the book and the ethical protest it provokes on her behalf, but also the memory - reluctant but overwhelming - of a scene of sexual violence to which she was subjected as a young girl. As well as, in perhaps the most powerful moment of the essay, an instant where, in a shocking identification, Elizabeth looks at her own naked body and imagines herself as one of those women victims of the Nazis 'at the lip of the trench into which they would, in the next minute, the next second, tumble, dead or dying with a bullet to the brain' (178). In an ironical twist which makes her objections more not less poignant, it is Elizabeth, not Paul West, who - we might say - does the best line in forced identifications, throwing the reader into the arms of evil, or into the pit.

The point is that her critique of the power of writing only works because of the power of her own; because she does to the reader - through the strength of her ability to convey her experience - exactly what she objects to having had done to her by Paul West's book. Of course, being in a story by Coetzee, she is only too aware of this. Costello argues with herself: 'Yet she is a writer too. She does the same kind of thing, or used to' (that 'used to' is sleight of hand since Costello - Coetzee as writer - is doing it to the reader *now*) (179). Writing forces unexpected, often unwelcome identifications, or it does nothing. Coetzee knows well that scenes like the one where Elizabeth was assaulted, however repugnant, will be compelling to the reader. Designed to shock, they make the reader intimate with fear. In this case there is an added pull because the violence is conveyed as an almost reluctant memory, the narrator's private musings on an event which she has never communicated before. We are the hidden, privileged party to a confession of something so devastating it has never, until now, made the passage into words. Nineteen years old, she has just been picked up by a docker and goes back to his room:

> 'I'm sorry,' she said,' I'm really sorry, can we stop'. But Tim or Tom wouldn't listen. When she resisted, he tried to force her. For a long time, in silence, panting, she fought him off, pushing and scratching. To begin with he took it for a game. Then he got tired of that, or his desire tired, turned to something else, and he began to hit her seriously. He lifted her off the bed, punched her breasts, punched her in the belly, hit her a terrible blow with his elbow to her face. When he was bored with hitting her he tore up her clothes and tried to set fire to them in the waste paper basket (165).

And so on ... 'It was', Costello comments, 'her first brush with evil' (165). She is convinced that he liked hurting her more than he would have liked sex. 'By fighting him off, she had created an opening for the evil in him to emerge' (165). I should perhaps add - as it will be relevant to the discussion later - that while I am happy (although 'happy' is not the right word) to reproduce these lines here, I found it very difficult and then impossible to read them out at the annual Conference of the Council for College and University English in Oxford and then at the Conference honouring Gillian Beer on her retirement in Cambridge last year.

It would, I think, be fair to describe such a moment as obscene (in the sense of what it wants to be). In fact Costello saves this epithet for the description of the bodies of the plotters on the point of execution, above all for the way the executioner humiliates and terrifies them, taunting them with the physical details of what is to come. Can there really, she asks, have been witnesses who wrote this down in such detail? Or is it West's fantasy - his passionate identification with the victims, but no less, of necessity if he is to render the scene faithfully, with the executioner - 'the butcher with last week's blood caked under his fingernails' - whom he brings so intensely to life? ('terrible that such a man should have existed, even more terrible that he should be hauled out of the grave when we thought he was safely dead', 158, 168). This is, for Costello, 'obscene'. Although it is not clear in the following sentence whether it is the grim abjection of the plotters or the no less grim perversity of the executioner which oversteps the bounds: '*Obscene. That is the word, a word of contested etymology that she must hold on to. She chooses to believe that *obscene* means off-stage. To save our humanity, certain things that we may want to see (*may want to see because we are human!*) must remain for ever off-stage*' (168-69. emphasis original). To rephrase: Obscenity must remain off-stage because, as humans, we want to see it so much. This, I would like to suggest to you, comes very close to making evil, if not the essence of writing, then no more than an exaggerated, or a kind of worse-case embodiment, of what compels us to read. Like evil, writing is enticing: 'He made her read, excited her to read' (179). We want to get inside other people's skins even if they are about to be fleeced alive. In the throes of identification - with victim *or* executioner - there is no limit to how far people are willing to go. What Costello seems to be objecting to is not evil so much, as its *temptation*: 'she had gone on reading, excited despite herself' (178).

The idea of evil as tempting has of course a long history (from the beginning, as one might say). One of the ways of thinking about the horrors of the last century - I leave aside for the moment those unfolding today - is as a transmutation in the age-old connection between these two terms. 'Evil in the Third Reich', writes Hannah Arendt in her famous *Eichmann in Jerusalem - a report on the banality of evil* of 1963, 'had lost the character by which most people recognise it - the quality of temptation'[5] (she is of course writing about the same history as West's book). In civilised countries, she continues, the law assumes that the voice of conscience instructs its citizens: 'Thou shalt not kill': 'even though man's natural desires and inclinations may at times be murderous'. But under Hitler, when the law changes sides, temptation follows suit: 'Many Germans and many Nazis, probably an overwhelming majority of them must have been tempted *not* to murder, *not*

5. Hannah Arendt, *Eichmann in Jerusalem - A Report on the Banality of Evil*, New York, Viking, 1963, Revised edition, Penguin, 1977, p150, hereafter cited parenthetically in text.

to rob, *not* to let their neighbours go off to their doom [...] and not to become accomplices in all these crimes by benefiting from them, but, God knows, they had learned how to resist temptation' (471). Imagine then a situation where the law instructs you to commit acts you would barely entertain in your wildest dreams. In Freudian terms, the law is always a problem because our psychic enforcer, the superego, draws its energy from the unconscious it is meant to tame; which is why the superego's edicts often seem fierce or cruel. Laced with perversion. But this is something else. Now the superego is instructing you to let the most terrifying components of your own unconscious go stalking. Faced with such an edict, the voice of conscience pales, becomes a ghost of its former self. Tempting, but impotent. Like the memory of someone you might once have been. But it would be wrong to think that this is anarchy, a release into freedom, no holds barred. The strength of Arendt's analysis is that she recognises that there is something deadly in the law. Hence her repeated emphasis on the 'reason of state' and its inherent violence: 'the rule of law, although designed to eliminate violence and the war of all against all, always stands in need of the instruments of violence in order to assure its own existence' (291). Likewise Chomsky, against the dominant rhetoric on terrorism, relentlessly charts acts of western-sanctioned state terrorism in the modern world.

Perhaps we are tempted by evil, find its literary representation so compelling, because evil is not just an outsider, nor just our guilty secret - the word 'transgression' won't do here - but belongs at the heart of the very mechanisms we deploy in order to restrain it. Violence is never more terrifying than when it believes itself justified by the highest law (Bush has stated quite clearly that he has known his divine mission since September 11). In Coetzee's story, it is the law - brazen, mocking - that produces the excessive energy which Costello describes as obscene: 'In his gibes at the men about to die at his hands there was a wanton, an *obscene* energy that exceeded his commission' (177). This energy is contaminating ('like a shock, like electricity', 176). If it weren't, Costello as reader would have no reason to object. West has thrust her, not just into the horror of what is still for many the worst atrocity of the twentieth century, but into its *mind*. Fiction's greatest offence becomes its ability to turn us into perpetrators, each and every one.

In their chapter on 'Concepts and Principles', the South African commissioners feel the need to justify their exploration of the 'Causes, Motives, Perspectives' of the perpetrators which appears in the final volume of Findings and Recommendations. Understanding can be seen as exonerating. Trying to get into the mind of the perpetrator is too risky: 'Without seeing offender accountability as part of the quest for understanding, the uncovering of motives and perspectives can easily be misunderstood as excusing their violations' (1, 130). Far from fiction, even in the most sombre conditions of political assessment and analysis, to allow a mind to the perpetrators of atrocity is, it seems, to risk one identification too far. In fact in the chapter itself, the perpetrators emerge as oddly without character. Psychological analysis is more or less eschewed: 'In such situations, people act primarily in terms of their social identities rather than personal attributes' (5,288). 'Political frameworks provide the fuel for atrocities' (5, 282). One by one, the Report rules out the argument from human nature (regression into atavistic behaviour), the argument from psychopathology (no psychological disfunction), the argument from authoritarianism (a collective phenomenon, not a personality type). In fact in a report that has been severely criticised for its emphasis on individual actors at the expense of a critique of state power, it is striking how in this chapter the whole analysis scrupulously, repeatedly, swerves in the direction of what Freud famously called group (or 'mass') psychology. Under apartheid, crime became the law: '[To paraphrase Hannah Arendt],' write the Commissioners at the end of the opening chapter on the historical context, 'Twentieth-century law in South Africa made crime legal' (1, 42). The perpetrators are best understood in terms of social coercion or 'binding' ('compliance', 'identification', 'internalisation') (5, 292). Only acts, not individuals, can be described as 'evil': 'While acts of gross violations may be regarded as demonic, it is counter-productive to regard persons who perpetrated those acts as demonic' (5, 274). In a strange mimicry of what collective identification is presumed to do to individuals (take away their personalities), it is as if there is *nobody there*.

And yet, by the account of the Commissioners themselves, these explanations are unsatisfactory. There is a factor that escapes. On authoritarianism: 'But does this offer an explanation for a predisposition to commit atrocities? Evidence is really rather thin' (5, 286); on social identity: 'It may be noted that social identity theory does not explain violence itself, but the preconditions of violence' (5, 289); on group identification: 'while these processes begin to explain why we become bound into groups, institutions and authorities, they do not yet suggest violence' (5, 292). 'Do not *yet*' - something has to wait. Without final cause, atrocity resists explanation, draws a blank. Attempting to explain the demonic, the Commissioners find something invisible, unnegotiable, sinister (demonic?) at play. Evil, it seems, is not just an absolute, not just a shifter; it is an empty place. This may seem like a failure of explanation. Or it may take us, I want to suggest now, to the heart of the matter. In her famous exchange with Gerschom Scholem over her book on Eichmann, Arendt writes:

6. Arendt to Scholem, letter of 24 July 1963, in Arendt, *The Jew as Pariah - Jewish Identity and Politics in the Modern Age*, New York, Grove Press, p251.

It is indeed my opinion now that evil is never 'radical,' that it is only extreme, and that it possesses neither depth nor any demonic dimension. It can overgrow and lay waste the whole world precisely because it spreads like a fungus on the surface. It is 'thought-defying,' as I said, because thought tries to reach some depth, to go to the roots, and the moment it concerns itself with evil, it is frustrated because *there is nothing* (my emphasis).[6]

Could there be a connection, I want to ask for the rest of this essay, between evil as nothing, and evil as subject to, or even as the violent, intransigent - obscene - embodiment of the highest law?

Arendt's analysis of Eichmann suggests there might be. She is best known for describing him as petty, banal (her phrase is cited by the Commission, and Arendt continues the quote above: 'That is its "banality"'). But in a less commented moment early in the book when she is introducing her main character, she tells of how he saw his birth as an 'event to be ascribed to "a higher Bearer of Meaning", an entity somehow identical with the "movement of the universe"'. She writes: 'The terminology is suggestive. To call God a *Höheren Sinnesträger* meant to give him some place in the military hierarchy, since the Nazis had changed the military "recipient of orders" the *Befehlsempfänger*, into a "bearer of orders," a Befehl*sträger*, indicating, as in the ancient "bearer of ill tidings", the burden of responsibility and of importance that weighed supposedly upon those who had to execute orders' (27). Eichmann is dismissive of metaphysics - the moment is passed over - but it is nonetheless central to Arendt's analysis that Eichmann's '"boundless and immoderate admiration for Hitler"' (in the words of a defence witness) played a major part in his accepting that Hitler's *word*, without having to be written, had the force of law (149). Hitler, or rather love of Hitler, comes close to the sacred. Evil is tempting because the devil, however despicable to the sanguine mind, takes on the aura of a god. There may be something mysterious, resistant to final explanation, in people's ability to commit evil acts (although to say that is already to run the risk of mystification); but mystery might also be intrinsic to the process which enables individuals to violate, even in the name of legality, the bounds of all human law. In *The Brothers Karamazov*, the Grand Inquisitor says to Ivan Fyodorovich:

> There are only three powers, only three powers on earth, capable of conquering and holding captive forever the conscience of these feeble rebels, for their own happiness - these powers are miracle, mystery and authority.[7]

Without depth - Arendt continues her letter: 'Only the good has depth, can be radical' - evil relies on transcendence. This is of course to invert the normal order of things in which the devil is presumed to exert all his power from below.

***

I am now going to take a detour via our most recent modern times before returning to Coetzee at the end. 'Fear is a great form of worship, and the only one worthy of it is God' - these words are from 'Atta's document', found in the baggage of Mohammed Atta 'the suspected ringleader' of September 11, thought to have piloted the first of the two planes into the Twin Towers

7. Fyodor Dostoyevsky, *The Brothers Karamazov*, London, New York, Quartet, 1990, p255.

and released by the FBI. Although its authenticity has been questioned by some (why wasn't his baggage on the plane?), and critiqued as a violation of Islam by others, it is such a bizarre mixture - in the words of *The Observer* who published it in full on 30 September 2001 - of the 'apocalyptic', 'dramatic', 'sometimes downright banal', that it is hard to imagine it invented even by someone, post 9/11, intent on the most violent slandering of Islam (in fact it has turned out that no less than 3 copies were found - one more in the wreckage of the plane that crashed in Pennsylvania, another in a car abandoned by the hijackers outside Dulles airport). 'It is [therefore] unlikely', write commentators Kanan Makiya and Hassan Mneimneh, 'that many of the hijackers did not know the suicidal nature of their mission'.[8]

8. Kanan Makiya and Havan Mneimeh, 'Manual for a "Raid"', *Striking Terror - America's new war*, edited by Robert B. Silvers and Barbara Epstein, New York, New York Review of Books, 2002, hereafter cited parenthetically in text.

The document is, as Makiya and Mneimeh put it, 'an exacting guide for achieving the unity of body and spirit necessary for success' (304). That God is the instructor is unsurprising. Returning to the spirit of the Prophet, to the brief period of his rule between 622 and 632, the manual calls for a return to the path of *ghazwah*, best understood as a raid on the path of God:

> Consider that this is a raid on a path. As the Prophet said: 'A raid ... on the path of God is better than this World and what is in it' (306).

More striking however, is the way the words work – divinely sanctioned performatives to be repeated at every stage: 'Recite supplications' 'Remind yourself and your brothers of the supplications and consider what their meanings are', 'Recite repeatedly the invocations to God (the boarding invocation, the invocation of the town, the invocation of the place, the other invocations)', 'When you arrive and see [the airport], and get out of the taxicab, recite the invocation of place', 'Recite the supplication', Wherever you go and whatever you do, you have to persist in invocation and supplication'. Like the God to whom they are addressed, these supplications are infinite but invisible: 'It should not be noticeable', 'If you say it a thousand times, no one should be able to distinguish whether you were silent or whether you were invoking God' (321-324).

The preparation for the body is no less crucial than that of the mind: 'Shave excess hair from the body and wear cologne', 'Shower', 'Tighten your clothes' (in square brackets we are told by the *Observer* translator, Imad Musa: 'a reference to making sure his clothes will cover his private parts at all times'), 'Tighten your shoes well, wear socks so that your feet will be solidly in your shoes' (321). The body must be perfectly in place so that it can most perfectly forget or let go of itself. Makiya and Mnemneih comment: 'True selflessness requires an acknowledgement of the flesh-and-blood self in order to become estranged from it' (312). If slaughter is, chillingly, a gift, it is not an act of aggression because there is precisely no-body there, only God: 'Fight for the sake of God those who seek to kill you, and do not commit aggression. God does not favour those who aggress' (315). This is for the commentators the most frightening aspect of the document, which inserts into the Muslim tradition the idea of the martyr who, void not just of personal but also of any communal purpose, acts solely to please God. Makiya and Mnemneih observe:

> Martyrdom is not something bestowed by God as a favour on the warrior for his selflessness and devotion to the community's defence. It is a status to be achieved by the individual warrior, and performed as though it were his own private act of worship (317).

Driven by fear of God - later developments of Islam relegate the most extreme forms of fear as worship to mystical experience, but not here - driven, then by fear of God, the martyr voids himself of all intention. The document relays the story of Ali Bin Abi Talib (companion and close relative of the prophet Mohammed) who, when spat on by a non-believer in battle, did not kill him immediately but raised his sword: '"When he spat at me, I feared that if I were to strike him, it would be out of vengeance, so I held my sword"(326). After he renewed his intentions, he went back and killed the man'. Without qualities - remember Arendt on Eichmann: 'he had no motives at all'- the document offers us an image of someone who purifies mind and body in the cause of slaughter and who then heads, in both senses, for the skies. Jane Smith, professor at Hartford seminary, Connecticut and author of *Islam in America*, comments:

> Apparently one can assume that what was done was done by people out of a genuine and sincere belief that they were helping bring about the will of God. And that, in turn, may be the most frightening thing about it.[9]

9. 'Atta's Document', the *Observer*, 30/09/01.

Or in the words of John Esposito, director of the Centre for Muslim-Christian understanding at Georgetown University, 'We have a certain need to explain what somebody does as totally irrational […] the fact that they might come out of a pious background stuns us'.[10]

10. Ibid.

It is often remarked that Freud did not live to witness the Holocaust. Refusing to lend his voice to Zionism in 1930, he shifted, after the rise of Hitler, and expressed support for the creation of the state of Israel by the end of his life. Today we are left with another perhaps more interesting question than what might have been his at once passionate and pragmatic forms of allegiance after the Second World War. In his last great work, *Moses the Man and Monotheistic Religion*, Freud attributed the 'rise in intellectuality' to the creation of the monotheistic faith in which he invested great hopes. Freud was eloquent on the subject of group insanity. But what would he have had to say about a superego carved so closely to the features of a monotheistic God that it would destroy half the world in His name? (a question, one should add, as relevant to Evangelical America - there are 70 million - as to fundamentalist Islam). Or was he already sentient of the dangers: '[in the history of religion] human beings found themselves obliged in general to recognise "intellectual [*geistige*]" forces - forces, that is, which cannot be grasped by the senses (particularly by the sight) but which none the less produce undoubted and extremely powerful effects'.[11] After all, in *Civilisation and its Discontents*, he gave what remains today perhaps the most persuasive account of fear as the driving force of social life. The child lives in fear of a superego whose aggression knows no bounds simply because it has inherited all the aggressiveness which the child would herself like to use against it. There is something unavoidably craven, abject, masochistic - self-abolishing - in every subject's relationship to the law. When we read Atta's document alongside Freud's text in an MA class this year, it did seem as if there was only one step from this analysis to the idea of obedience as a form of divinely sanctioned fear. 'Fear,' Freud writes, 'is at the bottom of the whole relationship'.[12] In the link between superego and ego, which is what we rely on for entry into our social identities, fear is the key.

11. Sigmund Freud, *Moses and Monotheism*, 1938, *Standard Edition of the Complete Psychological Works*, Volume 23, p114.

12. Freud, *Civilisation and its Discontents*, 1930, *Standard Edition*, 21, p136.

***

In his essay on 'The Structure of Evil', psychoanalyst Christopher Bollas describes evil as a form of transcendence. 'The killer finds a victim who will die his death'. The killer murders his victim, as it were, on his own behalf. Enacting death, he avoids his own subjection to its law. Every time the killer strikes, it is his own death that he avoids. In this analysis, murderousness is based on a passionate if involuntary identification. Like the term evil itself, killing serves to get rid of something felt as too threatening; you hand it over to someone else, and then destroy it so that you can wipe your hands of the affair. Evil represents: 'the unconscious need to survive one's own death'.[13] Onto the other you slough off this mortal coil. If we go back to Costello, we could therefore say that every time fiction enters the world of evil, it is our own death that we escape.

13. Christopher Bollas, 'The Structure of Evil', *Cracking Up - the Work of Unconscious Experience*, New York, Hill and Wang, 1995, pp189, 193.

Transcending one's own death might be a fair description of Atta's document. But Bollas's article can take us back to Elizabeth Costello in another sense. If we return to the passage of identification with the women victims of Nazism at the edge of the pit which I quoted earlier, it is a very specific body - the ageing, flagging body - that Costello finds herself in identification with:

> If there were a mirror on the back of this door instead of just a hook, if she were to take her clothes off and kneel here before it, she, with her sagging breasts and knobbly hips, would look little different from the women in those intimate, those over-intimate photographs from the European war, glimpses into hell, who knelt naked at the lip of the trench ... (178).

Go back through the essay and ageing and its humiliations are something of a refrain: 'Twenty million, six million, three million, a hundred thousand:

at a certain point the mind breaks down before quanta; and the older you get - this at any rate is what has happened to her - the sooner comes the breakdown'; 'She does not know how old Paul West is […] Might he and she, in their different ways, be not old enough to be beyond embarrassment?'; 'She does not like to see her sisters and brothers humiliated, in ways it is so easy to humiliate the old, by making them strip for example, taking away their dentures, making fun of their private parts' (159, 163, 178). And this at the heart of the most offending, *obscene*, chapter from West's book:

> fumbling old men for the most part […] their false teeth and their glasses taken from them […] hands in their pockets to hold up their pants, whimpering with fear, swallowing their tears, having to listen to this coarse creature, this butcher with last week's blood caked under his fingernails, taunt them, telling them what would happen when the rope snapped tight, how the shit would run down their spindly old-man's legs, how their limp old-man's penises would quiver one last time? (158)

If this is the ultimate degradation, whose writing - it seems fair to ask - Paul West's, Elizabeth Costello's, or the writing of J.M. Coetzee, is repeating the offence?

Is the ultimate evil then a dying body that no ablution or supplication can save? Is such a body - which of course means all bodies - the real disgrace? In Coetzee's prize-winning novel of that title, the central character, David Lurie, meets with his estranged wife after his sexual harassment of a young student has driven him from his University position: '"Do you think", she asks, "a young girl finds any pleasure in going to bed with a man of that age? Do you think she finds it good to watch you in the middle of your … "' Lurie muses: 'Yet perhaps she has a point. Perhaps it is the right of the young to be protected from the sight of their elders in the throes of passion'.[14] Again it is a refrain. Lurie takes tea with his daughter when he has just arrived at the farm: 'He is aware of her eyes on him as he eats. He must be careful: nothing so distasteful to a child as the workings of a parent's body' (61). Explaining to her later why he will not appeal against his dismissal: 'After a certain age one is simply no longer appealing, and that's that' (67). And perhaps most tellingly in the first chapter of the book:

14. J.M. Coetzee, *Disgrace*, London, Secker and Warburg, 2000, p44, hereafter cited parenthetically in text.

> He ought to give up, retire from the game. At what age, he wonders, did Origen castrate himself? Not the most graceful of solutions, but then ageing is not a graceful business. A clearing of the decks, at least, so that one can turn one's mind to the proper business of the old: preparing to die (9).

There is another point. In *Disgrace*, Lurie - following a violent assault by a group of black youths during which his daughter, Lucy, is raped - is forced to ask, when Lucy will not speak to him: 'do they think that, where rape is concerned, no man can be where the woman is?' and then later to take his own question further: 'He does understand; he can, if he concentrates, if he loses himself, be there, be the men, inhabit them, fill them with the ghost of himself. The question is, does he have it in him to be the woman?' (141, 160). But in the story of Costello delivered at the conference on evil, Coetzee defied his own caution. He gives us Elizabeth's scene of sexual violence, puts us in the room with her, goes - one might say - to places where, by his own previous account in the novel, the man should not, or cannot, tread. Is the worst offence of this story, therefore, not West's forcing us to enter - body and mind - into Hitler's executioners and the hangmen, not Costello letting us into a moment of sexual violence from her past, but Coetzee entering the mind of his female character at the very point which, in *Disgrace* - and it is not an aside, it is absolutely central to the dilemma explored by the novel - was not possible or permissible for the man? Is Coetzee, advertently - or in fact, as I am inclined to think in this instance, inadvertently - indicting himself?

Coetzee's preoccupation with the ageing dying body gives us the other face - or underside - of transcendence. It suggests that the issue, in *Disgrace* but not only in *Disgrace*, is not just one of moral turpitude but also of physical turpitude, a turpitude of the body - utterly effaced in Atta's document, taken on by Coetzee - to which one moralism, *in extremis* as it were, may be a possible reply. *Disgrace* ends with Lurie, having dedicated himself to the care of abandoned and stricken dogs, handing one of them over to die. Lurie's connection to these dogs is the key to his transformation in the book. Earlier, in a crucial moment of dialogue with Lucy, Lurie had made his view of the place of dogs in the scheme of things very clear: 'by all means let us be kind to them. But let us not lose perspective. We are of a different order of creation' (Lucy on the other hand is willing to envisage herself returning in her next life as a dog). Previously, like many other readers, I saw the last moment of the book as an act of compassion or mercy on the part of Lurie towards a degraded species: 'Are you giving him up?' 'Yes, I am giving him up'. Now I am more inclined to see it as an act of mercy towards himself. Nor do I think we can read this as simply a metaphor for a dying white South Africa and its language although both can be read into the book (a reading confirmed by the fact the Coetzee has now left South Africa). Through Lurie and Costello, Coetzee is giving us one of the barest accounts of the dilemma, for someone for whom transcendence is no option, of a body - ageing, dying - repelled by itself.

At a seminar organised by Pittsburgh University for its visiting students in London to mark the first anniversary of September 11, seven minutes of footage were screened, footage only shown once on American and British television and then pulled as too disturbing by CNN. It consists mainly of bodies - visible, almost recognisable - plunging from the burning buildings to their deaths. There is, commented one participant in the seminar, a taboo on death in American culture (in Russia, the image shown repeatedly was of people in the building waving white flags, an image never shown on US television - presumably because it could be seen to signify surrender). Above all a body must not be seen to die. Bodies that fail and fall. To efface, or pre-empt, such images George Bush - with the full backing of Tony Blair - went to war against Iraq. The infinitely superior killing machines of the West took to the skies. Another way of saying, perhaps, that the greatest evil lies within ourselves.

Strategic universalism?

Mary Baine Campbell

David Simpson, *Situatedness, or, Why We Keep Saying Where We're Coming From* (Durham, NC: Duke University Press), 2002, 302pp; £41.90 cloth; £14.50 paperback.

I am not David Simpson's Ideal Reader, and I think he might be glad, despite his arguments in *Situatedness*, that I have so situated myself. It is not really possible to write an 'unsituated' review of a book which so forthrightly aims to undermine the epistemological and rhetorical value of discourse located in the partialities of the speakers, so this review will constitute, as regards any communication with the author, a '*dialogue des sourds*.' Perhaps my response to Simpson's book will however be audible to some of his audience: if so it had better be clearly 'situated.'[1]

1. For a mostly different point of view from my own, see the review by Simpson's colleague Martin Jay, *London Review of Books* Vol. 24, No. 23 (28/11/02).

Speaking then 'azza' woman (Simpson's satiric locution is borrowed from Andrew Sullivan), a feminist, a teacher, a half-baked middle-aged American leftist who has experienced criminal court up close and personal from several sides, and speaking also as a cultural and literary historian of early modern epistemology and member of Knowledge and Belief, a research project under way at the Max Planck Institute for the History of Science which tends more to question and historicize than to share Descartes's anxious quest for 'clear and distinct' knowledge; speaking this veritable babble of tongues: I don't like this book. Speaking azza fellow toiler in the groves of academe, I do very much respect the thoughtfulness, the labour of mind (and, it seems from its insatiably unsatisfied tone, of heart) that went into this consideration of the contemporary rhetoric of 'situatedness' with its political and legal consequences and, importantly, lack of consequences. This is not a negligible topic, nor a negligible treatment of it. Whether it will itself have consequences I doubt. Most people worried about the issues that provoke the language of 'situation' are too busy trying to change the bits of the world they're up against to plough through 300 pages of hand-wringing over the philosophical sloppiness, the failure to explain the human world, that is attributed here to their operational lingo.

Simpson himself admits this: 'nothing I write here can of itself change the direction of the prevailing rhetoric of identification; but if those who read this are made more unsure about situating themselves and others, and more curious about alternatives [which go unmentioned in his text], then I will feel that I have been useful' (246). Few English professors are directly useful to the practical world of social policy primarily envisaged here as the world that counts, although Janet Halley's citation, for instance, of Eve Sedgwick's *Epistemology of the Closet* in her successful brief to the Supreme

Court in the case of the Colorado 'Amendment 2' (nullifying all gay rights legislation at state and local levels) makes this reader more hopeful about the effectiveness of situated discourse. I never was in a position to wish realistically for philosopher-kingship, and so perhaps I am affectively as well as ideologically outside the circle of Simpson's Ideal Readership, one that has come to feel strongly the contemporary loss of direct academic impact in the political arena. But I think a book that concentrates as hard as this one does on the intellectual areas most influential in social reality should be judged as a kind of action as well as a kind of argument. I will give a 'situated' example of my difficulties with the book later, but first, a summary.

The fundamental problem as Simpson sees it is that there can be no resolution to a debate that simply stages and restages the antinomy of liberal free will *vs* what he often calls Foucauldian determinism: 'it is the entire dialectic of free choice and determined response that is discredited by the obscurity of situatedness' (241). Simpson frequently describes his aims and locates his arguments: a very useful habit, though he is not always as good as his word. Certainly I could support the intentions described in this claim: 'The aim of my study here is to appeal for an understanding of the prescribed dead ends that result from taking the rhetoric of situatedness at face value, without giving way to the reactive frustration that wants to accord it no value at all' (211). To the degree that the book does this, it advances a conversation the history of which it also masterfully, if partially, surveys. *Situatedness* has a large chronological and disciplinary range. The long arguments of its chapters take in and critique social and epistemological theory from Descartes and Locke to (dismissively) Haraway and Benhabib, via Bentham, Clarence Darrow, Mill, Sartre and Habermas, from the high Enlightenment to the tired post-Postmodern, from jurisprudence to the realist novel (here discussed, too generally, as 'literature', in a brief chapter mostly on novelistic character). It provides a useful and in many ways credible conceptual history of situatedness - a term Simpson takes from Sartre - and the antinomies to which it belongs. The debate around determinism never presented an antinomy that caught my own imagination as a serious problem (we act as we act in urgent matters no matter how much Kant we've studied). Simpson has, however, provoked me to review my long-standing sense of the problem as one belonging mainly to zesty boys in first-year college seminars on Great Ideas. He is of course right that Enlightenment assumptions and their contemporary liberal-capitalist elaborations about individual responsibility have considerable weight and influence in the legal arena. And he is right to see that once we open up the question of what is wrong with the 'Twinkie defence' (a notorious American criminal law case of about ten years ago, in which a violent criminal was permitted to claim temporary insanity caused by high sugar and chemical content in his favourite snack), we have more to look at than merely the problem of going too far with exculpatory arguments from situatedness. A can of worms lies open here, and as citizen-intellectuals we ought to be engaged in the processes by which such open cans are partially closed again, or at least the worms are trained to dance.

But this big range has strange absences in it: lots on Sartre, nothing but a footnote to Simone de Beauvoir, and then only to a book *about* her. Lots on the pugilistic Harvard law professor Alan Dershowitz (post-9/11 a supporter of citizen identity cards and legal police and military torture), nothing at all on the remarkable efforts, in the area particularly of the legal concept of the 'reasonable man', of for instance Sarah Buel (University of Texas School of Law) to make the courts a more sensitive arena for battered women and children. Many references to the Twinkie case, none to the much more difficult and interesting case of the 'Framingham Eight', a group of women imprisoned in Massachusetts for killing boyfriends and husbands in self-defence, mostly in the immediate situation of being threatened with a lethal weapon or overwhelming physical force. And although Simpson includes among concrete cases of problematic situationism the notorious *Bell Curve* and Daniel Goldhagen's *Hitler's Willing Executioners*, the objects of critique most irritating to him are Donna Haraway's essay 'Situated Knowledges' (1988) and Seyla Benhabib's *Situating the Self* (1987), which (15-year-old) texts he takes as adequately representative of vast corpuses of critique in the general area of 'standpoint epistemology', an intellectual arena first mentioned on p218 and given next to no genealogy. A couple of times in earlier chapters he 'situates himself' ironically as a white middle-class male academic, but he does not make the effort to analyse what if anything that might have to do with the striking absence of women from his bibliography: there are twenty-five woman-authored or -edited works listed in the bibliography of a book on 'situatedness' of about 300 items, and Benhabib has to represent (along with a respectful paragraph on Gayatri Spivak's 'strategic essentialism') all non-European and non-Euroamerican thinkers and activists! I am not suggesting the bibliography of such a book programmatically match proportions of 'situated' theoretical and social policy work in the area of its subject. But it is noticeable in a work so irritated by the current mania, as Simpson sees it, for positionality, that he feels free to ignore so much of what has obviously moved him to demystify the ontologies subsumed within it.

It is in the area of ethics that Simpson is most daring, and seems most partial in his consideration of actual kinds of situation. 'Those of us in the habit of situating ourselves on a regular basis might stop to investigate the peculiar feeling of virtue we have as we do so, and ponder whether we have deserved it by any active connection with anything ...' (220). 'The imperative to situate oneself is perceived as ethical even as (or perhaps because) it is usually devoid of critical content and without consequences beyond the moment of utterance' (221). 'I might agree to respect my friend's declarations of situatedness as they succeed one another or accumulate ... but that is exactly where the process stops, with a gesture of respect ... [It] is one of recognition or interpellation rather than description: it will be useless to me if I am trying to assess my friend's eligibility for some kind of restricted benefit or his personal responsibility for some sort of crime ... These models of the self ... can encompass few if any of the problems that a politics or a jurisprudence must decide' (221-2). I well remember the interpellation 'My name is Geraldine Ferraro,' memorably pronounced on the occasion of the nomination of the first female vice-presidential candidate in American history. It certainly encouraged a lot of women to throw their energies into the kind of problem that a politics can decide.

On the problems a jurisprudence must decide, I'm going to start with an 'azza' because it invokes not only an experience but a source of information, and a good example of the difficult cases Simpson avoids confronting, perhaps because he is not forced to by his 'situation'. As one of the unlucky one in three American women who experiences the crime of rape in her lifetime, I was involved as chief witness for over fifteen years in a pair of aggravated rape cases that permitted me considerable first hand experience of jurisprudential changes in Massachusetts over that time period (1983-1998) - the period of the emergence of feminist involvement in social policy and the law; also the period of strong populist backlash against the rights of criminals. Some of the changes I had to deal with over that period were obviously for the good. The special (but hardly rare!) case of rape victims as chief witnesses in rape prosecutions has been recognized in ways that are transforming the social and legal consequences for women of reporting crimes of sexual aggression: the very term 'victim-witness' points to the inevitable undermining of the chief witness by her status as victim, and implies the exigency of handling such witnesses carefully, of not repeating physical aggression against them by means of public and verbal aggressions in the courthouse, of getting detailed accounts of the crime down as quickly as possible before traumatic amnesia sets in, and so on. On the other hand, the backlash in favour of victim's rights by 1997, when the second person charged in this case (who had jumped bail in 1983) had been apprehended, forced me indeed to state my situation in pre-trial considerations of sentencing. It was no longer effectively 'The Commonwealth of Massachusetts v. X,' but now 'Mary Baine Campbell v. X'. Azza victim in this case I had become a member of the prosecution's team. And anything I did, including refusal to consult, constituted a share of personal responsibility for the retribution of the state, while I myself oppose the concept of retribution in matters of criminal law. I had, in first taking action to pursue the case, considered the court an arena in which the participation of the Commonwealth in my situation gave me a solidarity with the whole population as a civic entity, rather than the vulnerable and provocative identity of an individual seeking revenge, and in particular a solidarity with the nearly 51 per cent of the population facing a high probability of sharing my situation (to which we must add the number of sexually abused children and overpowered men, such as the Haitian janitor

Abner Louima in the hands of the New York City police).

The women who had killed men to save their lives among the Framingham Eight were also compelled to state their situation, in a highly consequential drama pitting the prospect of life imprisonment against their difference from the legal model of the 'reasonable man'. The reasonable man, as Buel among others has argued, is usually considerably larger and stronger than the in many cases quite reasonable women being chased around their bedrooms by men with guns. Not always and everywhere of course, but the law is in fact capable of a certain amount of verbal precision, more than Simpson's habitual tone of near despair would suggest. I don't know how much peculiar 'virtue' they felt in situating themselves thus. I felt none in my own case, nor do I feel it now; the unpleasant facts are here to illustrate the difference experience and situation can make, not just to reason but to knowledge. But if I had felt virtue, perhaps he feels that as a rape victim I might have 'deserved it by … actual connection with' something (200). As a citizen and member of the same society Simpson lives so thoughtfully in, I am distressed to think that even a thoughtful man could imagine, even ironically, such a thing as 'deserving' a feeling of virtue in relation to the disenfranchised position of aggravated powerlessness some people, in some situations, are required by law or common sense to articulate. Is this really 'a modern form of casuistry that we deploy not only at the expense of others but on ourselves?' (246)

To be fair, Simpson's tone of near-despair, or of implacable refusal to find any account of the social or legal human being that is adequate to reality - or simply 'clear and distinct' – is the tone of a near-philosopher. Simpson might say it's not his job to be satisfied with the intellectual work of the past, nor is it his job to suggest those 'alternatives' to current antinomies of reason that could make for a better or at least more reasonable and articulable world. Those would be OK things to say. They would be more OK if his own refusal - consistent with his argumentative aims - to 'situate' himself did not simply leave him situated *despite* himself, unconsciously, and thus unable to critique his own critique. 'I have none of the qualifications', he says, 'that would permit me to hold a view on the adequacy of [Daniel] Goldhagen as a historian of the Holocaust, and I intend no comment on that topic and therefore no approval or dismissal of the book' (206). However, the English professor seems to feel fully qualified to dismiss primatologist Haraway, and professor of government and political science Benhabib, and to sympathize with the philosopher Habermas's nostalgia over our lost 'authentic privacy': 'solitary time within the patriarchal household once provided for the cultivation (through reading) of a critical reason that created the basis for a genuine *public* sphere' (180). Whose reading? Whose 'public sphere'? Alasdair MacIntyre's *After Virtue* (1981) is however rebuked for nostalgia, in its reliance on ethical narratives (224-5), as is Benhabib, whose own words are used against her: 'she wonders whether the whole tendency to declarations of situatedness might not emanate from a postmodern "nostalgia for home, for the certitudes of one's own culture and society" in a detraditionalized world' (203). Some nostalgias are more moving than others to Simpson, but he doesn't recognize it so can't tell us why.

In the end, while admitting uncomfortably that his arguments critical of situatedness 'could be taken to imply a basic comfort with the terms of our culture', Simpson decides not to take a position on this question: 'for to do so would of course be to situate myself and to encounter all the problems of so doing, the problems about which I have been writing' (245). No need to worry. The positions of a man who chooses the Twinkie defence and *The Bell Curve* as objects of critique, rather than the large-scale and responsibly theorized interventions in social policy and legal activism of collectively 'situated' persons and movements over the last 40 years of American history; who represents those interventions largely by way of a few disparaging remarks about a single 1980s article by Donna Haraway; and who without irony adopts his favourite word 'azza' from a right-wing journalist, are clear enough to any reader who does not share them.

In writing a book that finds fatal fault with most of the serious social thinking of white men over the last 300 years, and with, via a strangely negligent metonymy, all that of women in the last fifty (and which basically ignores both men's and women's theorizing in colonial and postcolonial societies), one should be careful not to leave oneself open to the attack of unselfconsciousness. Simpson has failed in that, and I have reacted strongly because it takes a long time to read a serious book, and in these demanding times I feel that the book should, as an action, account for what it says it will account for, rather than choosing targets on the basis of unacknowledged situation and unexamined personal irritation.

THE RARITY OF THE EVENT: ON ALAIN BADIOU

Andrew Gibson

Alain Badiou, *Infinite Thought: Truth and the Return of Philosophy*, Oliver Feltham and Justin Clemens (ed and trans), London and New York, Continuum, 2003, 208pp; £16.99 hardback, £9.99 paperback. Alain Badiou, *Saint Paul: The Foundation of Universalism*, Ray Brassier (trans), Stanford, Stanford University Press, 2003, 120pp; £8.99 paperback, £26.95 hardback.

If anything like a historical account of the Anglo-American intellectual world in the late twentieth and early twenty-first century ever comes to be written, one of the more important factors it should take into account is the history of the appearance of translations of French thought. The British and American reception of the thinkers in question has been comprehensively determined by this history. From the seventies to the nineties, this was strikingly the case with Deleuze. At the moment it seems likely that Badiou's career in the Anglophone world will be as patchy and erratic as Deleuze's was. If Badiou and Deleuze are the two great philosophical antagonists *de nos jours*, as some now see them in France, the similarity of their fates in translation is piquantly ironic. I don't mean to slight the dedication and expertise of the small group of (largely quite young) French-speaking philosophers and scholars who have been sedulously working on Badiou. Quite the reverse: apart from anything else, they have efficiently protected him against the prospect of being prematurely dumbed down - an issue I shall return to later - and we should be grateful for it. Beyond them, however, is a large readership that remains interested in contemporary French thought, if more fitfully and with less heady excitement than two or three decades ago. It is not clear, however, that this readership is being altogether well served by Badiou's English and American publishers. The corollary, of course, would be that Badiou is not altogether well served by them either. His progress in translation begins to look as though it might bear out some of his own more virulent polemics. For the problem is partly the increasing hegemony of a commercial logic to which he has always been fiercely opposed.

In the Anglophone world, Badiou's current reputation hinges chiefly on two volumes, his book on Deleuze and his *Ethics*.[1] This in itself is revealing: at the moment, Deleuze and ethics are sexy. A densely argued and extremely demanding book of mathematical philosophy (*Le nombre et les nombres*), apparently, is not.[2] Nor, *a fortiori*, is an extended post-Marxist meditation on politics as thought (*Peut-on penser la politique?*).[3] Yet the first two books are no more central to Badiou's thought than the second two, and in some

1. Alain Badiou, *Deleuze: The Clamor of Being*, Louise Burchill (trans), Minneapolis, University of Minnesota Press, 2000; and *Ethics: An Essay on the Understanding of Evil*, Peter Hallward (trans), London, Verso, 2001.

2. Alain Badiou, *Le nombre et les nombres*, Paris, Seuil, 1990.

3. Alain Badiou, *Peut-on penser la politique?* Paris, Seuil, 1985.

ways rather less so. Badiou's fundamental differences with Deleuze, Levinas, and the contemporary ethics of alterity are abundantly evident in both the Deleuze book and the *Ethics*. But the false if temporary pre-eminence of these two texts can be misleading. For it suggests that Badiou is readily assimilable to the terms of contemporary debates, when in fact he cuts right across them. The *Ethics* is actually a polemical anti-ethics. Such 'ethics' as it puts forward seems fascinating, but crude and unelaborated. This impression could not survive a better knowledge of the larger philosophy, but that knowledge cannot yet be gleaned from English translations. So, too, in isolation, the Deleuze book looks like an engaging critique of Deleuze's transcendental materialism as not only vitalist but monist. In fact, like Badiou's other brilliant and largely uncollected essays on major philosophers - from Spinoza, Nietzsche and Wittgenstein to Sartre and Althusser to Rancière and Françoise Proust - it is also part of an ongoing series of important philosophical self-differentiations.[4] These are painstaking, subtle and complex, but forceful and very clear. They are guided and spurred on by the belief that thought is above all conflictual: it begins in and steadily refines itself, makes itself exact, through divisions with others.

Some of the gaps are being filled in fast. The trouble is that other gaps are not, or not altogether satisfactorily. In some cases it's possible to imagine that they may not be filled in at all. On the one hand, we have a translation of Badiou's *Manifesto for Philosophy*. This book is a stirring but simplified version of ideas that take on more ample proportions elsewhere. It should really be set alongside Badiou's account of the importance of the modern manifesto itself (to be found in *Le Siècle*, due to appear in dual text from Seuil later this year).[5] On the other hand, whilst we now have Nina Power and Alberto Toscano's welcome translation of Badiou's writings on Beckett, his essays on Mallarmé are possibly even more central to his thought, illuminating, not least, the significance of the manifesto. Will full translations with the appropriate scholarly apparatus - necessary, given how much of Badiou's work on Mallarmé consists of extremely detailed philosophical readings of specific poems - ever be available to the Anglophone reader? It seems inherently unlikely: whilst Beckett remains a commercial proposition in the English-speaking world, Mallarmé has seldom if ever been one.

But isn't there a risk of overstating the problem? We have at present no English version of the great spine of Badiou's thought, *L'Être et l'événement* and *Logiques des mondes*. But the first is promised for next year, and, as for the second, well, he hasn't even finished it in French yet. The *Petit manuel d'inésthétique* and other major texts are on their way.[6] Isn't it pedantic and fussily purist to suggest that, as far as possible, the French Badiou should simply be 'made over' into English? The answer is, only up to a point. Firstly, the issue is more important in Badiou's case than, say, Deleuze's or Derrida's, because, alone among the best known recent French thinkers, Badiou is a systematic philosopher and in many ways a rationalist. His philosophy has a rigorous if extremely complicated structure into which all

4. See for instance 'L'ontologie implicite de Spinoza', in *Spinoza: Puissance et ontologie*, Myriam Revault D'Allonnes and Hadi Rizk (eds), Paris, Kimé, 1993, pp54-70; *Casser en deux l'histoire du monde?*, Paris, Le Perroquet, 1992 - on Nietzsche; 'Silence, solipsisme, sainteté: l'antiphilosophie de Wittgenstein', *BARCA! Poésie, Politique, Psychanalyse* 3 (Nov. 1994), pp13-53; *Jean-Paul Sartre*, Paris, Potemkine, 1981; 'Qu'est-ce que Louis Althusser entend par "philosophie"?', in *Politique et philosophie dans l'oeuvre de Louis Althusser*, Sylvain Lazarus (ed), Paris, PUF, 1993, pp29-45; 'Rancière et la communauté des égaux' and 'Rancière et l'apolitique', *Abrégé de métapolitique*, Paris, Seuil, 1998, pp121-27, 129-38; 'Sur le livre de Françoise Proust: *Sur le ton de l'histoire*', *Les Temps modernes* Nos. 565-66 (August-September 1993), pp238-48; and 'Depuis si longtemps, depuis si peu de temps', *Rue Descartes* 33 (2002), pp101-4 - on Françoise Proust.

5. *Le Siècle*, bilingual edition, translated with a reply by Alberto Toscano (Paris, Seuil, 2004).

6. Alain Badiou, *Petit manuel d'inésthétique*, Paris, Seuil, 1998.

aspects of his thought can in principle be fitted. He is not a dogmatist: one of his most beguiling qualities is that he is so willing to address the questions others raise for his system, and to modify its features if he sees the need. But he is, truly, a thinker: he teaches the meaning of thinking, not least because he is rightly intent on restoring the force of a crucial axiom: thought begins in the break with *doxa*. Because he is a systematic thinker, Badiou does not produce collections of essays, but coherent philosophical texts. They can be placed within his system as wholes. To break them up and redistribute the pieces, as English and American publishers have started to do, may sometimes be defensible, as in the case of Badiou's disparate essays on specific authors. But it is already to engage in a kind of misrepresentation.

Secondly, this redistribution makes it more likely that the non-expert will misconstrue the relationship between Badiou's thought and its most significant modern philosophical contexts, which Badiou himself identifies as German and hermeneutic, French and postmodern-deconstructive, Anglo-American and linguistic-pragmatic. Badiou neither identifies his thought with any one of these three camps, nor does he pit himself against their great champions. Precisely because his system is essentially complex, he continually discovers points of agreement as well as differences with other philosophers. To adopt one of his metaphors, he 'traces diagonals' across philosophy. Whilst his disputes with Heidegger and his insistence on a return to Plato are crucial to his thought, it makes no more sense to see him as categorically 'anti-Heideggerian' than it does simply to label him a 'Platonist'. Compare Badiou the great proponent of the Platonic account of mathematics with Badiou on the grimness of the Republic, as exemplified in the draconian treatment of the sophists and the banishment of the poets.

Again and again, attentive readers will find themselves on well-known ground only also to find it shelving beneath them, or in strange territory that turns out to be quite familiar after all. Thus, for example, with Being: Badiou both argues that philosophy should forget about the Heideggerian 'forgetting of Being', and yet, at the same time, that it must accept the Heideggerian premise: philosophy starts out from the question of ontology. As a philosophy not only of Being but of the event, his thought might seem close to that of some of his French contemporaries, notably Deleuze, Lyotard and Proust. But for Badiou, the event arrives as a supplement to Being, and is rare. One of his most powerful criticisms of Deleuze in particular is that Deleuze puts the event everywhere and thereby neutralises it (an argument, incidentally, that may do something to explain the strange eminence of Deleuzean philosophy in the neo-liberal and social-democratic phase of culture). Badiou vigorously resists the idea that a century of colossal disaster invalidates the philosophical enterprise: why should philosophers and not politicians, businessmen or the military shoulder the burden of guilt? But his call for an end to the thought of 'the end' does not mean that philosophy is not concerned with the consequences of the Holocaust, for example; rather, that such lessons as the Holocaust can teach are specific and, above all, political. How could the enemy ever really be the philosophical tradition, as compared for instance to the disposition of mind that produces the disingenuous and slack-minded journalistic and popular conflation of Hitler with Milosevic and Saddam Hussein?

These are of course just meagre little fragments from a formidable philosophical architecture, but they may give some small indication of the sheer intricacy of mind at stake in it. To reconfigure its internal relations is to run the risk of quite serious distortion. Badiou's philosophy involves a host of specific judgments, or better, decisions about thought. It is through this great array of decisions that he shows us how thought matters. A set of translations altogether adequate to a thought intended to matter would be a remarkable achievement. In Badiou's case, such a set of translations will not be available for some time to come, if at all.

Infinite Thought is a significant addition to Anglophone Badiou studies. It contains some important material, notably the interview with Badiou with which the volume ends. In particular, for anyone who might have been wondering precisely where Badiou was heading since the closing essays in *Court traité d'ontologie transitoire*,[7] Feltham, Clemens and their co-interviewers have skilfully extracted a succinct, clear and extremely interesting account of what is at stake for Badiou in *Logiques des mondes*. But - and in spite of the translators' rather good introduction - I am not sure that *Infinite Thought* is a very good introduction to Badiou's philosophy.

The problems begin with the great swirling nebula on the cover. This is presumably supposed to be an image appropriate to an infinite thought: 'thought, the final frontier'. It is precisely wrong for Badiou. If thinking infinity is crucial to him, it is only in rigorous contra-distinction to the theological or romantic uses of the concept. In the first instance, the concept of infinity is connected neither to a concept of time nor one of space. Infinity is banal and actual (in the Aristotelean and mathematical sense of 'actual infinity'). It is ready to hand, there at once. It is chiefly available to us through mathematics, as in the work of Cantor, Zermelo, Fraenkel, Gödel, Cohen and modern set theory in general. To think infinity in temporal or spatial terms is precisely to risk perpetuating the post-romantic 'pathos of finitude' that has dogged us since Hegel separated philosophy from mathematics.

Infinite Thought presents itself as a kind of sample of Badiou's thought, something close to a 'Badiou Reader'. It consists of a series of 'Philosophy ands' ... : 'Philosophy and Art', 'Philosophy and Politics', and so on. There is nothing inherently problematic about this: Badiou himself is responsible for some of the titles; indeed, he adopted the same format in his French text *Conditions*.[8] But to compare the two texts is to register the difference between a major philosophical work and the logic of a commercially-driven compilation. In *Conditions*, philosophy is linked to its four major conditions, the truth-domains: science (specifically mathematics), art (specifically poetry), love, and politics; and to psychoanalysis, which Badiou has long been tempted to declare a fifth domain. Each of these concerns is worked

7. See 'Groupe, catégorie, sujet', and 'L'être et l'apparaître', *Court traité d'ontologie transitoire*, Paris, Seuil, 1998, pp165-77, pp179-200.

8. Alain Badiou, *Conditions*, Paris, Seuil, 1992.

through meticulously and in relation to a key set of concepts. One such concept is 'the generic', which Badiou illustrates through a long final meditation on Beckett. Because it is so dense and so precisely organised, *Conditions* emerges as one of Badiou's half-dozen most important works. Yet it must be open to question whether we shall see it in English at all, save as parcelled out here and there in journals and 'collections'.

Set alongside it, *Infinite Thought* is a miscellany. It prises essays from the philosophical and discursive contexts in which alone they are properly comprehensible, and juxtaposes them with essays from different contexts. Thus 'Philosophy and Art', for example, comes from *Conditions*, but has been separated from the marvellous, detailed essays on Mallarmé and Rimbaud which follow it and reflect on its argument. 'Philosophy and the "War Against Terrorism"', by contrast, comes from an altogether different discursive world, that of Badiou's recent engagements with contemporary politics - Le Pen, Kosovo, Iraq, the headscarf debate and so on - particularly in *Circonstances*, 1 and 2.[9] These essays are a delight, not least in that they are pungent to the point of being scabrous. And they are important: Badiou is seldom as difficult as most of his French contemporaries - that is, if we leave the mathematics to one side. Yet he is as unashamedly mandarin and 'aristocratic' as they are. The essays in the two volumes of *Circonstances* seem part of an effort to marry serious thought to a more 'journalistic-intellectual' discourse than those Badiou usually chooses, without ever quite going pop. But philosophy does not belong with the 'war on terrorism' as it belongs with art. The two themes are not comparable. Whilst the editors clearly know this, the volume itself obscures the point. Insofar as *Infinite Thought* appears to suggest that the attack on the Twin Towers is of major importance for Badiou - and certainly insofar as it suggests that it might be important for him as, say, Celan or the mathematician J.P. Cohen are important - it is misleading. Part of Badiou's point about both the attack and the 'war on terrorism' is that both are philosophically insignificant. For they are encounters between nihilisms that bear no relation to any truth.

Infinite Thought should therefore be approached with a little care. It is more interesting to the already knowledgeable reader than it is illuminating for the beginner. If it is what the blurb calls it, 'a representative selection', it is so in a not altogether serious or helpful sense. I also have another reservation about it: some of the translation work is not especially good. There are more than a few clumsy Frenchisms of the kind that help to get French philosophers a bad name in the English-speaking world, and which are particularly unnecessary in Badiou's case: with the exception, perhaps, of Clément Rosset, he is the least difficult of contemporary French philosophers to translate. The problem is more worrying, in that Feltham is currently translating *L'Être et l'événement*. Given the extraordinary richness of that text, I hope he bears in mind the principle that English translations ought always to make sense as English to regular users of English.

Here he could learn from Ray Brassier, whose excellent translation of

9. Alain Badiou, *Circonstances, 1: Kosovo, 11 Septembre, Chirac/Le Pen*, Lignes, Éditions Léo Scherer, 2003; *Circonstances, 2: Irak, foulard, Allemagne/France*, Lignes, Éditions Léo Scherer, 2004.

Saint Paul is crystalline throughout. In fact, *Saint Paul* is a better introduction to Badiou than *Infinite Thought*. For *Infinite Thought* implies that Badiou's philosophy is best grasped as a loose set of grand abstractions, whereas *Saint Paul* is about a specific truth-procedure in its concreteness; and for Badiou all truth-procedures are specific and concrete. Paul is a key figure in Badiou's select pantheon, and a key element in the structure of his thought; many of his most important emphases are here. Paul is the subject of a truth: that is, in Badiou's terms, he is propelled towards a new way of being by an event that fractures an established order of things. A truth is an extension of this event in and by its subjects, a process of which Paul is a classic instance. Truth is not separable from a subjective trajectory. It demands commitment and must be sustained with a militant persistence - not least for others: the subject of a truth is a universal vector (the universality in question existing, of course, only in anticipation). Paul's truth determines its own specific modes of communication; that is, it requires the invention of new names. It also requires a subjective discipline. Paul subtracts his truth from established knowledge through the austere concentration involved in 'investigations' (*enquêtes*). He identifies his truth in the future anterior, in terms of the laws that 'will have structured' it. He also operates his own version of 'restricted action', a term Badiou gets from Mallarmé: everything must be organised around the few themes that matter.

The trouble with using *Saint Paul* as a starting-point, however, is that it really needs to be precisely placed in the context of Badiou's thought. In this respect, it is a pity that his publishers did not urge Brassier to provide a succinct introduction. For in some ways, *Saint Paul* invites misconstruction. Its historical and scholarly detail is part of what makes it so accessible. But the detail is untypical of Badiou, and is even at odds with his larger philosophy, which is resolutely ahistorical. History has no objective content and does not supply explicatory contexts. It is a subjective discipline of time founded on events. Indeed, although the point is not immediately evident, *Saint Paul* does say this: Paul's truth cannot be named from within established discourses. He adamantly resists any dissolution of truth into opinion, into the perspectival world of historicity and 'culturalism'. This specifically involves him in a work of radical dehistoricisation. Thus the book does not exactly bear out its own theory of history in its practice.

Even more importantly, there is the initially perplexing matter of Badiou and Christianity. Serious readers can already be heard grumbling that there is too much residual Christianity in the philosophy for comfort. No doubt at some level the residue is perceptible. But deconstructing Badiou is a project of negligible interest and value, certainly at the current time: there are other, much more important things that we can be doing with his thought. One crucial point in *Saint Paul* is that the Pauline truth is not that of the Damascene conversion. It is not the truth of a *coup de foudre*, a revelation or a moment of illumination. The Pauline event has an intellectual structure, the structure of a fable. The fable in question is the resurrection, understood

10. Alain Badiou, *Court traité d'ontologie transitoire*, op cit., pp9-24.

as 'a mythological assertion'. The logic here can only be fully grasped in the context of Badiou's great essay 'God is Dead'.[10] Apart from anything else, that essay effectively provides us with an axiom the force of which runs right through the philosophy: no thought is possible save on the further side of the atheist decision. It is not often that we can ignore this point in Badiou's work; but we might do so in reading *Saint Paul*.

11. Peter Hallward, *Badiou: A Subject to Truth,* Minneapolis, University of Minnesota Press, 2003.

In the end, the character of Badiou's philosophy is such that it might be better not to start with one of his books at all, but with Peter Hallward's *Badiou: A Subject to Truth*;[11] or perhaps with Hallward's book alongside the *Manifesto for Philosophy*, the *Ethics* and *Saint Paul*. Hallward's book is a remarkable achievement: erudite, richly informative about the relevant philosophical, mathematical, political and historical contexts, precise, accurate and extremely well-written. It is an excellent base to set out from, but it also leaves room for further exploration, not least of Badiou's aesthetics. Hallward, incidentally, provides a great example of how to fight the current pressures to trivialise, formidable as they are, in the UK at least. In this he is faithful to Badiou; for Badiou's work enters a plea that can also be heard coming, in one form or another, from various uniquely powerful voices of the time, from Agamben, Proust and Rancière to Coetzee, Morrison and Sebald. Quite simply, without resorting to any of what Badiou calls the current set of 'spiritual supplements' - from the doctrine of rights to the self-deceiving sentimentality of contemporary humanitarianism, to obscurantist chatter or quasi-religion - it is time we started getting serious again.

This essay was funded by a Leverhulme Trust Research Fellowship for 2003-2005.

THE MODERN PRINTS

Jon Klancher

Terry Cochran, *Twilight of the Literary: Figures of Thought in the Age of Print*, Harvard MA, Harvard University Press, 2001, 288pp; £27.95 hardback.

This is a demanding meditation on the concept of modernity, a lucid and carefully orchestrated book that ranges among Italian, French, German, Spanish and even Portuguese texts, and from the fourteenth to the twenty-first centuries, as well as between humanist, materialist, and poststructural vocabularies. Its aim is to seek a better grounding for materialist, critical thought in a global situation where the fundamentals of modernity - the subject, the national, vernacular writing - no longer hold together in a coherent 'world picture'. Theories of modernity have ranged widely in recent years, from substantive efforts to define the logic of a historical era, to a sceptical reluctance to credit this category as more than a narrative device used in countless ways to affirm the modern (or capitalist) age as such (as Jameson argues in *A Singular Modernity*). Cochran presses the sceptical view in a different direction. To recognise how the category of modernity functions narratively or ideologically is not to 'dispel its necessity, for it rests on the conceptual needs of secularisation, on the need to show that human beings largely control their own fate'. Humans control their fate in modernity by inscribing their thought in a particular and complex material form, print - a medium that has required complex institutions for steering thought into modes of effectiveness and power over time. And though the twentieth century introduced powerful new media (film, digital, and so forth) that disturb and bid to displace the centrality of print, Cochran makes the provocative case for a prolonged 'twilight' in which our thought continues nonetheless to be figured by print and the modern institutions printed knowledge has required.

Cochran grasps this process by attempting to link the complexity of figuration with the needs of hegemony in the modern. He links 'figures' in the poststructuralist sense (*prosopopeia* is the most extended instance) with the historical meaning given to 'figura' by Erich Auerbach, where the divine is shadowed forth into the human as the shape of its history. In a chapter on 'The Use and Abuse of the Human' Cochran considers modernity's project to ground knowledge in the human subject by reading Kant's *Anthropology from a Pragmatic Point of View* in the light of Heidegger's 'Age of the World Picture'. Much of this illuminating discussion is retrospective, clarifying how an Enlightenment anthropology dispelled the figuration entailed by religion and myth by means of the secularising notion of *anthropomorphism*. '"Nothing whatsoever could be thought" about the cause of the world', as Cochran cites Kant, without the anthropomorphic centring in human imagination. Even when we no longer believe in the gods or divine origins, this account goes, we maintain in the anthropological idea the same discursive framework while adopting the figure itself 'from the prosaic world'. Pragmatic anthropology - the human sciences more broadly - pushes the figurative to the ornamental edges of discourse and 'dispenses with personification [as a figure] because the (human) object can be experienced daily as a living referent'. Thus figuration lives on, unacknowledged, like a god lurking in the materials of the everyday. Late twentieth century questioning of this process exposes it by criticising transcendent or ahistorical essences, rendering them immanent, explained as resulting from historical or epistemological circumstances and interests.

Turning to Baudrillard's pessimism about the ensuing loss of a transcendent place for critical reflection, Cochran then asks why genuinely critical thought needs a 'transcendental fiction' (the human) at all. What, dispensing with that fiction, would a 'truly secular historical vision' be like? Evidently it would have to leave behind not only the anthropomorphic subject, but the central place of print as well. In a fascinating chapter on 'The Collective Culture of Print', Cochran considers some little-read writings of Gramsci on print and communications technologies, contrasting Gramsci's situation - and embeddedness in the national vernacular history of print and 'tradition' - with Benjamin's. Gramsci understood print as radically democratising, the basis for 'a new culture on a new social base' that had not yet, by the early twentieth century, been fully realised. He associated, on Cochran's reading, the traditional intellectual with an aristocratic oral culture where education and speaking are absorbed, as Bourdieu would say, through the class habitus and not formal education. Among the media, he dismissed journalism as more or less a transcription of 'oratory and conversation', not a fundamental print genre. The contrast with Benjamin's placing of print and oral-visual media at the centre of 'social, political, and cultural agency' is indeed striking.

For Benjamin the global perspective, not the national vernacular language, was the point of departure. Cochran cites a passage in Benjamin that attributes the power of the sound film to its merger of 'new capital from the electrical industry with that of the film industry. Thus, viewed from the outside, the sound film promoted national interests, but seen from the inside it helped to internationalise film production even more than previously'. Since sound films appeared, unlike silent film, to limit the reach of film to a national audience sharing its (spoken) language, Benjamin's shift of analytic register to the connection between industries rather than filmmakers and spectators jarred the familiar grounding of language-based media in national forms of union. Both film and electrical industries *were*, of course, mainly national in the 1930s; retrospectively, Benjamin anticipated the globalisation of mediatic relationships in a way

Gramsci's assumptions, deeply grounded in the transcendent value of the national vernacular, could not.

Much of this book reworks critical insights that have been won in the past three or four decades, from Benjamin and Heidegger to Said and de Man, by placing them in a larger framework, not the 'end' of modernity but the transformation, globally and mediatically, of its framing conditions. Not only critical thinking but a range of humanist disciplines of knowledge are at stake here. Critical thinking itself, Cochran concludes, 'results from the struggle to detach thought from the means of thinking; that is, it is the sediment from the effort to think the figures of thought'. If we need figures in order to think, and we can only think in language, then the question of how language, discourse and print is inscribed institutionally becomes fundamental. Cochran offers perhaps the most imaginative and serious reading of Gramsci since Raymond Williams, finding in his work both the recognition of the powers of figuration and the means of 'institutional critique'.

The discrediting of transcendence by way of contextualist or historicist 'debunking' today marks the dominant method across the range of knowledge production, from literary studies and art history to the cultural history of science and other disciplines. As they expose this situation, however, the humanities disciplines find they are simultaneously 'losing their own objects of knowledge'. I wish Cochran had pursued an analysis of this disciplinary crisis further in this book, an issue which has something to do with how a book like this will be read now and who will read it. *Twilight of the Literary* speaks cogently across several conceptual divides - poststructuralist and materialist, the printed and the mediatic, 'figuration' and 'hegemony' - and especially to a literary discipline that does not seem to know what to do in the twenty-first century with its own humanist, theoretical, and cultural-historical legacies of thought. But it speaks hesitantly, and much less clearly, to the 'what now?' question. At most there is a cautious hopefulness here that the perspective that Cochran calls 'linguistic materialism' may give us a 'new approach to historical intervention'. The shape and point of that intervention remains elusive in this book; nevertheless *Twilight of the Literary* offers an indispensable critical reflection on what modernity *has* entailed, an unusually rich resource for the critical imagination at a disorienting turn of the modern.

MAKING IT NEWER

David Cunningham

Jane Goldman, *Modernism, 1910-1945: Image to Apocalypse*, Basingstoke and New York, Palgrave, 2004, 312pp; £45 hardback, £14.99 paperback.

What's in a date, or rather a pair of dates? For the contemporary scholar of something called 'modernism', apparently everything. How wonderful it must be to work, by contrast, in a cultural field named 'Victorian', where everything is apparently so clear: 1837-1901, coronation to death. So little ambiguity or doubt in that. Even a less obviously 'periodising' category like Romanticism seems subject, at least in literary and art history, to an agreed historical 'placing' that allows everybody to know (roughly) what they're talking about when the term pops up in conversation. But for 'modernism', beginnings and endings are a different matter. Even if we can agree that it must surely begin at some point, we can never seem to agree when. And as to its ending - well, we can't agree on that at all (nor even whether it has yet, or can ever, occur).

For Anglo-American literary studies, Malcolm Bradbury's and James McFarlane's dating of modernism from 1890 to 1930, in the title of a much reprinted collection of essays from the late 1970s, has (despite numerous challenges over the years) proved most persistently influential - an influence reflected in hundreds of undergraduate course syllabuses throughout the English-speaking world. The immediate interest in Jane Goldman's new book - published in Palgrave's *Transitions* series (the stated editorial aim of which is 'to address anew questions of literary history and periodisation') - comes therefore from the historical situating (and shift) that its title points up: lopping off twenty years at the beginning, and extending Bradbury and McFarlane by fifteen at the end. It is, for me, the impact that these last bonus years have on the field more generally that proves to be the most fascinating and productive aspect of this book.

Let us begin at the 'beginning' though. Goldman's rationale for starting a decade into the twentieth century, rather than in the dying embers of the nineteenth, is clearly articulated, and is not without pedagogical persuasiveness: '[T]o approach the heights of modernism gently via the foothills of Symbolism and the Yellow period ... tends to defer and diffuse rather than sharply define the specific topics and shock tactics of the various movements in modernism ... [so that] new readers and students of the period often find it difficult, in my experience, to discern the "modernist" aspects of this complex narrative' (22). The 'potency' of 1910, as the more precise inaugural date, is reinforced by both its 'mythical' status in Virginia Woolf's essay 'Mr Bennett and Mrs Brown' – the moment when 'human character changed' - and (more originally) the connection Goldman suggests it might have to the political context of the suffragette movement and the demand for 'material improvement for women workers' (159). (Goldman is particularly good on the 'gendering' of modernism throughout, while rightly questioning any 'gender apartheid' in its theorisation). Regarding 'Mr Bennett and Mrs Brown', as is usual Goldman links Woolf's historical caesura to the impact of the London exhibition of Post-Impressionist painting organised by Roger Fry in that year. And this is certainly not unconvincing, if we accept Bloomsbury as being at the centre of modernism as a cultural moment. But it risks - despite Goldman's own detailed attention to figures like Paul Celan and Kurt Schwitters elsewhere in the book - a certain provincialism in relation to what was a very 'international' and 'cosmopolitan' era. For if the Yellow Period might well seem 'tame' by comparison with the likes of Pound, Joyce or Lewis, the same surely cannot be said - to take a few French examples - of Baudelaire, Lautréamont, Nerval, Jarry or Rimbaud. Moreover, as Goldman acknowledges, Fry's 1910 exhibition presented work that was itself 'not strictly *contemporary* "modern" art. Cézanne, Gaugin and Van Gogh … were all by 1910 dead' (43). Meanwhile, continental Europe had already seen Picasso's *Demoiselles D'Avignon* three years earlier.

As for Goldman's posited closing date: in a book which concludes (in some of its most interesting passages) with the 'apocalypse movement', centred around poets like Dylan Thomas, David Gascoyne and W.S. Graham, 1945 makes obvious sense as an ending: *Modernism, 1910-1945* concludes with the sound of the atom bomb exploding. In terms of the book's general coverage its immediate effect is very welcome. For it works to disturb a critical *doxa* concerning the 1930s which has been allowed to stand for far too long: that this is a decade dominated by a 'retreat' from the dynamics of modernism, a 'return' to 'realist reportage' legitimated by a crude conception of 'political commitment'. As Goldman shows, in many ways this is, rather, a period of 'further flourishing', with the belated arrival of Surrealism on British shores and the formal experiments of a new generation of poets. Considering the 1930s from this perspective, Goldman is wonderfully rude about the likes of Orwell, whose work is often taken (like that of Larkin and Amis later) to represent English Literature's return to the straight and narrow after its 'avant-garde' flirtations. For Goldman, Orwell's is rather 'a dreary, melancholic residual modernism … mutilated by liberal guilt, worthiness, and didacticism' (xxii).

While Goldman's re-readings of Eliot, Woolf and Pound, in the first half of her book, are well-judged and often novel - particularly in her contextualisation of their work by re-placing it within the pages of the little magazines and journals where it was first published - it is, then, the second half of the book, introducing the likes of Gascoyne and the remarkable 'Renaissance man' of modernism John Rodker, that is the most rewarding and inspiring. The downside is that it leaves you wanting more. Perceptive as is her reading of *The Waste Land*, I would happily have sacrificed the space it takes up here for more of Goldman's thoughts on marginal figures like David Jones, Hugh Syke Davies, Basil Bunting or Mary Butts.

Nonetheless, Goldman's book does a good deal more than one can usually expect from a book of this type, aimed as it is at an already over-saturated 'introductory' market. Insightful in its readings, this is a book which is never dull, manifests an entirely infectious enthusiasm, and is at times downright funny. If it is most obviously aimed at an undergraduate audience, it also has a lot to say - perhaps most - to those who have been working in this area for a long time, and who might consider themselves to be largely familiar with all it has to offer.

And as for those irritatingly fluid historical co-ordinates of its subject? Well, perhaps the problem lies less in the difficulty of fixing the co-ordinates themselves than in the scholarly and pedagogical assumption that periodisation is what is actually required here. For 'modernism', after all, is not a term like 'Victorian', and cannot be made such, since its *temporal* implications as a concept - concerning the production of the historically 'new' through a non-identity to tradition - will always be in tension with the historicising, chronological logic of periodisation itself. It is entirely to her credit that, somewhat slyly given the stated aims of the series in which this book appears, Goldman clearly recognizes as much. She refuses the usefulness, for example, of the epithet 'postmodernist' (22) and reiterates the ways in which 'avant-garde' and 'modernist' movements 'themselves' have always manifested a dynamic energy resistant to any reduction to a 'fixed category of aesthetic qualities', or an 'impoverished sense of historicism and periodisation' (xvi). Despite the implication of the title, 1945 emerges here not as the 'end' of modernism *per se*, but as 'a post-war place from which modernism's and the avant-garde's new ladders start' (xxii). As Goldman states: 'Transitions continue'.

QUEERING THE SPHERES

Judith Surkis

Eric O. Clarke, *Virtuous Vice: Homoeroticism and the Public Sphere*, Duke University Press, Durham and London, 2000; 233pp; £11.95 paperback. Michael Warner, *Publics and Counterpublics*, Zone Books, Cambridge, MA and London, 2002, 334pp; £19.99 hardback.

Eric Clarke's book *Virtuous Vice* and Michael Warner's collection of three new essays and five previously published articles *Publics and Counterpublics* draw upon a well-established body of literature on the uses and abuses of 'the public sphere'. They do so, however, in a way that seeks to break with the normative ideal that has guided the field of Habermas criticism to date; namely, of public discourse as a domain consecrated to the 'public exercise of private reason'.

Since the 1989 English translation of Habermas's classic text *The Structural Transformation of the Public Sphere*, Habermas's model of the institutions and associations of bourgeois civil society has circulated widely in the writings of Anglo-American critics interested in the past, present and future of participatory democracy. In seeking to appropriate this model, critics called attention to the exclusions upon which the historical emergence of the bourgeois public sphere was based, while themselves remaining largely beholden to the ideal of '"critical-rational" debate"'praised by Habermas himself. They brought into relief the limitations of Habermas's account, its lack of attention, on the one hand, to the bourgeois public sphere's marginalization of women, the working-class, and racialised subjects, and, on the other, to efforts by those who were so excluded to enter into "the public sphere"', or to form subaltern spheres of their own. In other words, numerous critics sought to demonstrate how Habermas's vision of the public sphere was at once too large and too small - in any case not quite right. Responding to these challenges, Habermas concurred that his 1962 text was both overly homogenising in its class analysis and insufficiently critical of how the consignment of women to the realm of private domesticity had structuring significance for political and public life. He nonetheless re-affirmed his commitment to the normative ideal of public rational-critical debate which emerged, in his view, with bourgeois humanism, and, further, reiterated his concerns regarding the erosion of this ideal by market-driven, mass media culture and politics.[1]

Eric Clarke and Michael Warner extend these analyses of the public sphere's constitutive exclusions. They do so, however, in order to lay bare the heteronormative presumptions which structure access to socially

1. See Jürgen Habermas, *The Structural Transformation of the Public Sphere: an Inquiry into a Category of Bourgeois Society*, Thomas Burger (trans), Cambridge, MA, MIT Press, 1989. For a good introduction to the existing body of criticism on the Habermasian public sphere, see Craig Calhoun (ed), *Habermas and the Public Sphere*, Cambridge, MA, MIT Press, 1992. This volume includes Habermas's essay 'Further Reflections on the Public Sphere', pp421-461.

2. For a particularly
good account of how
the public sphere is
frequently described
in spatialised terms,
see Harold Mah,
'Phantasies of the
Public Sphere:
Rethinking the
Habermas of
Historians', *The
Journal of Modern
History* 72 (March
2000), 153-182.

legitimate publicity and privacy. Both authors focus their attention on the
sexual norms and proprietary codes of publicness. This emphasis takes their
analyses in a new direction: towards a rhetorical rather than spatial
understanding of social marginalisation.[2] For Clarke and Warner, the
limitation of the Habermasian model is less a question of capacity (that is,
of inclusiveness) and more one of socially acceptable language and behaviour.
Both writers are suspicious of political endeavours which emphasise more
and better representation for women, the working-class, people of colour,
and gays and lesbians within the existing framework of publicness. They
point to the risks involved in strategies which adhere too closely to reigning
norms of acceptable public representation. And finally, they express concern
that such tactics reinforce reified conceptions of identity and perpetuate
the social exclusion and political abjection of 'queers' who do not conform
to these norms.

The creative power of language is also central to the arguments of both
authors. The essays collected in Warner's volume highlight the 'performative'
or animating character of public discourse by emphasising how modes of
address constitute and call into being the very publics that they imagine as
addressees. Warner is consistently critical of how the 'language ideology' of
the public sphere - as a dialogue between disembodied and theoretically
interchangeable subjects - obscures this poetic function (146). For Warner,
the idealisation of 'rational-critical debate' by Habermas and his critics poses
limits to social movements - like those around gender, sexuality or race -
which directly engage issues of embodied subjectivity and identity. The self-
abstraction and disembodiment required in order to participate in this model
of the public sphere, supposedly available to all, is in fact a privilege of the
few. Warner explores the socially transformative possibilities of the
'counterpublics' which he discerns in seventeenth-century British satirical
texts, Christopher Street bars, nineteenth-century African-American theatre,
and Walt Whitman's poetry. These contexts create, in his view, 'new
individuals, new bodies, new intimacies, and new citizenships', and, in the
process, remake publicness itself by giving it 'a visceral resonance' - as well
as, one might add, a certain erotic charge (62).

Clarke's book similarly identifies a performative fiction, or what he refers
to as a 'subjunctive mood', which is constitutive of 'bourgeois publicity'.
That is, he highlights how participation in public debate demands that
'one act *as if* the material practices and organisations associated with the
public sphere unproblematically embody the ideals of democratic publicness'
(7). Clarke examines the familial and material value judgements that,
according to Habermas's own analysis, have historically structured legitimate
publicness and its exclusions. He further claims that gay and lesbian public
visibility - in, for example, the popular television show *Ellen*, or as a valuable
consumer market with an expensive 'lifestyle' and disposable income - is
often mistaken for political and civic equality. What is more, he suggests
that these mediatised representations may provide ideological cover for

the perpetuation of inequities and normalising valuations of gender and sexuality. Like Warner, he interrogates how and whether a social movement which seeks to promote 'fair' and 'true' representations of gays and lesbians as 'normal' rather than, as Ellen Degeneres remarked, 'scary homosexuals' (32), and hence deserving of rights (to marry, to serve in the army, as viable consumers), recapitulate the at once moralising and commercial value judgements on which bourgeois publicity is based. He does not reject these rights claims *per se*. He does, however, express concern with how the 'erotic indeterminacy' characterising queer subjectivity and ethics is remarginalised and, indeed, 'demonised' by such representations.

In interrogating the heteronormative character of dominant conceptions of legitimate publicity - historically and in contemporary political debate, in both literature and social theory - Clarke and Warner's texts have much in common. Yet there are significant differences in their approach to and analysis of publicness itself. As the titles of their books suggest, Warner is largely concerned with 'publics' and similarly plural 'counterpublics', while Clarke examines 'the public sphere'. Warner's model of publicity insists on multiplicity and open-endedness, taking as its point of departure the circulation of texts in print culture. Clarke figures 'the public' as an ideological totality and notably deploys a rhetoric of vision and visibility. Both authors point to how the power of public discourse is founded on a paradoxically real fiction. Warner tends, however, to highlight the creative potential of this performativity, while Clarke understands its mystificatory potential. This difference in focus has important implications for their respective arguments.

Clarke concentrates on how the ideological fiction of democratic publicness, and the proprietary values - at once moral and economic - which it frequently sustains, obscure and perpetuate social inequality and marginalisation. His argument, laid out in two opening theoretical chapters, appeals to Marx's reading of commodity fetishism and Adorno's discussion of the public sphere as an instrument of bourgeois hegemony. Clarke here critiques the moral and economic value judgments which inform dominant notions of personal worth and which often structure access to representative publicity. His third chapter provides a compelling reading of Kant's writings on morality in order to illustrate how the master-thinker of the Enlightenment public sphere correlated human dignity, citizenship, and married, monogamous (hetero)sexuality. Two final chapters are devoted to nineteenth-century English literature and canon formation. 'Inseminating the Orient' examines how authors such as Lord Byron, at the beginning of the century, and Arthur Symonds, at the end, reclaimed ancient Greek homoeroticism as virile and Western, while projecting the feminising aspects of pederasty onto the Orient. In the process, Clarke suggests how 'affective historical reflection' (131) may consolidate and sustain national, sexual, and racial identity. The last chapter illustrates how late-nineteenth century literary critics negotiated and managed highly ambivalent, passionate attachments to Percy Bysshe Shelley as a figure and writer, by attempting to pass off their risky perversion (known as 'Shelley love') as 'normal' and culturally valuable humanistic scholarship. He here interrogates the ambivalent character of strategies of cultural legitimation, and insists in an epilogue that an outright rejection of 'publicity' in and through a celebration of 'romantic alterity' (170) is at once unworkable and politically unproductive. He rather aims, in this work devoted to demystifying the dissembling claims of the dominant public sphere, towards a more far reaching transformation of the terms of public- and, by extension, political and civic legitimacy.

Warner's book, by contrast, opens with the striking claim that 'publics are queer creatures' (7). He works to identify a 'queerness' at the heart of publicity itself. The essays that follow attempt to demonstrate how and why this is the case. In other words, they seek to 'out' the promiscuous 'stranger-relationality' (75) that is at work, in Warner's view, every time 'a public' is called into being by an address. Warner argues that critiques which remain focused, for example, on the dominant whiteness or maleness of the public sphere, obscure the 'fruitful perversity' (113) of public discourse, a perversity that he seeks to celebrate. Indeed for Warner it is impossible to grasp the creative and transformative 'world-making' possibility of counterpublics without seizing upon how they reveal and exploit the promiscuous relationship to strangers that characterises all kinds of public address. Warner's vision of the queer dynamics of publicity are thus implicitly informed by an ethic of stranger-intimacy that one might associate with those privileged tropes of queer criticisms: cruising or bathhouse subcultures.

Warner's more theoretical and programmatic chapters, devoted to critical overviews of the relationship between 'Public and Private' and 'Publics and Counterpublics', are complemented by essays with a more precise focus. A chapter on recent debates about the status of the public intellectual and the valorisation of 'clear writing' provides an occasion for reflection on the politics of styles of address, especially in the work of leftist academics. Another essay, 'The Mass Public and the Mass Subject', contrasts the historical public sphere's ideal of self-abstraction with the kinds of iconic embodiment mobilised in the modern 'mass public'. 'Sex in Public', co-written with Lauren Berlant, provides a concrete articulation of how sexual subcultures or counterpublics implicitly critique a heteronormative privatisation of intimacy, and can hence be seen fundamentally to rework the relationship between private and public life. In 'Something Queer about the Nation-State', Warner proclaims the affinity between the norms of liberal modernity, as instantiated by the ideal of a civil society independent of the state, and queer politics, in order to caution against the largely state-oriented character of recent struggles for gay and lesbian rights. Another co-written, scrupulously documented essay discusses a performance which almost certainly took place at the first African-American theatre in the United States (established in New York in 1821), entitled 'Soliloquy of a Maroon Chief in Jamaica'. The little noticed speech, according to Warner, addressed its audience as a 'counterpublic', and may thus be read as intervening in and commenting upon wider contemporaneous debates surrounding the racialisation of citizenship. Warner's final chapter on the author of a mid-century temperance tract, who turns out to be Walt Whitman, suggests how Whitman's early engagement with that major American social movement sheds light on the kind of stranger-relationality that, Warner suggests, subtends all forms of public discourse. The book ends with an evocative reading of how Whitman's 'To a Stranger', in its apostrophe to a vacillating addressee (a 'you' that is either a 'he' or a 'she'), simultaneously invokes the codes of intimacy *and* the anonymity of print circulation. For Warner this text, 'like so much of Whitman's poetry ... mimes the phenomenology of cruising' (287).

In their mixing of history and literature, theory and politics, both Clarke's and Warner's texts bring about a creative interaction between genres and disciplines. In the process, both engage in a challenging project to interrogate and remake the norms and forms of cultural legitimacy and democratic public participation. Like Habermas himself, they construct 'the public sphere' as an object of critique and a site for the elaboration of political and ethical ideals.

Clarke and Warner seek to counter the charge that queer theory and politics are overly invested in a kind of blind anti-normativity that refuses affective bonds and social attachment, arguing that such a charge is hopelessly bound up with an ideological construction of privatized subjectivity or identity.[3] Both authors put forward a seemingly paradoxical ethics - in Clarke's case, of 'erotic indeterminacy' and in Warner's, of 'stranger relationality' - that is suspicious of psychic interiority, and which appears to privilege a paradigm informed by male homosexuality. While they invoke new kinds of social relations created by queer counterpublics, their texts fail to provide sustained explorations of the affects and attachments that these relations might involve. In a current context in which debate over the right to marry more than ever structures the terms of acceptable gay and lesbian representation, the exploration of the political implications of this alternative ethics require even greater clarification and specification. While 'erotic indeterminacy' and 'stranger relationality' are seductive and suggestive formulations for what this might entail, they remain, here, largely allusive and elusive. What these books do successfully demonstrate, however, is the significance of queer theory for any effort to rethink the norms of democratic public life.

3. For critical analyses of this anti-normative tendency see Biddy Martin, 'Extraordinary Homosexuals and the Fear of Being Ordinary', *differences* vol. 6, issue 2-3 (1994), 101-125; Brad Epps, 'The Fetish of Fluidity', *Homosexuality and Psychoanalysis*; Tim Dean and Christopher Lane (eds), Chicago, IL, University of Chicago Press, pp412-431.

BACK ISSUES

1 Peter Wollen / Denise Riley / Dick Hebdigeís / Laura Marcus / John Tagg / Franco Bianchini / Homi K Bhabha / Stephen Feuchtwang and Barbara Harlow

2 Mary Kelly, Elizabeth Cowie and Norman Bryson /Greil Marcus / Georgina Born /Geoffrey Nowell-Smith / Ien Ang / Alan Sinfield / Tony Bennett

3 *TRAVELLING THEORY* Julia Kristeva / David Edgar / Kobena Mercer /Jacques Ranciere / Peter Hulmeís /Bill Schwarz / Ginette Vincendeau / Steve Connor / Christopher Norris

4 *CULTURAL TECHNOLOGIES* Out of print

5 *IDENTITIES* Out of print

6 *THE BLUES* Jacqueline Rose / James Donald / Benita Parry / John Silver / Mitra Tabrizian and Andy Goldingís / Barbara Creed / Joseph Bristow /Graham Murdock / Edmond Wright

7 *MODERNISM/MASOCHISM* Victor Burginís / Linda Williams / John Tagg o/ Geoff Bennington / Emilia Steuerman / Paul Crowther / Mark Cousins / Iain Chambers / Adrian Forty / Lisa Tickner

8 *TECHNO-ECOLOGIES* Peter Wollen / John Keane / S.P. Mohanty / David Kazanjian and Anahid Kassabian / Paul ThÈberge / David Tomas / Felix Guattari / Margaret Whitford

9 *ON ENJOYMENT* Slavoj Zizek / PeterOsborne / Rachel Bowlby / Joseph Bristow / Gail Ching-Liang Low / Christine Holmlund / Line Grenier / Mark Cousins / Simon Critchley

10 *RADICAL DIFFERENCE* McKenzie Wark / Paul Hirst / Cindy Patton / Anna Marie Smith / Tracey Moffatt / Susan Willis / Hazel V. Carby / David Lloyd / Peter Redman

11 *SUBJECTS IN SPACE* Dick Hebdige / Iain Chambers / Meaghan Morris / Sam Appleby / Raphael Samuel / Peter D. Osborne / Victor Burgin / Donatella Mazzoleni / Ann Game / Nicholas Green

12 *NATION, MIGRATION AND HISTORY* David Morley and Kevin Robins / Renata Salecl / McKenzie Wark / Peter Wollen / Victor Burgin / Elizabeth Grosz / Mitra Tabrizian / Gail Ching-Liang Low / Peter Middleton

13 *NO APOCALYPSE YET?* Angela McRobbie / Slavoj Zizek / Geoffrey Nowell-Smith / Paul Du Gay / Colin Mercer / Peter Nicholls / Lyndsey Stonebridge / Jenny Taylor / Joseph Bristow

14 *ON DEMOCRACY* Chantal Mouffe / Renata Salecl / Joan Copjec / Mladen Dolar / Slavoj Zizek / Zdravko Kobe / Bill Schwarz exorcising the general / Patrick Parrinder Leeds

15 *JUST LOOKING* Kevin Robins / Charlotte Brunsdon / McKenzie Wark / Sarah Kember / Gill Frith / Christopher Norris

16 *COMPETING GLANCES* Out of print

17 *A QUESTION OF 'HOME'* Ariel Dorfmann / Doreen Massey / Tzvetan Todorov / Jamie Owen Daniel / Aine O'Brien / Celia Applegate / Jeffrey M. Peck / Helen Fehervatu / Jenny Bourne Taylor / Bill Schwarz / Theodor W. Adorno / Mary Ellen Hombs / Mananna Torgovnick / Irena Klepfisz

18 *HYBRIDITY* Christopher Norris / John Frow / Annie Coombes / Simon Frith / Andreas Bjørnerud / Rod Giblett

19 *PERVERSITY* Out of print

20 *WALTER BENJAMIN* Out of print

21 *POST-COLONIAL INSECURITIES* Benita Parry / Kenneth Parker / Jon Stratton / McKenzie Wark / Kevin Robins / John Borneman / Anne Beezer / Marcia Pointon

22 *POSTCOMMUNISM* Vitaly Komar and Alex Melamid / Michael / Ted Levin / Mark Slobin / Svetlana Boym / Mikhhail Yampolsky / Katerina Clark / Nancy Condee and Vladimir Padunov

23 *LACAN AND LOVE* Joan Copjec / Renata Salecl / Juliet Flower MacCannell / Mladen Dolar / Alenka Zupancic / Miran Bozovic / Jane Malmo / Slavoj Zizek

24 *ON NOT SPEAKING CHINESE* Ien Ang / Ghassan Hage / Rob Wilson / C.J.W.-L. Wee / Julia Emberley / Iain Chambers / Neil Roughley / Gillian Swanson / Johan Fornas

25 *MICHEL FOUCAULT: J'ACCUSE* David Macey / John Rajchman / Kate Soper / Alan D. Schrift / Sue Golding / James Miller / Robert J.C. Young / John / Wendy Wheeler / Nick Couldry

26 *PSYCHOANALYSIS AND CULTURE* Malcolm Bowie / Lesley Caldwell / Dominique Scarfone / D.W. Winnicott / Jim Hopkins / Clare Pajaczowska / Alex

Tarnopolsky / Christopher Wintle / Special Section - Revisiting Psychoanalysis and Feminism:Ann Scott, Juliet Mitchell, Margot Waddell,Joanna Ryan, Joan Raphael-Leff

27 *PERFORMANCE MATTERS* Simon Frith / Lydia Goehr / Nicholas Cook / Martin Stokes / Sally Banes and John F. Szwed / John Stokes / Gill Frith / Karen Lury / Les Back

28 *CONSERVATIVE MODERNITY* Harriet Guest / Geoff Eley / Janet Wolff / Paul Gilroy / Lynne Segal / Bill Schwarz / John Kraniauskas / Peter Osborne

29 *TECHNOSCIENCE* Rosi Braidotti / Andrew Barry / Nell Tenhanf / Terri Kapsalis / Simon Penny / Tiziana Terranova / Sue Owen / Cheryl Sourkes / Janine Marchessault

30 *CULTURAL MEMORY* Michael Rowlands / Tony Kushner / Anna Vidali / Susan Taylor / Imruh Bakari / Sylvie Lindeperg / Mamadou Diouf / Erica Burman / Tricia Cusack

31 *UNCIVIL SOCIETIES* Jeremy Gilbert / Drew Hemment / Richard Cavell / Ien Ang and Jon Stratton / Michael Humphrey / Albert Paolini / Fiona Nicoll / Vicki Callahan / Lee Grieveson

32. *LEGAL FICTIONS* Josephine McDonagh / David Glover / Ian Ward / Stella Swain / Ruth Robbins / Philip Leonard / Joseph Valente / Sally Munt / Timothy Bewes

33 *FRONTLINE BACKYARDS* Phil Cohen / Stuart Hall / Bill Schwarz / Mary Chamberlain / Les Back / David A Bailey

34 *DREAMING IN THEORY* Rachel Bowlby / Sara Ahmed / Nicholas Daly / Laura Chrisman / Maureen Moynagh / Benita Parry / Michael Pickering and Keith Negus / Simon Frith / Wendy Wheeler / Simon Wortham

35 *THE ETHICS OF VIOLENCE* Étienne Balibar / Henrietta Moore / Renata Salecl / Juliet Flower MacCannell / Parveen Adams / Alain Abelhauser / Mladen / Slavoj Zizek / Alenka Zupancic / Cecilia Sjöholm / Jane Malmo / Marinos Diamantides

36 *DIANA AND DEMOCRACY* Jacqueline Rose / Ruth Richardson / Carol Watts / Anthony Barnett & Jenny Bourne / Mark Gibson / Nick Couldry / Heather Nunn / Lisa Blackman / Clare Birchall / Jude Davies

37 *SEXUAL GEOGRAPHIES* Miles Ogborn / Christopher Breward / Mica Nava / Frank Mort / Marcia Pointon

38 *HATING TRADITION PROPERLY* Neil Lazarus / Graham Pechey /Andrew Edgar / Barbara Engh / Herbert Schnadelbach / Sean Homer / Deborah Parsons / Graeme Gilloch / Esther Leslie / Eamonn Carrabine and Brian Longhurst / Kate Soper

39 *COOL MOVES* Dick Pountain and David Robins / Rita Felski / Steven Connor / Mariam Fraser / Guy Hocquenghem / Bill Marshall / Fred Botting / Anny Brooksbank Jones Avonís / Gregory Stephens / Syed Manzurul

40 *CULTURE/CHINA* Stephanie Hemelryk Donald / John Cayley / Wanning Sun / Audrey Yue and Gay Hawkins / Souchou Yao / Katie Hill / Shu-mei Shih / Richard Read / Harriett Evans / Tamara Jacka

41 *THE FUTURE OF DIALOGUE* Michelle Barrett / Stephen Bygrave / Denis Flannery / John Hood-Williams and Wendy Cealey Harrison / Lucy Hartley / Ken Hirschkop / Simon Jarvis / Laura Marcus / Nicky Marsh / Peter Middleton /Saul Newman / Sujala Singh

42 *THE RUINS OF CHILDHOOD* Adam Phillips / Douglas Oliver / Vicky Lebeau / Bernard O'Donoghue / David Marriott / Tanya Horeck / Marian Partington / John Wilkinson / Vincent Quinn / Lindsay Smith / Christine Clegg /Bernard O'Donoghue / Sebastian Mitchell / Stephanie Hemelryk Donald

43. *MOBILITIES* Tim Cresswell / Ginette Verstraete / Don Mitchell / Vikki Bell / Alan Finlayson / Eleanor Byrne and Martin McQuillan / Rebecca Beasley / Eluned Summers Bremners

44 *MASS-OBSERVATION* Laura Marcus / Dorothy Sheridan / Rod Mengham / Tyrus Miller / Steven Connor / Drew Milne / Nick Hubble / Jeremy MacClancy / Elizabeth Cowie / Margaretta Jolly / Karen Fang

45 *'THE RENDEZ~VOUS OF CONQUEST'* Meyda Yegenoglu and Mahmut Mutman / Kelwyn Sole / Salah D. Hassan / Elliott Colla / Ben Carrington / Peniel E. Joseph / James T. Campbell / Madhu Dubey / Wendy Hui Kyong Chun

46 *THE PROSTHETIC AESTHETIC* Bernard Stiegler / Raiford Guins / Suhail Malik / Joanne Morra / Fred Botting and Scott Wilson / Marquard Smith / Aura Satz / Andrew Patrizio / Mandy Merck / Kate Ince

47 *AFTER FANON* Neil Lazarus / Vikki Bell / Timothy Bewes / Benita Parry / Kwadwo Osey-Nyame Jrn / Azzedine Haddour / Priyamvada Gopal / Gautam Premnath / Robert Spencer / MarÌa Josefina Saldaña-Portillo / David Kazanjian / Rajeev Pakte / Fabio Vighi/ Lisa Trahair / Ben Highmore / Nick Prior / Jane Kilby / Michael Calderbank

48 *JEAN LAPLANCHE AND THE THEORY OF SEDUCTION* John Fletcher / Jean Laplanche / Jacqueline Lanouziére / Dominique Scarfone / Jacques André / Guy Rosolato

49 *COMPLEX FIGURES* Philip Tew / Wendy Wheeler / Christopher Norris / Patricia Waugh / Merja Polvinen / Peter Hallward / Lisa Lynch / Steve Baker / Kate Soper / Debra Benita Shaw / Roger Luckhurst / Deborah Philips / Megan Stern

50 *REMEMBERING THE 1990s* John Tomlinson / Michael Bracewell / Roger Luckhurst / Roger Hampson / Peter Middleton / Wendy Wheeler / Steven Connor / Joe Brooker / Andrew Gibson / Lynn Segal

51 *THE SHORT CENTURY* Simon Gikandi / Uzoma Esonwannc / Steven Nelson / Parvati Nair / Sara Wills / Ian Buchanan / Jon Stratton / Neil Turnbull / David Dwan / Ben Highmore

52 *CULTURES AND ECONOMIES* Boris Vejdovsky / Paul Smith / Stephen Maddison / Anne Barron / Mandy Merck / Cora Kaplan

---

Back issues cost £14.99 each plus £2 post and packing
You can pay by cheque, made out to Lawrence & Wishart, or by credit card (VISA or Mastercard only). Send cheques and credit cards details to: Lawrence & Wishart, PO Box 7701, Latchington, Chelmsford CM3 6WL you can also send your credit card details to: landw@btinternet.com

---

Why not Subscribe?

New Formations is published three times a year. Make sure of your copy by subscribing.

SUBSCRIPTION RATES FOR 2004/2005 (3 ISSUES)

Individual Subscriptions
UK & Rest of World   *£40.00*

Institutional Subscriptions
UK & Rest of World   *£125.00*

Back issues: *£14.99 plus £2 post and packing for individuals*
                   £34.99 plus £2 post and packing for institutions

Please send one year's subscription
starting with Issue Number ————————————————

I enclose payment of ———————————————————————

Please send me ———— copies of back issue no. ——————————

I enclose total payment of ————————————————————

Name ————————————————————————————————

Address ——————————————————————————————

————————————————————————— Postcode ——————————

Please return this form with cheque or money order (sterling only) payable to
***Lawrence & Wishart* to: Lawrence and Wishart (Subs), PO Box 7701, Latchington,**
Chelmsford, CM3 6WL. Payments may also be made by Visa or Mastercard.